Theologies of Guadalupe

Theologies
of Guadalupe

From the Era of Conquest to
Pope Francis

TIMOTHY MATOVINA

OXFORD
UNIVERSITY PRESS

OXFORD
UNIVERSITY PRESS

Oxford University Press is a department of the University of Oxford. It furthers the University's objective of excellence in research, scholarship, and education by publishing worldwide. Oxford is a registered trade mark of Oxford University Press in the UK and certain other countries.

Published in the United States of America by Oxford University Press
198 Madison Avenue, New York, NY 10016, United States of America.

Library of Congress Cataloging-in-Publication Data
Names: Matovina, Timothy, 1955– author.
Title: Theologies of Guadalupe : from the era of conquest to Pope Francis.
Description: New York, NY : Oxford University Press, [2019] |
Includes bibliographical references and index.
Identifiers: LCCN 2018015453 (print) | LCCN 2018039573 (ebook) |
ISBN 9780190902766 (updf) | ISBN 9780190902773 (epub) |
ISBN 9780190902759 (hardcover) | ISBN 9780190902780 (online content) |
Subjects: LCSH: Guadalupe, Our Lady of. | Mary, Blessed Virgin,
Saint—Theology. | Mexico—Religious life and customs.
Classification: LCC BT660.G8 (ebook) |
LCC BT660.G8 M355 2019 (print) | DDC 282/.72—dc23
LC record available at https://lccn.loc.gov/2018015453

1 3 5 7 9 8 6 4 2

Printed by Sheridan Books, Inc., United States of America

for my mother, Barbara

Contents

Illustrations

Acknowledgments

THE GENESIS OF this volume was a doctoral seminar called Guadalupe: Faith, Theology, and Tradition that I team taught for over a decade at the University of Notre Dame with a treasured friend and mentor, the late Virgilio Elizondo. To our knowledge, it is the only doctoral seminar dedicated entirely to Guadalupan studies. We read many of the principal theological texts examined in this book with scores of bright students whose insights deepened my understanding of the individual texts and the overall Guadalupe tradition. The term papers of one group were so excellent that we collaborated with the students after the semester to publish their work in a coauthored volume, *New Frontiers in Guadalupan Studies.* Findings from each of their essays are cited in this work. The students we taught over the years are too many to mention here, and our conversations were too lively to credit particular interpretations and ideas to one single discussant. But I want to acknowledge that those conversations shaped both the overall thesis and particular claims in every chapter of this book. I also want to highlight how great an honor it is to have taken part in forming these talented and dedicated scholars. Most of all, I thank you, Virgilio. *Gracias hermano, por todo. Que en paz descanses.*

Drafts of chapters for the book received critical commentary from colleagues at the annual meetings of the Academy of Catholic Hispanic Theologians of the United States and the U.S. section of the Comisión para el Estudio de la Historia de la Iglesia en Latinoamerica. At the University of Notre Dame I received similar feedback from colloquia in the Department of Theology and the Institute for Latino Studies. The support and acumen of colleagues from a variety of disciplines and areas of theological expertise enhanced this project and made it more enjoyable, and I am thankful to them all.

Several generous friends and colleagues read and conversed with me on chapter drafts and the overall project. I am especially grateful to Michelle

Gonzalez Maldonado, Daniel Groody, CSC, Matt Kuczora, CSC, Nancy Pineda-Madrid, Tom Tweed, and Neto Valiente. In particular, Chris Tirres provided invaluable recommendations in our ongoing conversations about the scope and focus of the book. My very deep gratitude to Bill Taylor. Not only did I draw extensively from his lifetime of research and profound insight on religion and devotion in New Spain, but he graciously lent his expertise to a critical reading of the entire manuscript, in some cases a first and successive draft of the same chapter. And for bringing the manuscript to final publication and improving it in the process, I offer thanks to Theo Calderara and his colleagues at Oxford University Press and to Mary Reardon for her skillful preparation of the index.

I am also grateful to colleagues who provided expert guidance and assistance on the illustrations for the volume: Nadia Rodríguez Alatorre and Ilsse Odile Romero Mata of the Museo de la Basílica de Guadalupe in Mexico City; Maribel and Rachel Parroquín; Jason Bourgeois and Sarah Burke Cahalan of the Marian Library at the University of Dayton; Carlos Cortez of the UTSA Institute of Texan Cultures in San Antonio; and Erika Hosselkus, Natasha Lyandres, Sara Weber, and the late David Dressing of the University of Notre Dame Hesburgh Library and Rare Books and Special Collections. Artists Catherine Kwon and Anita Valencia graciously allowed that their creations be reprinted as illustrations. The Institute for Scholarship in the Liberal Arts within Notre Dame's College of Arts and Letters provided funding support for the reprints and for the volume index. Allison Collins, Patti Guzowski, and Melody Kesler helped gather and format the illustrations with the usual efficiency they lend to administrative matters in Notre Dame's Department of Theology. Finally, student research assistants at Notre Dame—Grace Girardot, Alma Marquez-Montero, Sasha Nakae, and Sadie Yates—performed admirable work that helped advance the research and the search for illustrations.

An earlier version of chapter 1 appeared as "Guadalupe at Calvary: Patristic Theology in Miguel Sánchez's *Imagen de la Virgen María* (1648)," *Theological Studies* 64 (December 2003): 795–811. Chapter 2 was published in an earlier form as "The First Guadalupan Pastoral Manual: Luis Laso de la Vega's *Huei tlamahuiçoltica* (1649)," *Horizons: Journal of the College Theology Society* 40 (December 2013): 159–177.

Introduction

EVERY COUNTRY IN Latin America and the Caribbean has a national
Marian patroness that served as a protagonist in the spread of Christianity.
The Dominican Republic's Our Lady of Altagracia (Highest Grace) is
recognized as "the first evangelizer of the Americas" since she is associated with the first place Spanish Catholics sought to spread their faith in
the New World. Others include Our Lady of Charity (la Caridad del Cobre)
in Cuba, Our Lady of Divine Providence in Puerto Rico, Our Lady of Luján
in Argentina, Our Lady of Suyapa in Honduras, and Our Lady of Peace in
El Salvador. Like the famous Marian shrine at Lourdes in France, various
prominent Latin American images are associated with the Immaculate
Conception, such as Our Lady of the Miracles of Caacupé of Paraguay, Our
Lady of Aparecida of Brazil, and Nicaragua's Our Lady of the Immaculate
Conception of El Viejo.

Yet Our Lady of Guadalupe is the only Marian apparition tradition in
the Americas—and indeed in all of Roman Catholicism—that inspired a
sustained series of published theological analyses. Theologians in each
successive epoch since the mid-seventeenth century have plumbed the
meaning of Guadalupe for their times. Their theological formulations are
grounded in two realities: the first is the relationship between Guadalupe
and her faithful, and the second is her power to shape their lives and their
world. The contemporary theologian Virgilio Elizondo has avowed that
"today devotion to Our Lady of Guadalupe continues to grow, to be explored,
and to be rediscovered. Our explanations do not make it powerful. It is
powerful because it lives in the minds and hearts of the people."[1] The primary purpose of *Theologies of Guadalupe* is to examine the way theologians
have understood Guadalupe and sought to orient her impact in the lives of
her devotees. Illuminating the foundation of those theological reflections,

this book also assesses the spread of Guadalupan devotion over nearly half a millennium as Guadalupe's faithful interacted with their loving mother and expanded the sphere of her influence.

Guadalupe emerged in New Spain as a living presence and patroness. From the Eurocentric perspective of the first Guadalupan theologians, she was a celestial protector who providentially defended the Spanish colonial enterprise and facilitated the Christian effort to convert native peoples to their religion. Their maximalist Marian theology placed Mary—the mother of Jesus Christ—at the center of a universal history of Christian salvation. But it also encouraged indigenous and other devotees to imagine Mary of Guadalupe as a powerful celestial being whose appearance in the New World signaled she was willing to advocate for her native sons and daughters. Intentionally or not, by the nineteenth-century era of Mexican independence the ideas the first Guadalupan theologians had expounded stirred their successors to deem Guadalupe the progenitor for the establishment of the Mexican nation. Guadalupe's acclaim as the emblem and conscience of the new republic led preachers to identify her more narrowly with the nation and its historical processes. Though they continued to accentuate Guadalupe's presence and power, their theological proclamations shifted the focus from the beneficent spread of European Christianity to a covenant with her chosen people of Mexico. These orators' insistence that Mexicans rejuvenate their nation subsequently resounded in theologies of Guadalupe that call for personal conversion and social change. However, theologians of the twentieth and early twenty-first centuries have cultivated yet another shift in the development of Guadalupan theologies. They tend to adopt the perspective of marginalized persons as their point of departure, often with the intent of eschewing the perceived Eurocentric and elite biases of their predecessors. Consequently their interpretations focus on Guadalupe's encounters and empowerment of the poor native Juan Diego as the hermeneutical key to understanding her transformative interventions in the lives of the lowly and the social injustices that afflict them.

The generations of Guadalupan theologians—along with numerous devotees—have contemplated the Guadalupe image, the narrative of her apparitions to Juan Diego, and testimonies of her miracles and her faithful's veneration. They meditate on these three sources of theological reflection—image, narrative, and devotion—as holy mysteries that unveil God's saving plan for them and their communities. From patristic-based theological writings in the colonial era down to contemporary formulations shaped by the emergence of liberation theologies in Latin America, the theologies under study here reveal how Christian concepts and scriptures initially imported from Europe developed in dynamic interaction with the new contexts in which they took root. The historical, scholarly, and theological background for this study illuminates the importance of Guadalupan theologies and the overall Guadalupe tradition for understanding the saga of Christian faith and theology in the Americas.

Historical and Scholarly Background

Debates about the documentary evidence for the 1531 Guadalupe apparitions to Juan Diego have in many instances overshadowed theological writings in Guadalupan studies. The first published account of the apparitions was in Miguel Sánchez's 1648 book *Imagen de la Virgen María*. However, many commentators and most devotees contend the foundational source for the apparition tradition is the Nahuatl-language *Nican mopohua* (a title derived from the document's first words, "here is recounted"), a parallel narrative first published in Luis Laso de la Vega's 1649 treatise *Huei tlamahuiçoltica* (By a great miracle). Both accounts relate Juan Diego's encounters with Guadalupe, who sent him to request that Juan de Zumárraga, the first bishop of Mexico, build her a temple on the hill of Tepeyac. At first the bishop doubted the celestial origins of this request, but he came to believe when Juan Diego presented him with exquisite flowers that were out of season and the image of Guadalupe miraculously appeared on the humble *indio*'s *tilma* (cloak). Though millions of devotees have an unwavering conviction in the historical veracity of this account, scholars have contested the issue for centuries. No one doubts that a shrine dedicated to Guadalupe at Tepeyac, originally situated north of Mexico City (though today within the domain of the since expanded metropolis), has been active since at least the mid-sixteenth century. The disagreement is whether the shrine or the apparition tradition came first. In other words, did reports of Juan Diego's miraculous encounters with Guadalupe initiate the shrine and its devotion, or is the apparition narrative a later invention that provided a mythical origin for an already existing image and pious tradition? Infrared photography, fiber analysis, and other "scientific" studies of the *tilma* are an important component of this debate, which most prominently resurfaced when Pope John Paul II canonized Juan Diego in 2002, renewing arguments about whether Juan Diego ever existed.

Well-known episodes from the controversy about the historicity of Juan Diego and the Guadalupe apparitions are briefly addressed in this current volume. But far greater attention is afforded to an equally vital historical question that is less frequently engaged: given the plentiful miraculous images of Christ, Mary, and the saints that dotted the sacred landscape of colonial Mexico, how did the Guadalupe cult rise above all others and emerge from a local devotion to become a regional, national, and then international phenomenon? Put in simplest terms, why Guadalupe? What were the historical circumstances, devotee motivations, and theological understandings that facilitated Guadalupe's rise to prominence? The *Nican mopohua* states that news of Guadalupe's miraculous presence on Juan Diego's *tilma* immediately attracted people from "everywhere" who came "to see and marvel at her precious image."[2] Extant primary sources and scholarship on the historical evolution of Guadalupan devotion, particularly the work of William B. Taylor, reveal a more measured, uneven growth. Taylor has documented nearly five hundred shrines and miraculous images in colonial New Spain. While most devotees and more than a few scholars anachronistically project Guadalupe's singular acclaim in contemporary times back into the sixteenth century, Taylor's work clearly demonstrates the need to situate Guadalupan devotion within the broad context of the numerous local and regional holy sites and images within which Guadalupe's eminence gradually emerged. Moreover, "these shrines are not all the same, and they did not amount to a network of sacred sites, hierarchically organized, with Tepeyac—the shrine of Our Lady of Guadalupe outside Mexico City—at the apex."[3]

Thus Taylor highlights the need to examine the rise of the Guadalupe tradition—its devotional expressions, visual representations, meanings, and miraculous manifestations—within the patterns of continuity and change that marked the sacred landscape of New Spain during the colonial era. Today the Guadalupe basilica is the most visited pilgrimage site on the American continent, with pilgrims journeying there from throughout the hemisphere and beyond. After Jesus of Nazareth, Guadalupe's image is the most reproduced sacred icon in the Americas. But the temptation to project her present distinction back into the past must be avoided at every turn. Only then can we appreciate more fully the various factors that eventually contributed to Guadalupe's protracted ascent, such as her multivocal appeal to diverse castes, the urban networks that linked other municipalities to the trend-setting center of Mexico City, the influence of sermons on the spread of the devotion, her later role in the formation of the

Mexican nation, and especially her devotees' multitudinous testimonies about her compassion and miraculous aid. Careful examination of such factors reveals that Guadalupe's national prominence evolved over the entire span of the colonial era and only reached full fruition after independence in the nineteenth century.

Similarly, Guadalupe was not the first holy figure from the New World who gained renown in the Old World. Reverence for Santa Rosa de Lima, a lay member of the Dominican order revered for her asceticism and her dedication to the sick and the poor, began during her lifetime and expanded after her death in 1617, five years before the completion of the first major church edifice dedicated to Guadalupe at Tepeyac. Santa Rosa became the first American-born person to be canonized a saint in 1671, garnering international eminence at the Vatican and elsewhere more than eighty years before Guadalupe was even declared the official patroness of New Spain, the viceroyalty in which she appeared. Guadalupe's rise to hemispheric and global prominence occurred still later, largely over the course of the twentieth century, culminating in her official designation as the patroness of America by the century's end.

No previous book has presented a history of published Guadalupan theologies within the broader context of the changing devotional and social worlds that shaped and were shaped by those theological discourses from the mid-seventeenth to the early twenty-first centuries. Nor has any single study examined Guadalupan devotion across the full range of that time span as it evolved from a local to a regional and then national and international phenomenon. David Brading's monumental work, *Mexican Phoenix: Our Lady of Guadalupe, Image and Tradition Across Five Centuries*, presents an intellectual history of the Guadalupe tradition that includes the major contributors to the debate about the historicity of the apparitions, as well as theological treatises, devotional histories, and sermons. Unlike a number of other historians who conclude their analyses with the close of the colonial era, Brading examines Guadalupan writings down to the present. He directs considerable attention to political history: court intrigues, power struggles, and shifting relations between church and state. His greatest innovation vis-à-vis the religious history of Guadalupan writings is to frame his analyses around the theology of images. He summarizes the debates over images from the first millennium down to the Reformation, a historical backdrop that sets the context for his exploration of the Guadalupe image in Mexico. Brading concludes that "as much as any icon, the Virgin of Tepeyac silently taught the truths of revelation as effectively as scripture since, like the gospels, the image was conceived through the inspiration of the Holy Spirit."[4] Yet Brading's primary focus is not the development of Guadalupan theologies, and he gives little attention to the concurrent evolution of Guadalupan devotion and the mutual influences among theological writings, pious practices, and visual representations.

Other scholars have examined Guadalupe from a range of disciplines and perspectives. In addition to the works of Taylor and Brading, historians' writings explore topics such as Guadalupe's formative role in the emergence of Mexican national consciousness, Guadalupe sermons, and Guadalupe in art.[5] Documentary collections present sources from the origins and development of the Guadalupe tradition, as well as key issues and topics such as Guadalupe and nationalism, culture, society, sanctuaries, and institutions.[6] Scholars of ethnographic and performance studies have examined elements of Guadalupan devotion such as pilgrimage, dance, the influence of feast-day celebrations on social hierarchies and collective identity in Mexican villages, and the transnational creation of sacred spaces.[7] Still other scholars have assessed Guadalupe through the lens of Chicana feminism, immigrant activism and integration, and types of religious experience.[8] And these are merely a sampling of the many books, essays, dissertations, and other investigations of Guadalupe as an historical, cultural, gendered, social, and religious phenomenon. But the array of multidisciplinary scholarship on Guadalupe has arisen only since the late twentieth century. This volume enriches the growing field of Guadalupan studies through its analysis of the foundation and development of the Guadalupe tradition, especially the theological writings that shaped the hermeneutical framework for that tradition for more than three centuries preceding the recent rise in Guadalupan scholarly interest.

Theologies of Guadalupe

Theologians are well represented within the contemporary surge in Guadalupan writings, producing more book-length investigations of Guadalupe since the 1980s than in the previous three centuries combined. Yet while many of these works examine Guadalupan devotion as a primary source for their inquiries, none of them treat comprehensively the historical evolution of Guadalupan devotion, and in fact a number of them presume that the pervasive veneration of Guadalupe today has been extant since the early colonial era. Moreover, rarely do these authors

examine the ways their contemporary interpretations enhance and contest the formulations of their predecessors. Indeed, most contemporary
theologians who examine Guadalupe do not cite the vast majority of their
forebears who composed treatises prior to the mid-twentieth century.

Theology is traditionally understood as "faith seeking understanding."
Though theological formulations are occasionally the starting point for
a believer who embraces faith, typically faith precedes theology. As Pope
Francis has often avowed, faith stems from an encounter: with believers,
with holy beings like Guadalupe, and for Christians ultimately with Jesus
Christ. Typically those who theologize have already had an encounter of
faith and are now seeking a deeper understanding of that encounter and
its implications. But this does not reduce faith to some private feeling
about ourselves and our relationship with God. Rather, believers see faith
as a fundamental relationship, received through a gift, with God, with the
saints, and with one another. Theology seeks to understand this gift through
an ongoing discernment that places contemporary experience in conversation with the long tradition of Christian thought and faith communities.
In the case of Guadalupe, amid the joys and pains that influenced their
daily lives, theologians and devotees have assessed their faith and their
Guadalupan encounters against the backdrop of the wider Catholic tradition. They have understood, affirmed, and contested Guadalupe's significance with appeals to that tradition: its iconic representations of celestial
beings; sacramental and devotional rites; proclamations on morality, justice, and human dignity; and biblical and theological teachings. They have,
as Orlando Espín has succinctly put it, engaged tradition as "an interpretation of the past, made in and for the present and in anticipation of an
imagined future."[9] Convinced that Guadalupe illuminates the mystery of
invisible realities that sustain their daily existence, they have sought to
understand those realities in light of their faith tradition and their relation
with their celestial mother.

Though rooted in a religious tradition that shapes and is shaped by the
lives of everyday believers, published theological analyses of Guadalupe
overwhelmingly derive from clerical and scholarly elites. While these same
elites frequently influence devotional culture, their efforts to do so are
contingent on developing collaborative relations with grassroots devotees.
Numerous pastors who sought to alter treasured local images or customs
in New Spain and later Mexico have encountered stern resistance from the
communities they were charged to serve. More than a few met physical
opposition or expulsion from the community. The most common means

of devotees' influence is their level of support for clerical attempts to en-shrine new sacred images or promote particular devotional expressions. Moreover, devotees' collective behavior, as well as their initiatives and those of artists, regularly shape devotional practices and their meanings as profoundly as the ministrations of priests and the writings of theologians. In some cases, their initiatives also shape published theological discourse. For example, artistic renderings of holy figures like Guadalupe are not solely employed to illustrate textual claims. Rather, as the insightful works of scholars such at Jaime Cuadriello and Jeanette Peterson have demonstrated, in many cases popular and professional artists visually posit their own claims about faith and the divine.[10] The Guadalupe *tilma* clearly illustrates the influence of the visual on the textual, as it has been both examined as a primary source for written theological analyses and artistically engaged as a theological expression itself.

Seen in this light, *Theologies of Guadalupe* complements my earlier work, *Guadalupe and Her Faithful: Latino Catholics in San Antonio, from Colonial Origins to the Present*,[11] to date the only volume that explores Guadalupan devotion in a single faith community from Spanish colonial times into the twenty-first century. That earlier work focuses primarily on San Fernando Cathedral in San Antonio, Texas, a parish community that for nearly three centuries has sustained its Guadalupan devotion. The study of San Fernando parishioners' devotion to Guadalupe accentuates the interconnections between faith expressions and the social constructions, cultural horizons, and bodily existence of their practitioners. Most impor-tantly, in addition to describing religious traditions, that previous volume also probes the theological worldview that underlies them. Amid the often harsh realities that influenced their daily lives—drought, conflicts with Native Americans, changes of national government, poverty, racism, exile, family discord, social hierarchies, and struggles for their own dignity and advancement, to name but a few—Guadalupan devotees at San Fernando consistently assessed their situation against the backdrop of their Catholic faith. In this way everyday devotees engaged in theology—faith seeking understanding—through their conversations, veneration of holy images, prayers, and personal reflections. The attempt in *Guadalupe and Her Faithful* to uncover local Guadalupan theologies in individual reflections and collective behavior illuminates the most pervasive but often unac-knowledged form of theological reflection: that of everyday believers. *Theologies of Guadalupe* examines the writings of believers trained in the-ology and consciously engaged in theological analysis of a faith tradition.

It extends the analysis of *Guadalupe and Her Faithful* through a study of published theologies within the context of their dynamic interplay with their social world and the evolution of Guadalupan devotion.

Scholarly efforts to retrieve written theological works produced in the Americas have expanded since the 1990s. For example, within my own area of specialization, Latino Catholicism, writers who have sought to re-cover such theologies from the colonial era include Luis Rivera Pagán on the sixteenth-century theological debates about the evangelization of the New World; Gustavo Gutiérrez on the famed defender of the native peo-ples, Bartolomé de las Casas; Alejandro García-Rivera on the mulatto saint of the poor, Martín de Porres; Claudio Burgaleta on the missionary and naturalist José de Acosta; and Michelle Gonzalez and Theresa A. Yugar on the self-taught New Spain intellectual and poet Sor Juana Inés de la Cruz.[12] Latina and Latino scholars have also begun to critically examine hemi-spheric trends in theology and religious studies, such as Alex Nava's explo-ration of the sense of wonder and displacement that spans five centuries of exploration, conquest, intermingling of peoples, and literary output in the New World; Michelle Gonzalez's analysis of religious studies and liberation theology discourse on religion in the Americas; and Christopher Tirres's comparative study of pragmatists and Latino/a liberationist theologians.[13] As Gonzalez explains, "the *ressourcement* movement in twentieth-century Roman Catholic theology was an appeal for theologians to return to histor-ical sources to inform contemporary understandings." This does not mean merely examining ancient sources in their historical context, but rather "a revival of historical sources" that enables a critical engagement between past formulations and present realities.[14] Thus, just as renewed study of the church fathers was a key intellectual precursor to the Second Vatican Council (1962–1965) within the Roman Catholic Church, the *ressourcement* of theological works such as those of Latinos is a crucial step in the project of developing theologies that are rooted both in the wider Christian tradi-tion and in the life, faith, and struggles of communities on the American continent.

Yet studies like those just mentioned overwhelmingly tend to examine select figures from the early colonial era, particularly those deemed to have a liberationist bent. Ample scholarly investigation is also given to the rise of liberation theologies over the past half century, but there is comparatively scant attention given to the intervening centuries. A few scholars have attempted a more comprehensive history of theology in Latin America, such as the collaborative project of the Comisión para el

Estudio de la Historia de la Iglesia en Latinoamerica, which resulted in a book that Pablo Richard edited, and an ensuing and also collaborative project led by Josep-Ignasi Saranyana, the director of the Institute of Church History at the University of Navarre in Pamplona, Spain.[15]

Significantly, the centuries-long lacuna in most scholarship on Latin American theology omits analyses of what could be considered some of the most problematic constructions in the overall history, such as theologians whose works buttressed colonial rule or those whose writings linked biblical revelation with narrow articulations of nationalism during the rise of Latin American nation states. At the same time, this lacuna obscures theological insights that can enhance the contemporary project of *ressourcement*. This can leave the unintended impression that the sole purpose of historical recovery is to find "usable" exemplars from the past to bolster positions taken in current debates, rather than to learn what our ancestors can teach us from their responses to the world they inhabited. Since all theological formulations have both strengths and weaknesses vis-à-vis their articulations of a vision for a life based on Christian tradition, a more comprehensive attempt to recover Latin American theologies enriches our knowledge of how the Christian tradition can be manipulated and coopted, as well as how it offers resources for human flourishing and deepening faith. The specific strengths and weaknesses of any given formulation are a matter of debate, of course, including whose interests are reflected and served in those formulations. But the consideration of theological constructions across generations provides a richer opportunity to learn from our forebears in faith and theology. *Theologies of Guadalupe* addresses the lacuna in Latin American theological studies through its presentation of the first book-length examination of Guadalupan theologies from the colonial era to the present.

Plan of Work

Collectively the chapters that follow examine chronologically major developments in the theological and devotional trajectory of the Guadalupe tradition within the shifting historical context in which they were enacted. Though the Guadalupe tradition is presented throughout as complex and multilayered, each chapter highlights a primary theme from theological reflection on Guadalupe's presence and capacity to shape devotees' lives. The initial two chapters explore the first published writings on Guadalupe, those of Sánchez and Laso de la Vega. These two priests and the devotional tradition on which they sought to reflect laid the foundation for Guadalupan theologies, Sánchez with his engagement of early church theologians and the theme of salvation history and Laso de la Vega with his treatise on Guadalupe and the evangelization of native peoples. The remaining chapters successively examine the colonial, independence, and contemporary periods and the shifts in the understanding of Guadalupe's meaning and impact in these eras, from divine providence to covenant to personal and social transformation. Not surprisingly, theologians and devotees did not all endorse these themes to the same degree, and some even contested them or accentuated other interpretations. But the themes presented are arguably the most significant understandings of Guadalupe in a particular foundational work or time period. Critical exposition and analysis of primary theological sources—books, published sermons, essays, devotional expressions, and artistic works—as well as secondary sources on devotional, art, and social history provide the basis for presenting the evolution of the Guadalupe tradition in relation to the changing historical context. The influence of the foundational works of Laso de la Vega and especially Sánchez on subsequent authors and eras is explored. Throughout the book illustrations present artistic expressions of Guadalupe's significance and theological meaning. Each chapter concludes with analysis of the core insights and weaknesses of Guadalupan theology in the historical work or era under consideration, as well as links between that theology and contemporaneous developments in Guadalupan art and devotion.

The first chapter assesses Sánchez's *Imagen de la Virgen María* as well as the origins and formative phase of Guadalupan devotion. A local devotion to Guadalupe in Mexico City and the communities surrounding it had developed over the century preceding the volume of Sánchez, a learned and respected Mexico City priest. Sánchez's intent was to provide a theological foundation for this pious tradition. Yet the earliest interpreters of his work focused narrowly on its place in documenting the origins of belief in the Guadalupe apparitions. Later analysts linked *Imagen de la Virgen María* to Sánchez's patriotic pride that Guadalupe appeared on the American continent of his birth. Such readings of Sánchez occlude his principal purpose of illuminating the Guadalupe tradition through the lens of the premier sources of Christian revelation, especially the Bible and the writings of Saint Augustine and other church fathers. Sánchez addressed a fundamental issue: the place of the Guadalupe event and, more broadly, the Spanish encounter with the peoples of the American continent in salvation history. This chapter illuminates the influence of patristic thought and theological methods on Sánchez, as well as the frequently ignored but foundational role of his theology and that of the church fathers on the Guadalupe tradition.

Laso de la Vega was also a Mexico City priest. He served as vicar at the Guadalupe sanctuary and was among the first readers of *Imagen de la Virgen María*, acknowledging its influence on him and his *Huei tlamahuiçoltica*. His publication was one of many writings composed to enhance the evangelization of native peoples, and the first to focus on engaging Guadalupe in such an apostolic endeavor. A number of scholarly analyses have examined the *Nican mopohua* first published in *Huei tlamahuiçoltica*. Yet no previous scholar has presented a theological evaluation of Laso de la Vega's work as a whole, despite its importance for understanding Guadalupan evangelization efforts, particularly among Nahua natives. By the time Laso de la Vega published his treatise, the Nahuas had already been under the rule of the Spanish newcomers for over a century. But the natives' capacity to shape the practice of the Catholic faith propagated among them was greater than is often acknowledged. Their participation in Guadalupan devotion since its inception illustrates this capacity. Chapter 2 treats Laso de la Vega's pastoral treatise within the context of the early evolution of natives' devotion and their response to Christian evangelization efforts. *Huei tlamahuiçoltica* provided Laso de la Vega's fellow pastors with Nahuatl-language pastoral aids for their ministrations. A close reading of the treatise reveals the ways European missioners sought to ground Christian faith in the everyday realities of natives' lives, as well as the limitations of their evangelizing initiatives. Like *Imagen de la Virgen María*, the theological issues raised in *Huei tlamahuiçoltica* had an enduring resonance in theological analyses, as well as on pastoral initiatives related to Guadalupe. In particular, Laso de la Vega and many pastors since have urged that devotees relate to Guadalupe not only as a means to gain heavenly favors but also as a way to grow in faith and Christian life.

Colonial preachers developed the foundational concerns of Laso de la Vega and especially Sánchez during the century and a half following their publications. The preachers also introduced new theological perspectives on Guadalupe as liturgical celebrations in her honor proliferated and received papal approbation. By the mid-eighteenth century, the considerable growth of Guadalupan devotion and her celebrated intervention in the alleviation of a severe epidemic led to her official designation as the patroness of New Spain. Preachers played a major role in the expanding devotion and its significance, as sermons had a formative impact not only on Christian believers but also on colonial society. Though his full corpus of Guadalupan writings has not been examined in previous inquiries, no colonial Guadalupan preacher was more influential than Bartolomé Felipe de Ita y Parra, a native of Puebla who became an influential priest and preacher in Mexico City during the first half of the eighteenth century. Ita y Parra delivered four published Guadalupan sermons from 1731 to 1746, a crucial period in Guadalupe's ascent as the most widely venerated holy image in the viceroyalty. His orations illustrate the theological claims articulated in colonial sermons like those dedicated to Guadalupe, especially the central claim that divine providence guided society and its inhabitants. Such claims tended to sanctify extant social hierarchies and the general social order. But for numerous devotees living the fragile existence of colonial life, patron saints like Guadalupe embodied in a deeply relational way the support of celestial protectors who watched over them and could transform their life situation. Chapter 3 examines the theological concept of divine providence through the lens of Guadalupan devotion and the sermonic discourse of Ita y Parra.

The succeeding chapter documents the continuing rise of Guadalupan devotion, including an unprecedented increase among native peoples, as well as the conflicting appeals to Guadalupe's aid among insurgents and royalists who combated during the nineteenth-century war of Mexican independence. Preachers on opposing sides even stated unequivocally that Guadalupe allied her power with their respective causes, and insurgent priests as well as crown loyalists led troops who fought under Guadalupe's banner and attributed their victories in battle to her. As in the colonial era, sermons were the major source for Guadalupan theologies before and after independence. Guadalupe's strong association with national identity led many interpreters to emphasize that her appearance in their land established a singular election of Mexico as her chosen nation. Preachers addressed a variety of national concerns through allusions to biblical notions of covenant, avowing that Guadalupe had established a pact with the Mexican people in similar fashion to God's covenants with Noah, David, and especially Moses and the people of Israel. While no single figure stands out as the predominant theologian of Guadalupe during this period, a number of nineteenth-century Guadalupan preachers addressed the theme of covenant as Mexicans won their independence, struggled to establish a new nation, and mounted a successful campaign for papal authorization of a Guadalupe coronation. Their theological discourse and the widespread devotion to Guadalupe as Mexico's national symbol encapsulate the strengths and limitations of engaging Guadalupe through the biblical lens of covenant.

Guadalupan devotion has expanded well beyond the bounds of Mexico over the course of the twentieth and early twenty-first centuries. Devotees have dedicated shrines and churches to her in numerous countries and on every continent. Her image has also proliferated globally. Even believers from other religions and those who profess no religion have been attracted to Guadalupe. Theological analyses have expanded in conjunction with her growing acclaim. So too has the range of Guadalupan interpreters, which now includes significant numbers of women, laity, and persons from beyond Mexico. Responding to the increasing consciousness of injustice and poverty and the advance of popular movements for social change, over the past half century Guadalupan writers have addressed Guadalupe's prophetic call to personal and social transformations grounded in the struggles of groups such as marginalized persons, women, and everyday believers who all are called to be agents of evangelization. In sharp contrast to the presumption of the first Guadalupan theologians that Guadalupe abetted the Spanish colonial enterprise, today Guadalupe is frequently associated with the efforts to overcome the negative effects of the conquest of the Americas as well as the hope for a new future of greater justice and conversion. For the first time theologians have examined Juan Diego as a protagonist in the struggle of oppressed peoples for survival and dignity. The final chapter of the book examines these new trends in Guadalupan theologies and devotion, with concluding thoughts about the trajectory these trends present for the future of the Guadalupe tradition.

In her study of Guadalupe in the lives of Mexican American women, the contemporary theologian Jeanette Rodriguez writes that when she asked an indigenous woman in Mexico what makes Guadalupe different from other images of Mary, the woman simply responded "se quedó" (she stayed).[16] Like this woman, numerous devotees have been attracted to Guadalupe because they see her as a loving mother who has ever accompanied and defended them and their people. Theologians across the centuries have sought to comprehend that potent presence and its significance for the lives of devotees and the societies they inhabit and construct. My hope for this volume is that it will enable readers to grasp more fully the evolution and the importance of that theological and devotional trajectory.

PART I

Foundational Works

The New World in Salvation History

MIGUEL SÁNCHEZ'S *IMAGEN DE LA VIRGEN MARÍA* (1648)

DEVOTION TO OUR Lady of Guadalupe on the hill of Tepeyac progressively grew in stature within the vicinity of Mexico City during the century before Miguel Sánchez penned his 1648 work *Imagen de la Virgen María*.[1] Sánchez avowed that his book was intended to provide a theological foundation for this local tradition. Yet readings of Sánchez's work have tended to encompass positivist condemnations for his lack of historical documentation about the Guadalupe apparitions or, conversely, laudatory praise for his defense of that pious tradition. Beginning in the mid-twentieth century, a new interpretation of *Imagen de la Virgen María* stressed his patriotism as expressed through his adulation of Guadalupe and the baroque culture of New Spain. These interpreters underscored Sánchez's background as a *criollo*, a technical designation in the Spanish caste system for persons of Spanish blood born in the New World, a term that over time was employed more broadly to encompass other American-born Spanish subjects.[2] Rarely do readers of Sánchez accentuate that he was a pastor and theologian renowned for his knowledge of Saint Augustine and other church fathers. Nor do they emphasize that the primary focus of *Imagen de la Virgen María* was to examine the Guadalupe narrative, image, and devotion within the context of the evangelization of Mexico and the wider Christian tradition, particularly the patristic writers and the biblical image of the "woman clothed with the sun" in Revelation 12.

Imagen de la Virgen María employed a European worldview to address the encounter and clash between the inhabitants of two continents previously unknown to one another. These encounters had set off intense debates in sixteenth-century Spain. Attempts to legitimize or protest military conquest on religious grounds were only one major concern of these arguments, as opponents contested issues such as slavery, sin, sacramental absolution, the autonomy of native peoples and nations, indigenous religions, and the humanity of the natives they confronted in the Americas.[3] Sánchez did not explicitly refer to any of the sixteenth-century debates in his volume, but his understanding of native inhabitants and their pre-Columbian history clearly reflects these debates' broad Eurocentric presuppositions. Deeply rooted in the conviction that the Christian scriptures were the only source that could unlock the hidden meaning of momentous human events, Sánchez followed his theological contemporaries in presenting a decidedly Eurocentric interpretation of the Spanish imperial project and its place in world history, which for Sánchez was equivalent to salvation history. Consistent with other colonial works like figure 1.1, his book set an enduring pattern of engaging Old World sacred texts and theological discourse to examine Guadalupe as a New World chapter in the spread of Christianity.

Miguel Sánchez studied at the Royal and Pontifical University in Mexico City and was a diocesan priest—that is, a clergyman who was not a member of a religious order but rather under the obedience of a bishop in a specified ecclesiastical territory called a diocese. Though his efforts to secure a teaching position at the university were unsuccessful, he was respected for his learning and preaching. He was also a member of the Congregación de San Pedro (Congregation of Saint Peter), an association of diocesan priests with whom he participated in religious, civil, academic, and other public celebrations in Mexico City. When he joined a community of Oratorians (the Oratory of Saint Philip Neri) in 1662 he was serving as chaplain of the sanctuary near Mexico City dedicated to Nuestra Señora de los Remedios (Our Lady of Remedies), the Spanish Virgin whose image Hernán Cortés and his men brought as their protector and patroness in the conquest of Mexico. Subsequently Sánchez retired to the Guadalupe shrine, where he lived a quiet life of prayer until his death and celebratory funeral.[4] At his own request he was laid to rest "in the Holy Chapel of Our Lady of Guadalupe," specifying that he did not mean the new church edifice blessed in 1622 but, rather, "the old one, that of the natives." He stated that he made this request "because, from my first having the use of reason I have had tender devotion, affection, and yearning for that holy place." His last will and testament also made provision for the continued adornment of the Guadalupe chapel.[5]

FIGURE I.I. Anonymous, *Virgen de Guadalupe con San Miguel arcángel como atlante*, second half of 18th century. The depiction of Guadalupe and Juan Diego amid details like God the Father in the upper right, Christ with the cross in the upper left, the dove representing the Holy Spirit above the Guadalupe image, the twelve apostles at the bottom with the keys of Saint Peter in the lower right, and angelic figures throughout underscore the conviction that Guadalupe propagated Christianity in the New World. Courtesy Archivo del Museo de la Basílica de Guadalupe.

Sánchez's known publications include several sermons, an account of the procession and ceremony to renew the oath to defend the doctrine of the Immaculate Conception at his alma mater, and a Marian novena (nine days of devotions) designed for prayer at the sanctuaries of both Our Lady of los Remedios and Our Lady of Guadalupe.

The full title of his major work was *Imagen de la Virgen María, Madre de Dios de Guadalupe: Milagrosamente aparecida en la ciudad de México; Celebrada en su historia, con la profecía del capítulo doce del Apocalipsis* (Image of the Virgin Mary, Mother of God of Guadalupe: Miraculously appeared in the city of Mexico; Celebrated in her history, with the prophecy of chapter twelve of the Apocalypse). This book won Sánchez acclaim as the first of four authors whose seventeenth-century writings led to their recognition as the Guadalupan "evangelists." Luis Laso de la Vega's *Huei tlamahuiçoltica* (1649) was followed by two works renowned for arguing the historical foundation of the Guadalupe apparition tradition: Luis Becerra Tanco's 1675 *Felicidad de México* (Felicity of Mexico) and the Jesuit Francisco de Florencia's 1688 *La estrella del norte de México* (Polestar of Mexico).[6] Though the latter two works were more widely cited during the colonial era, particularly among preachers and writers who wanted to underscore the historical foundations of the Guadalupe apparitions and tradition, Sánchez's volume shaped theologies of Guadalupe more than any other publication.

Imagen de la Virgen María was both the first published theology of Our Lady of Guadalupe and the first published account of Guadalupe's apparitions to Juan Diego. As such it merits critical examination within the context of the evolving devotion to Guadalupe, as well as the contested status of the Guadalupe apparitions in the genesis of that devotion. The reading of Sánchez's volume as a *criollo* patriotic oration also merits further scrutiny. But most of all *Imagen de la Virgen María* needs to be assessed from the perspective which its author himself intended, that of theology. An erudite and somewhat convoluted treatise primarily intended for the clergy and other learned readers of Mexico City, the book was abbreviated to a more popular version in a 1660 volume by the Jesuit Mateo de la Cruz: *Relación de la milagrosa aparición de la santa imagen de la Virgen de Guadalupe de México* (Relation of the miraculous apparition of the holy image of the Virgin of Guadalupe of Mexico).[7] The extensive influence of Sánchez's *Imagen de la Virgen María* on the Guadalupe tradition stems both from the appeal of de la Cruz's condensed volume and Sánchez's direct influence on prominent New Spain clergy and other *criollos*. Recognizing the scriptural and patristic influences on Sánchez is essential for understanding the foundational role of these premier Christian sources on his theology and its subsequent impact on the evolution of the Guadalupe tradition.

An Evolving Local Devotion

Depositions from a 1556 investigation into a controversial oration are the first uncontested primary sources that illuminate devotion to Guadalupe at Tepeyac. Fray Francisco de Bustamante's sermon on the feast of the Nativity of the Virgin Mary criticized the Mexico City archbishop Alonso de Montúfar for promoting Guadalupan devotion. Bustamante feared such devotion would induce indigenous neophytes to offer Guadalupe worship that in Christian belief is solely rendered to God, or induce them to abandon or waver in the Christian faith if their pleas to her for help went unanswered. Though the investigation Archbishop Montúfar ordered resulted in no punitive action, the nine witnesses who testified illuminated the contours of Guadalupan devotion. Favorably comparing Guadalupan devotion to that of Nuestra Señora de Atocha in Madrid and Nuestra Señora de Prado in Valladolid, Spain, one crown official stated that he had been to the Guadalupe chapel "many times," heard of the miracles that occurred there, and observed how visits to this sacred site had replaced more frivolous and "illicit pleasures" among the residents of Mexico City. A lawyer related that he had seen a number of people enter the chapel "with great devotion, many of them [proceeding] on their knees from the door to the altar where the blessed image of Our Lady of Guadalupe is located." He also noted that the stream of women and men, the healthy and the infirm who went from Mexico City to pray, attend Mass, and hear sermons at the shrine was so continuous it induced young children to "agitate [their elders] to take them there." Another witness urged that the Guadalupan cult be further promoted since "in this land there is no other devotion so celebrated, to which the people have offered so much fervor." The final interviewee testified that he had been to the chapel more than twenty times and his young daughter was cured of a bad cough after he prayed with her there. He also added that Bustamante's sermon "had not stopped the devotion, but rather it had increased even more" in the weeks following his oration.[8]

Subsequent sixteenth-century sources attested to further claims of miraculous cures, testimonies that of course are typically integral to the growing aura of holy sites and images. A 1575 letter of Viceroy Martín Enríquez to the Spanish king Felipe II stated that the chapel at Tepeyac emerged from the claim of a herdsman that he "had recovered his health" when he visited the Guadalupe image in an original hermitage on the site. One of Hernán Cortés' soldiers, Bernal Díaz del Castillo, noted in his chronicle of the conquest that at Tepeyac one can "observe the holy miracles which she [Our Lady of Guadalupe] has performed and is still doing every day." Similarly, the 1589 historical chronicle of Juan Suárez de Peralta observed that Our Lady of Guadalupe has "produced many miracles." Guadalupe's reputation for miracles was also evident in the first known Guadalupe painting that copies the original. The 1606 work of Spanish-born Baltasar de Echave Orio, who was widely regarded as the most prestigious artist in New Spain at the time, depicts both the image and the cloth of the *tilma* on which it appears, suggesting that the cloth itself was considered a relic. Indeed, as the art historian Jeanette Peterson has noted, the painting "replicates the model's [the original Guadalupe image's] proportions with scrupulous care, going so far as to simulate the sewn panels of the *tilma* painting." The inclusion in this painting of Juan Diego's cloak on which the image of Guadalupe is believed to have miraculously appeared has led historians to infer that for at least some early devotees the *tilma* was "as much the object of veneration as the image."[9]

Devotees propagated the Guadalupe cult through their patronage of new facilities and construction projects. Increased involvement of archdiocesan authorities in the development and oversight of the Tepeyac shrine enhanced such efforts. The Mexico City archbishop Juan Pérez de la Serna sponsored the initiative to enlarge the road from the city to Tepeyac. By the 1620s *casas de novenarios*—accommodations for devotees who came to complete nine consecutive days of prayer at the shrine—were operative.[10] Construction efforts reached a high point with the completion and 1622 dedication of a more imposing Guadalupe church built in proximity to the original chapel constructed on the site. In the wake of Guadalupe's acclaim for providing relief from a devastating Mexico City flood during 1629 to 1634, a Mexico City devotee, Magdalena Pérez de Viveros, donated an impressive new altarpiece that was installed at the church in 1637.[11]

Nonetheless, indicators such as the dispersal of copies of the Guadalupe image suggest the devotion evolved only gradually. Most early residents of New Spain, especially the native peoples, came to know Guadalupe through word of mouth and visual representation. Peterson rightly contends that "to appreciate more fully the impact of Guadalupe's imaging, we must take into account the central role of images in cultures where low literacy rates and language barriers made oral and pictorial communication essential." Thus it is significant that the only known image that is a possible Guadalupe replica from the

sixteenth century is a silver statue Alonso de Villaseca donated to the
Guadalupe shrine in 1566; though available sources do not indicate
whether the image was of Guadalupe or another Marian figure, scholars
such as Peterson presume the statue was Guadalupan. The first extant
painting that replicated the revered Guadalupe image was the Echave
Orio work, which was not produced until the early seventeenth century.
Samuel Stradanus, a Flemish artist and New Spain resident, made an
engraving (c. 1613–1615) that depicts the Guadalupe image surrounded
by eight scenes of miracles that devotees attributed to her, apparently drawn from supplicants' testimonies or from ex-votos they had
enshrined at the Guadalupe chapel (see p. 73). Promoters distributed
prints from this plate as part of a fundraising campaign for the new
Guadalupe church.[12] Reproductions of Guadalupe's image became more
widespread around Mexico City after devotees acclaimed her intervention during the 1629–1634 floods. However, the ecclesiastical council of
the cathedral deemed many of these copies of "inferior quality," issued
a 1637 edict establishing norms for future likenesses of the image, and
announced their intention to confiscate existing copies they judged to
be defective. Moreover, the geographic range for the distribution of such
images was largely confined to the Mexico City area.[13]

The measured growth of Guadalupan devotion is confirmed in other
sources. In 1574 Diego de Santa María, a Hieronymite friar from the popular shrine of Our Lady of Guadalupe in Extremadura, Spain, visited the
Tepeyac Guadalupe sanctuary to investigate why its caretakers had not
deemed it a "satellite" shrine and paid a portion of the alms received to the
more ancient Guadalupe establishment of his religious order. While his
financial concern suggests a growing prominence of the Tepeyac chapel,
he also opined that "it is not decorated and the building is very poor" and
predicted that "divine worship and the service of God [there] cannot increase."[14] The following year Viceroy Enríquez noted that a Guadalupe
cofradía (confraternity or pious society) associated with Tepeyac reportedly had four hundred members who supported the shrine and provided dowries for orphaned girls. But he did not deem the influence of
the Guadalupe cult sufficiently widespread to merit the establishment of
a monastery or even a parish church on the site, recommending that a
priest appointed as chaplain of the shrine would suffice.[15] The ebb and
flow of financial contributions to the Guadalupe shrine further reveals
an ongoing but uneven evolution of Guadalupan devotion. Moreover, by
all indications devotees were overwhelmingly residents from Mexico City

and native communities in the immediate vicinity, a pattern of primarily local patronage that continued for at least a century after the devotion's genesis.[16]

The limited geographic range of Guadalupan devotion is consistent with other religious traditions that emerged in the Spanish colonial period. Jennifer Hughes's study of the Cristo Aparecido (Christ Appeared), a graphic carved image of the crucified Christ enshrined in the Mexican village of Totolapan, narrates the emergence of a local devotion to the Cristo after its initial "appearance" in 1543, when a mysterious Indian visitor presented it to Augustinian friar Antonio de Roa. Similarly, María Elena Díaz and Jalane Schmidt recount the early stages of devotion to Our Lady of Charity, Cuba's national patroness, among seventeenth-century slaves in the mining settlement of El Cobre. The local character of such traditions in the New World reflected established patterns of religious life on the Iberian Peninsula, as William Christian has shown in his studies of religion in late medieval and Renaissance Spain. Christian summarizes one mid-seventeenth-century inventory that listed 182 Marian shrines in Catalonia alone. Apparition narratives tended to be transmitted through local oral traditions, such as one apparition "in a Segovian village around 1490 [that] was quite fresh when recounted to an ecclesiastical investigator over 120 years later." Christian's conclusion that such apparitions were "predominantly rural events" with a circumscribed sphere of influence is consistent with analyses of religious phenomena in the Spanish colonies of the New World. In the early colonial period, patterns of local and regional devotion inhibited the cult of Guadalupe or any single image from ascending above all others in the viceroyalty.[17]

Indeed, as William Taylor has shown, Guadalupe's ascent as the premier holy image in Mexico evolved over centuries. Presumptions that her current renown stems from a spontaneous sixteenth-century eruption of devotion that encompassed all of New Spain are unsubstantiated. Distant pilgrimages to Tepeyac increased in the late nineteenth century in tandem with the advent of the railroad, but through the colonial era the difficulty of travel, government regulation of people's movement from place to place, and the focus on local and regional religious centers of devotion deterred such pilgrimages. Moreover, notwithstanding evidence of local devotion to the Guadalupe *tilma* as a sacred object, religious sensibilities of the era made little distinction between the miraculous qualities of such original sacred objects and copies of them venerated in a local church or sanctuary. Ultimately "the catchment area of practiced belief in divine presence through the Guadalupan image [both reproductions and the original] was far greater than the attraction of the Tepeyac shrine." Taylor's meticulous mapping of holy images and shrines during the colonial era charts the rise to prominence of both the Guadalupe image and Tepeyac:

> While the image of the Virgin of Guadalupe became the most widely known object of faith in New Spain by the late eighteenth century, before the mid-nineteenth century Tepeyac . . . was not much more appealing beyond its vicinity than were eight or nine shrines to other miraculous images, not to mention the hundreds of shrines to yet other images of Mary and Christ that were regarded as essential to the well-being of people living nearby [each particular image].[18]

Even within the local area of Mexico City, during the sixteenth and seventeenth centuries Guadalupe was but one among many pious invocations and practices. Taylor's documentation of shrines and miraculous images in colonial New Spain includes fifty-five Marian images and forty-nine of Christ or the cross in Mexico City and the environs. Moreover, Our Lady of los Remedios enjoyed precedence over Guadalupe in the capital. A shrine in her honor was located in a settlement called Naucalpan about ten miles northwest of Mexico City. According to tradition, one of Cortés' soldiers left a small image of Remedios at Totoltepec during the *noche triste* (sad night) after the natives defeated them in battle. Devotees built a small chapel there when the image was rediscovered in the mid-sixteenth century. While the Guadalupe image continued to be housed in a modest chapel at Tepeyac until the following century, in 1574 municipal officials of Mexico City received the king's permission to exercise patronage over the Remedios shrine. Subsequently members of the city council provided the funding for a new and larger church structure. They also oversaw its maintenance, served as officers for the Our Lady of los Remedios *archicofradía* (archconfraternity), sponsored the annual Remedios feast day, organized periodic processions of the Remedios image from the shrine to the Mexico City cathedral, and in general promoted the devotion. Consequently the Remedios shrine had greater revenue and more furnishings than its Guadalupan counterpart.[19]

Devotion to Remedios was also more conspicuously prevalent among the general populace of Mexico City. Civil and ecclesiastical records pertaining to a deadly outbreak of *matlazahuatl*[20] in 1576 state the devout in Mexico City and its environs called on Remedios for protection, but those same sources do not mention appeals to Guadalupe to alleviate the epidemic. Remedios was accredited with ending the contagion, as well as with halting a drought two decades later, an occasion when once again Mexico City residents apparently did not collectively invoke Guadalupe in their hour of need.[21] A 1621 petition to the city council summarized Remedios's stature with the observation that "one finds in this [her] shrine more devotion and feeling than in any other."[22]

The Mercedarian friar Luis de Cisneros's history of the image of Our Lady of los Remedios in Mexico, the first devotional history of a Mexican holy site, documented her prominence as an intercessor. Published posthumously in Mexico City in 1621, just as the new Guadalupe church was nearing completion at Tepeyac, Cisneros's book surveyed the development of multiple pious traditions among New Spain devotees and what some analysts have exaggeratingly deemed a pitched rivalry between the Spanish Remedios and the Mexican Guadalupe. While Cisneros stated that Guadalupe was the oldest Marian sanctuary in New Spain, he also enumerated the various Marian images that received significant veneration. Moreover, given his primary focus on Remedios, his work recounted her many favors to her devotees, such as a heavy rain in 1616 Mexico City that occurred following a citywide invocation of her intercession to end a drought.[23] Overall, extant records suggest that devotees in the Mexico City area invoked Remedios more often than Guadalupe for over a century after the traditional 1531 date for the Guadalupe apparitions. Their preference for Remedios was due in part to her association with help during droughts, as well as during epidemics and in meeting other communal needs, while typically they called on Guadalupe for relief from the less frequent occurrence of floods.[24]

Even when the Guadalupe image was brought from Tepeyac to the Mexico City cathedral to combat the 1629–1634 flood—an occasion that scholars such as Jacques Lafaye assert was pivotal in Guadalupe's rise to eminence over other celestial patrons of the city—Guadalupe's "triumph" over other holy images invoked during this disaster was by no means absolute. The procession of the Guadalupe image to the cathedral was the only time it has ever been publicly removed from Tepeyac, yet the Guadalupe novena at the cathedral did not bring immediate relief from the flood. Furthermore, devotees were not unanimous in acclaiming Guadalupe as the guardian who ended the flood, as some observers at least partially attributed the celestial aid received to a Marian invocation other than Guadalupe or to saints such as Saint Dominic or Saint Catherine.[25]

The publication of Sánchez's 1648 book abetted the growth of a devotion that at the time was gradually evolving in stature but still largely confined to the immediate Mexico City area. As we shall see in chapter 3, after *Imagen de la Virgen María* was released Guadalupe shrines and church edifices, artistic representations, feast day celebrations, and sermons increased and expanded to various locales beyond the capital vicinity. Sánchez's codification of the Guadalupe tradition provided the theological foundation on which subsequent ecclesial leaders, preachers, artists, and devotees extended the veneration of Guadalupe.

The Apparition Tradition

While a local devotion to Guadalupe at Tepeyac was evident from at least the mid-sixteenth century, Sánchez was the first to publish an account of the Guadalupe apparitions to Juan Diego as the originating event in the devotion. A number of sixteenth-century sources make no reference to the Guadalupe apparition tradition, such as the decrees of the bishops who met at the 1555 First Mexican Provincial Council, the writings of the famous Dominican advocate for native peoples Bartolomé de las Casas, those of the renowned Franciscan missioner Pedro de Gante, and the works of the Franciscan chronicler of Nahuatl history and culture Bernardino de Sahagún. The most unexpected of these documentary silences is in the extant primary sources of Bishop Juan de Zumárraga. Some analysts have correctly noted that the absence of Guadalupe references in Zumárraga's records could result from the fact that not all of them survived. Their opponents reply that, given Zumárraga's supposed foundational role in the Guadalupe event and devotion, the inattention to Guadalupe in primary sources such as his will is puzzling, particularly since various sixteenth-century Spanish Catholic wills include bequests for Masses dedicated to a special celestial patron.

Several sixteenth-century indigenous chronicles mention a Guadalupan appearance at Tepeyac during the mid-1550s. The annalist Juan Bautista's comment is typical of these brief references, noting, "In the year 1555: at that time Saint Mary of Guadalupe appeared there on Tepeyacac." Similarly, Domingo Francisco de San Antón Muñón Chimalpahin Quauhtlehuanitzin wrote, "12 Flint the year 1556 . . . And likewise in this year was when our precious mother Saint Mary of Guadalupe appeared at Tepeyácac." However, such references do not describe any particularities of an apparition story and conceivably could refer to the placement of a Guadalupe image in the shrine at Tepeyac rather than an apparition.[26]

Given this dearth of early documentation, it is not surprising that debates about the significance of *Imagen de la Virgen María* for the Guadalupe apparition tradition have been prominent in analyses of the work. As with other fields of scholarly inquiry in New Spain and abroad, the intellectual challenges of the Enlightenment shaped Guadalupan studies, with some thinkers employing the tools of modern scholarship and others ardently contesting these thinkers' methods and findings. Though Sánchez later insisted that he had been researching the Guadalupe tradition since the early decades of the seventeenth century, the vague statement about historical sources in the opening pages of his book was a precipitating factor in this debate:

> With determination, eagerness, and diligence I looked for documents and writings that dealt with the holy image and its miracle. I did not find them, although I went through the archives where they could have been kept. I learned that through the accident of time and events those that there were had been lost. I appealed to the providential curiosity of the elderly, in which I found some sufficient for the truth. Not content I examined them in all their circumstances, now confronting the chronicles of the conquest, now gathering information from the oldest and most trustworthy persons of the city, now looking for those who were said to have been the original owners of these papers. And I admit that even if everything would have been lacking to me, I would not have desisted from my purpose, when I had on my side the common, grave, and venerated law of tradition, ancient, uniform, and general about the miracle.[27]

Arguments against the apparition tradition were first systematized by Juan Bautista Muñoz, whom the Spanish monarch Charles III appointed as official historian of the Indies. Muñoz's 1794 address to the Royal Academy of History in Madrid laid the foundation for subsequent *antiaparicionistas*. He argued that the lapse of over a century between the 1531 date given for the apparitions and Sánchez's published account and the lack of documentation about the Guadalupe apparitions during the intervening years demonstrate the apparition tradition was not extant in the sixteenth century.[28] For more than two centuries this historical debate has continued to revolve around disagreements about the existence of sixteenth-century evidence for the apparition tradition. The controversy resurfaced among scholars and in numerous media reports during the years leading up to the 2002 canonization of Juan Diego.[29]

The standard argument against a foundational apparition tradition is exemplified in the work of Stafford Poole, whose writings are unsurpassed in their influence in making these historicity debates known among English-language readers. Noting the lack of sixteenth-century documentation about an apparition tradition, Poole contends that "an argument from silence is not usually persuasive in itself, but it is very strong when the sources would logically be expected to say something." However, he and others who have proposed this argument fail to account for the fact that relatively few primary sources mention Guadalupan devotion in the sixteenth century (which we know existed), including documents from various informants who might logically have been expected to speak of the Guadalupe shrine and its devotion. Moreover, those who propose an argument from silence never make an explicit connection between the still developing and decidedly *local* character of the Guadalupe tradition during the sixteenth and early seventeenth centuries and the presumption that historians should expect to find ample documentary evidence about Guadalupe from the sixteenth century onward if it is indeed, as Poole states, "the foremost religious event of Mexican history."[30] In other words, since the significance of Guadalupe for Mexican history was still in its nascent stages during the first century of devotion to her, it is inconsistent to expect that chroniclers and noted figures of the period would necessarily have written about her. This inconsistency does not completely invalidate the argument from silence. Nonetheless, the extent to which Guadalupan devotion was locally circumscribed decreases the likelihood that extant sources will answer all the questions that scholars, devotees, and the curious pose retrospectively about a tradition that only later came to have a pervasive impact on Mexican history and Catholicism.

Poole is one of a succession of analysts who have opined "that the apparition story, as it is now known, was largely the work of Miguel Sánchez." He allows that Sánchez's "primary source . . . seems to have been some form of oral tradition among the natives." He even hypothesizes that "in all probability" Sánchez "popularized one version of the native tradition." But he contends that, whatever the precise content of this oral tradition (or traditions), Sánchez liberally modified it in his written version. In one publication Poole even goes so far as to contend that "Juan Diego is a pious fiction, a figure out of literature who has no more historic reality than Captain Ahab or Sherlock Holmes."[31] Thus, he asserts that Sánchez was not only the first published author but also the primary architect of the apparition story and of the claim for its foundational status in the genesis of Guadalupan devotion.

Conversely, those who uphold the foundational status of the apparition tradition argue that the Spaniards' disdain for the allegedly inferior native peoples accounts for the delay of over a century before an official inquiry recorded indigenous testimony about Guadalupe and Juan Diego. They further contend there is early written documentation for the apparitions, such as a recently discovered codex that the Jesuit Xavier Escalada argues is Juan Diego's 1548 death certificate depicting his encounter with Guadalupe.[32] These commentators tend to argue, or simply presume, that Sánchez's publication is based on oral testimony or on an earlier written version of the apparition narrative. In an obituary of Sánchez, for example, Antonio de Robles credited his friend with writing a "learned book" that reinvigorated a "forgotten" tradition and "seemingly has been the means by which devotion to this holy image has spread throughout all Christendom."[33]

No available records from Sánchez's contemporaries recount any accusations that he contrived the apparition account. Nor did his publication produce debate as the Bustamante sermon did a century earlier. Nonetheless, while not doubting the veracity of Sánchez's account, some later Guadalupan writers bemoaned his failure to clearly cite his sources, such as José Patricio Fernández de Uribe, who stated in a late eighteenth-century treatise on Guadalupe that "this respectable author [Sánchez] would have done a great service to posterity had he left us with a precise record of the documents used in his volume." Others asserted that Sánchez had access to an unpublished version of the apparition narrative, an argument first advanced by the nineteenth-century journalist Agustín de la Rosa, who claimed that Sánchez relied on a dramatized version of the apparitions, which he mistakenly accepted as literal truth. While such assertions are plausible, no known primary source from Sánchez or his contemporaries substantiates them.[34]

The heart of the apparition debate is disagreement about the viability of historical arguments from silence; the role of oral testimony and of Sánchez in the development of the apparition tradition; and, especially, the authenticity, authorship, proper dating, and significance of crucial documentary sources. Polarization has dominated the apparition debate—the opposing views that either the apparitions occurred as a singular transformative event in 1531 or Sánchez invented them 117 years later—resulting in a stalemate that largely ignores significant evidence about the gradual evolution of the Guadalupe tradition. Disputants tend to employ a decidedly all-or-nothing approach: either there are documents verifying that the standard apparition story and the current Guadalupe image existed at the very outset of the devotion, or these traditions are later inventions and therefore lack credibility.

An often overlooked consideration is that demonstrating Guadalupe did not have an immediate and vast impact in New Spain does not eliminate the possibility that a tradition of an apparition experience emerged alongside the gradually developing practice of Guadalupan devotion. After all, there are numerous examples in the Spanish Catholic world (and beyond) of religious traditions with miraculous origins that never received more than local acclaim. The still nascent evolution of the Guadalupe apparition tradition as a pivotal event in Mexican history is consistent with Sánchez's claim that his published account drew on a relatively obscure apparition tradition that had developed previously within the vicinity of Mexico City.

Most importantly, interlocutors on both sides of the debate consistently fail to note that Sánchez was not a historian and certainly not so according to the modern standards of the discipline. Attempts to read his work as a source for the origins of the Guadalupe tradition pose questions that his writings were never intended to answer. In the end, the only clue Sánchez offers regarding the genesis of the apparition narrative is that he presumed it was a local pious tradition, which he sought to make known and interpret theologically.

La Criolla

Francisco de la Maza opened a new chapter in the interpretation of Sánchez's work, if not in the understanding of the Guadalupe tradition itself, with the 1953 publication of *El guadalupanismo mexicano*. A renowned art historian, de la Maza contended that "Guadalupanism and baroque art are the only authentic creations of the Mexican past."[35] Unlike previous commentators, his fascination with New Spain's baroque period enabled him to see beyond Sánchez's failure to cite written documentation for the apparition tradition, as well as beyond Sánchez's ornate writing style and theological audacity. De la Maza's sympathetic treatment of Sánchez; his fellow Guadalupan "evangelists" Laso de la Vega, Becerra Tanco, and Florencia; and the Guadalupe sermons preached and published in the wake of Sánchez's volume revealed a bold new thesis: the *criollo* clergy's intrinsic association of patriotism and religious piety was the core and unifying theme for their energetic promotion of Guadalupan devotion.

Jacques Lafaye expanded de la Maza's thesis in one of the most influential twentieth-century books on Guadalupe, *Quetzalcóatl and Guadalupe: The Formation of Mexican National Consciousness, 1531–1813.* Examining a wide range of historical actors and forces from the Spanish conquest of the indigenous peoples to the outbreak of the war for Mexican independence, Lafaye sought to uncover the role of myth and symbol in the rise of Mexican national consciousness. Significantly, the subtitle of his book delineates the years of 1531, the traditional date for the Guadalupe apparitions, and 1813, the year in which Lafaye contends Mexican leaders crystallized the independence movement under Guadalupe's protective mantle. He posits that a central theme in Sánchez's work is his *criollo* claim of New Spain's divine election, as is evident in Sánchez's biblical references such as the identification of Tepeyac with the Garden of Eden and, most importantly, the parallel between the woman of Revelation 12 in the birth of primitive Christianity and the appearance of Guadalupe at the dawning of the church in the New World. Lafaye concludes that Sánchez is "the true founder of the Mexican *patria*, for on the exegetic bases which he constructed in the mid-seventeenth century that *patria* would flower until she won her political independence under the banner of Guadalupe. From the day the Mexicans began to regard themselves as a chosen people, they were potentially liberated from Spanish tutelage."[36]

Some more recent scholars such as Poole have gone so far as to categorize *Imagen de la Virgen María* as "a florid, complex celebration of *criollismo*" and to contend that "criollismo is the central theme of the book." Poole goes on to argue that Sánchez is significant both for providing the genesis of the apparition narrative and for "bonding it to criollo identity." Thus he concludes that "the story of the apparitions is little more than a framework on which Sánchez can build his criollo interpretations" of the providential election of New Spain's native sons and daughters revealed through the singular blessing of nothing less than the Virgin Mary's "second birth" in their homeland. According to this line of argument, if Sánchez is indeed largely the creator of the apparition narrative, his motive in crafting the story was to foster *criollo* patriotism.[37]

Various arguments reveal that such claims overstate the case. As Poole and others note, one dilemma is the "strange" juxtaposition in *Imagen de la Virgen María* of an apparition story "directed toward the Indians" with Sánchez's "unrestrained criollo interpretations." In other words, "Sánchez took a cult story that should have been exclusively Indian and appropriated it for the criollos." Why would Sánchez have made Juan Diego the protagonist in the apparition narrative if indeed he largely invented the account to foment *criollo* patriotism? Poole contends that "nobody knows or will know this side of the grave why he downplayed the indigenous role in what was essentially an Indian miracle tale."[38] But if we don't know *why* Sánchez invented an indigenous protagonist, what evidence is there *that* he did so? It is at least as plausible to conclude Sánchez adopted a local account that already had an indigenous protagonist—as Sánchez himself claimed—than to conclude he invented the account and for some inexplicable reason contrived an indigenous protagonist.

Textual evidence from *Imagen de la Virgen María* does not support an overblown interpretation of the *criollo* emphasis that de la Maza and Lafaye unveiled in a more nuanced way from Sánchez's writing. For example, Sánchez recounts the healing of an indigenous convert he identifies as Don Juan, whom he introduces as the one who found the Remedios image that according to tradition one of Cortés's men had hidden among maguey plants on the *noche triste*. Significantly, Juan's illness was not healed in response to prayers offered before the Remedios image, for which he had served as caretaker for a number of years. Rather, he had his loved ones carry him a distance of over two leagues to the Guadalupe sanctuary. There Guadalupe affected his cure and sent him back to Naucalpan to build the first chapel for Remedios. Yet despite the seeming priority of Guadalupe evidenced in Don Juan turning to her rather than to Remedios in his hour of need, Sánchez goes on to assert that among Marian images the *criolla* Guadalupe complements the Spanish Our Lady of los Remedios in a manner that parallels the biblical figures of Naomi and Ruth. Like Naomi, the native of Bethlehem, Guadalupe was a native of Mexico; like Ruth, Remedios was a foreigner who migrated to provide her love and assistance in a new land. Both Virgins are equally deserving of veneration. Moreover, like many of his contemporaries Sánchez was a devotee of both Remedios and Guadalupe, as is evident in his periods of residency at both their shrines and in his authorship of a 1665 series of novena meditations intended for interchangeable veneration of both these Marian images. It is also noteworthy that the seven Guadalupe miracle accounts Sánchez narrates in *Imagen de la Virgen María* encompass various identified Spanish and indigenous beneficiaries. While the terms Spanish and *criollo* were sometimes used interchangeably during this era to distinguish those of European ancestry from mixed-race *castas*, despite identifying Guadalupe as a *criolla* Sánchez does not recount by name any particular *criollos* who received favors from her.[39]

Most strikingly, Sánchez dedicated the entire first section of his volume to Guadalupe's role in the Spanish conquest of Mexico. Although he professed Guadalupe as "a native of this land and its first creole woman" (257), he also presumed that the Spanish conquest of Mexico was an act of divine providence, deeming Guadalupe Spain's "assistant conqueror" (179) and attesting that the "heathenism of the New World" was "conquered with her aid" (191). Thus Sánchez presumed that God blessed the colonial enterprise of the *criollos'* nemesis, the *peninsulares*, or Old World Spaniards from the Iberian Peninsula. He stated the angel who descends from heaven to deliver a scroll as described in Revelation 10 is none other than "the king of Spain" and attested that "God had chosen this monarch as the universal sun of the planet and put in his hand the book of God's law so he could diligently promulgate it all over the world, as he has done" (166). According to Sánchez, God's design was that "in the light and warmth of the Catholic sun of Spain, this land of Mexico might have a great number of children gloriously called children of the sun Felipe [King Philip]" (166). Furthermore, Cortés and his "miraculous warrior army" that conquered Mexico were nothing less than "an army of angels for the conversion of this New World and the foundation of the church, who like angels destroyed the dragon" that had led the native peoples into idolatry and sinfulness (170).

While these are among the most audacious claims Sánchez makes about Spain and the purported biblical validation of its imperial project in the New World, similar quotations could be multiplied. It is not surprising that Sánchez presented such a favorable view of the Spanish crown and the Spanish conquest of Mexico, since no doubt he would have been censored (or worse) had he criticized either. Still, Sánchez's numerous explicit statements of support—indeed adulation—of the Spanish conquest and king as divinely ordained in their shaping of Mexican history vastly overshadow the comparatively small number of passages in which he mentions *criollismo*. As Martinus Cawley has argued, "the praises he [Sánchez] showers on the *criollos'* fatherland are couched in complex allegories" that in no way comprise a conscious nationalist movement. Indeed, Sánchez "certainly" could not even conceive of "a rebellion against a king whom he accepts without reservation."[40] While there is a definite undercurrent of *criollo* patriotism in Sánchez's book, the explicit focus of his work is clearly not a *criollo* contestation of peninsular Spanish dominance in New Spain. Rather, the general tone is an implicit *criollo* native pride alongside an explicit and far more pronounced validation of Spanish rule and evangelization.

Moreover, the extensive—and no doubt largely unforeseen—subsequent effects of Sánchez's ideas among his fellow *criollos* do not constitute evidence regarding his intentions when he actually composed his volume. Alicia Mayer's study of the Guadalupan sermons published in the wake of Sánchez's book notes that, while numerous *criollo* preachers identified Guadalupe as a *criolla* and the native-born residents of Mexico City and later all New Spain as her chosen people, until the very end of the colonial era these preachers also continued to laud her as the defender of the Spanish monarch and empire. Cornelius Conover concurs that for fully a century after the publication of *Imagen de la Virgen María* the spread of Guadalupan devotion was "less determined by the triumphant rise of creole consciousness than by such factors as her reputation for miraculous power, changes in the cult of saints in Mexico City, the support of high-ranking men, and excellent timing" in the history of the devotion's evolution (a fortuitous timing that is examined in chapter 3).[41] The link between Guadalupan devotion and *criollo* consciousness has its origins in *Imagen de la Virgen María*, but a number of later developments—most of them a full century after the publication of Sánchez's book—affected the eventually pervasive *criollo* adoption of Guadalupe as a patriotic symbol.

Thus a conventional but nonetheless important insight about *Imagen de la Virgen María* is it should first be understood in light of the Guadalupan devotion that preceded it and shaped Sánchez at the time of its composition, not the posterior influence of the book on *criollo* consciousness. Though the seeds of *criollo* patriotism planted in Sánchez's text would in time bear fruit among his fellow American-born priests and their compatriots, reading *Imagen de la Virgen María* merely as a *criollo* patriotic oration by no means exhausts the meaning of this crucial work in the development of the Guadalupe tradition. The *criollo* emphasis in Sánchez is a subtext to his primary contribution: his is the first and arguably the most influential theological attempt to examine the Guadalupe tradition in light of Christian scriptures and teachings, particularly as filtered through the interpretive lens of the church fathers.

Imagen de la Virgen María

Though the majority of commentators on Sánchez have been historians, journalists, and public intellectuals, Sánchez himself was first and foremost a pastor and theologian. His obituary boldly asserted that "it was the common opinion of many learned men that he knew all St. Augustine by heart."[42] Notwithstanding the hyperbole of such a claim, even a cursory reading of Sánchez's work reveals his admiration and extensive study of the fathers of the early church, especially Augustine. Though he cited a wide range of thinkers from Aristotle to Aquinas to his own theological contemporaries, Sánchez referred to Augustine more than two dozen times and also liberally quoted from other leading theologians of the early church such as Ambrose, Jerome, Tertullian, John Chrysostom, Cyprian, Basil the Great, Gregory Nazianzen, and Clement of Alexandria, among others. In various passages his allusions to Augustine included panegyrics, such as his statement that "to Saint Augustine the archive of divine things I attribute my desire, determination, and calling to celebrate the miraculous apparition of the Most Holy Virgin Mary Mother of God, in this her holy image of our Mexican Guadalupe" (198).

At times Sánchez followed the theological consensus of his era by incorrectly attributing to Augustine and other leading church fathers statements that subsequent scholarship has shown are from other sources. Most notably, Sánchez's foundational thesis that the woman in Revelation 12 is identified with the church and Mary and, by extension, with Guadalupe (160) does not come from Augustine's instructions to catechumens, as Sánchez claimed. The correct source is Augustine's contemporary Quodvultdeus, who became bishop of Carthage around 437.[43] Nonetheless, Sánchez gleaned numerous authentically Augustinian insights to guide his analysis. Most importantly, he imitated Augustine's theological method, particularly through engaging biblical typologies and presuming that the church embodied the ongoing fulfillment of biblical prophecy. Sánchez also followed Augustine and other patristic theologians by exploring biblical narrative and imagery as the primal lens through which to interpret historical and contemporary events.

As was customary at the time, *Imagen de la Virgen María* opened with letters of approbation from ecclesiastical censors. It also contained a brief prologue from Sánchez and concluded with three testimonial letters lauding the volume's accomplishments. The author of one letter was Luis Laso de la Vega, at the time the chaplain of the Guadalupe sanctuary. Another was Francisco de Siles, an ardent Guadalupan devotee who subsequently led the Mexico City cathedral chapter's 1665–1666 inquiry of the Guadalupe apparition tradition, in which Sánchez also participated as a witness. Sánchez divided the body of the work into five major sections: Guadalupe's role in the conquest of Mexico; the apparition account; a theological reflection on the image itself; a summary of postapparition developments in the Guadalupe site and tradition; and a narration and analysis of seven miracles attributed to Guadalupe. Collectively, these five sections are intended to incite the reader toward a deeper contemplation of Guadalupe: in Mexican history, in the apparitions, in her image, in the providential site of her sanctuary, and in the favors she bestows on those who turn to her. Put another way, *Imagen de la Virgen María* is a theological odyssey from chaos to Calvary. Sánchez opens his work with his overwhelmingly negative perspective on pre-Christian Mexico and ends at the foot of the cross with echoes of Jesus's voice admonishing the Mexican people to take the place of the apostle John in the biblical crucifixion scene. Just as John remained with Mary beneath the cross and received Jesus's invitation to "behold your mother" (John 19:27),[44] Sánchez's readers are urged to behold Guadalupe, the loving mother who now accompanies them.

The first major section of *Imagen de la Virgen María* argued that Guadalupe's appearance during the conquest of Mexico is foretold in Revelation 12. Consistent with an Augustinian theology of history that posits a divine plan and purpose working through human events and even human frailty and failings, Sánchez lauded the conquest as a providential occurrence that defeated Satan and idolatry and paved the way for the destined appearance of Mary of Guadalupe and the establishment of the church in Mexico. Like the woman in Revelation 12, the birth of the Mexican church occurred "in pain" (Revelation 12:2) and, as a later artist depicted in figure 1.2, entailed a cosmic battle between the dragon and Michael and his angels (12:7), whom Sánchez respectively identified with Satan and the indigenous "Gentiles," Cortés, and his fellow conquistadors. The woman escaped the dragon when she was "given the wings of a gigantic eagle" (12:14), a verse Sánchez correlated with the sacrament of baptism: just as the eagle (here associated with the classical Phoenix) is

FIGURE I.2. Anonymous, *San Miguel arcángel con estandarte guadalupano*, 18th century. The archangel Michael appears with a Guadalupan banner battling the seven-headed dragon from Revelation 12, which Miguel Sánchez associated with the idolatry of pre-Columbian Mexico. Courtesy Archivo del Museo de la Basílica de Guadalupe.

the only bird with the capacity to renew itself, so too the indigenous peoples were re-created in the waters of baptism and then could "shelter and protect themselves in the nest of the church" (172). The dragon's pledge "to make war on the rest of [the woman's] offspring" (12:17) revealed the reason Mexico was so plagued with idolatry. But Mary of Guadalupe's appearance in Mexico overshadowed this grave misfortune. Declaring that the most faithful image of God in this world was that of the Virgin Mary, a pseudo-Augustinian insight he incorrectly attributed to Augustine,[45] Sánchez concluded that "although [the natives] have the general consolation that each person is an image of God," their confidence was reassured once they were "accompanied by the image of Mary [who] appeared to defend them from the dragon" (177).

Next Sánchez recounted the apparition narrative itself. He structured this second major section of his work around five Guadalupe apparitions, which encompass Juan Diego's movement back and forth from Tepeyac to the residence of Bishop Zumárraga. Though the prelate is depicted as skeptical when he first heard Juan Diego's message that Guadalupe wanted a temple built at Tepeyac, he repented of his unbelief when Juan Diego presented him Guadalupe's signs of flowers that grew out of season and the miraculous *tilma* image. The healing of Juan Diego's uncle, Juan Bernardino, was attributed to Guadalupe's intercession and added further credence and cause for amazement among the bishop, his household, and devotees from throughout Mexico City who came to pray before the miraculous image once the bishop moved it from his private oratory to the cathedral.

Whatever his historical sources (or lack thereof) for this account, Sánchez's exposition reads like a series of biblical and theological reflections on a received pious tradition. When Juan Diego returned to Guadalupe dejected after the bishop's initial incredulous response to his request, for example, the Virgin's refusal to heed Juan Diego's plea that she send a "more credible" (182) messenger led Sánchez to cite and then paraphrase Luke 10:21 (and its parallel in Matthew 11:25): "Virgin Mary my sovereign mother, lady of heaven and earth, I confess, celebrate, and thank you that, though you could commend this work of such celestial mysteries to superior and excellent subjects, you have commended it to one who is humble, poor, and unlearned" (182). He also compared Juan Diego to Moses, Tepeyac to Mount Sinai, and Mary of Guadalupe to the Ark of the Covenant, which bore the Ten Commandments as Mary bore the Christ child. Sánchez observed that Juan Diego ascended the Mount Sinai of the New World to bring down the blessings of the "true ark of God" (195). His primary purpose was to evoke wonder and awe in his readers at the "most holy image, appeared and born for universal joy" at Tepeyac (196). He concluded this section with the contention that those who gaze on the Guadalupe image have the singular blessing of experiencing the fulfillment of Saint Augustine's prayer: "My heart communicates with you in secret, saying that it desires no other reward than to see you, and that it must live persevering in the diligences of seeking you and the hope of seeing you" (197).[46]

Next Sánchez dedicated the lengthiest and most complex section of his volume to an analysis of what pious believers can see as they gaze upon the incredible "beauty, grace, and loveliness" of the Guadalupe image (200). Once again he structured this part of the work around select references from Revelation 12, a scriptural link to Guadalupe repeatedly echoed in subsequent eras, as is illustrated in figure 1.3. The Revelation passage has clear parallels to various details in the Guadalupe image: "a woman clothed with the sun, with the moon under her feet, and on her head a crown of twelve stars" (12:1), who was accompanied by the arch-angel Michael and "was given the wings of a gigantic eagle" (12:14). While depictions of Mary cloaked with stars and sun rays and with the moon under her feet were widespread well before the publication of *Imagen de la Virgen María*—particularly for depictions of the Immaculate Conception—Sánchez focused on the biblical text that gave rise to such imagery.[47] From a Christian theological perspective, this section on the Guadalupe image is a Mariological tract designed to maximize what can be said of Mary of Guadalupe, pressing the boundaries of doctrinal orthodoxy to their limit before ending with a properly Christological affirmation of Mary's role to support and illuminate the saving work of her divine son.

Despite his concurrent claim about Guadalupe's complementarity with Our Lady of los Remedios, at times Sánchez argued for Guadalupe's primacy over other Marian images, as in his avowal that "in all of Christendom" Guadalupe is the "unique, singular, only, and rare" mirac-ulous image of Mary "painted with flowers" (206). Recounting various biblical images associated with Mary such as the ark, the burning bush, Jacob's ladder, and the rose of Jericho, he contended that, in her image that remains on Juan Diego's *tilma*, Guadalupe is also the "Vesture of Christ" (214). Expanding on Augustine's comment that the torn and divided gar-ment of Christ represents the dissemination of the church throughout the world,[48] Sánchez asserted that the divided garment also represents the distribution of miraculous Marian images like Guadalupe throughout all of Christianity (214). But this miraculous image is also a new Eve in a singular way: she appears in the new paradise of Tepeyac, which, un-like the original Garden of Eden, is not sealed off to humanity. In fact, at Tepeyac God relinquished the precious relic of Guadalupe's image so that Christianity and the grace of her favor could flourish among the "new Adam" (229) Juan Diego and all the inhabitants of Mexico.

FIGURE 1.3. Anonymous, *La Virgen de Guadalupe con los arcángeles Miguel y Gabriel, escenas de las cuatro apariciones y visión apocalíptico-guadalupana de san Juan evangelista*, 18th century. The Guadalupan image is surrounded by the archangels Michael and Gabriel and four scenes of her apparitions. At the bottom of the painting in the middle is Saint John the Evangelist, whose vision of the woman clothed with the sun in Revelation 12 is visually linked with Guadalupe. Courtesy Archivo del Museo de la Basílica de Guadalupe.

Sánchez's varied reflections on the Guadalupe image concluded with the observation that the cross of Christ is represented both by the eagle's wings around the angel at the base of the image and by a small insignia on Guadalupe's tunic. In these symbolic representations Sánchez saw a great reversal: Adam and Eve hid in shame under the shadow of a tree in Eden, but now the devotees who stand before Guadalupe come under the protective shadow of the cross. He then marveled at the wondrous way the image of Guadalupe fulfills the words attributed to Saint Cyril of Alexandria, "Through you, O Mary, the cross of Christ is celebrated and adored in all the world" (235).[49]

The fourth section of Sánchez's volume continued the apparition narrative of section 2 by briefly outlining subsequent developments in the Guadalupe tradition: the procession from the Mexico City cathedral two weeks after the miraculous apparitions to enshrine the image in a hastily constructed chapel at Tepeyac, Juan Diego's service as a caretaker at the Guadalupe sanctuary until his death in 1548, and the growth of the devotion and the facilities at the shrine. Theologically, Sánchez professed that these developments and even the site of the sanctuary itself reflected the guiding hand of divine providence. As had various authors since the famous sixteenth-century Franciscan chronicler Bernardino de Sahagún, Sánchez identified Tepeyac as a pre-Christian pilgrimage site. Unlike Sahagún, however, who opposed Guadalupan devotion as a thinly veiled continuation of indigenous religion, Sánchez claimed that Guadalupe's appearance on Tepeyac enabled her to providentially replace a Nahua deity previously worshiped on the site and thus win the natives for the Christian faith. Moreover, he observed that the hill of Tepeyac was strategically situated at a crossroads that enabled Guadalupe's benefits to be extended "throughout the diverse roadways of all New Spain" (240). A well at the base of Tepeyac marked the site of Guadalupe's fourth apparition to Juan Diego and, as in the case of numerous other shrines, provided medicinal waters to which devotees attributed miraculous cures. In a word, Sánchez concluded the sanctuary, site, and piety at Tepeyac reflected a celestial plan to provide a sacred ambiance in which, to paraphrase 1 Corinthians 13:12, "Now we see and contemplate the Virgin Mary in mirrors and obscurely, hoping we will clearly see her, accompany her, and rejoice with her in heaven" (245).

Following established conventions for writings about miraculous images and their sacred sites, in the final section of his work Sánchez narrated various miracles attributed to Guadalupe's intercession. He contended that Guadalupe bestowed many favors on the natives during the early years of the Spanish evangelization in order to "inspire, teach, and attract them to the Catholic faith and the shelter of her intercession" (246–247). Significantly, in this section he narrated seven miracles: the first three benefited indigenous devotees, the next three involved persons of Spanish heritage, and the final miracle was the rescue of Mexico

City from the flood of 1629–1634, a rendering of celestial aid that indiscriminately saved residents of indigenous, Spanish, *criollo*, and caste backgrounds. His relatively lengthy explication of Guadalupe's intervention in this deluge, which Sánchez apparently experienced firsthand, encompassed an emphasis on the image of Mary of Guadalupe as the ark which, as in the time of Noah, served as protection from the raging flood. Then he echoed another theme, Mary as the Vesture of Christ, in this case Christ's garment that the woman with the flow of blood touched in order to receive healing (Mark 5:25–34 and parallels). Noting that the Mexico City archbishop Francisco Manso y Zúñiga temporarily had the Guadalupe image transferred to his cathedral where devotees asked that her intercession abate the floodwaters, Sánchez professed that with the Guadalupe image "attending, accompanying, abiding, and touching the infirmed city, she healed it, dried it out, liberated it, redeemed it, restored it, and conserved it" (253).

Dramatically, Sánchez ended the volume with a reflection on the ongoing cosmic battle for the soul of Mexico. He extended his earlier analysis of Revelation 12 into the first verses of the thirteenth chapter, in which the Antichrist arises as a wild beast out of the water, supersedes the powers of the dragon, and seduces the whole world with his might. In response to the perceived threat of this false idol and deceiver, Sánchez invited his readers and all the peoples of New Spain to take their place at Tepeyac, the Calvary of the New World, as the apostle John took his place at the foot of the cross. There they would hear Christ say to them an extended version of what he had said from the cross to John (John 19:27): "Behold your mother; behold her image of Guadalupe . . . behold the protector of the poor; behold the medicine of the infirmed; behold the comfort of the afflicted; behold the intercessor for the suffering; behold the honor of the city of Mexico; behold the glory of all the faithful inhabitants in this New World" (260).

Sánchez and the Guadalupe Tradition

Sánchez's obituary eulogized him correctly. He is best remembered not as a baroque *criollo* patriot, nor as a historian. Rather, he was primarily a seventeenth-century pastor and theologian who, not surprisingly, privileged biblical and other Christian sources in his analyses of the Guadalupe cult and the Spanish Catholic enterprise in the New World. Sánchez's published account of the Guadalupe apparitions, which was disseminated through Mateo de la Cruz's abbreviated version, shaped the centrality of the apparitions within the overall Guadalupe tradition. But his most pronounced influence was to systemize that tradition in light of the Bible and Christian theology, particularly the church fathers.

Imagen de la Virgen María also marked a transition between a tradition that initially evolved among indigenous and Spanish devotees and then grew among *criollos* as they became more demographically and socially prominent in New Spain. Preachers, many of them *criollos*, advanced some of Sánchez's core theological ideas in the century and a half following his book's publication. Though the contents of *Imagen de la Virgen María* itself have not been widely known, much less the patristic theology that shaped it—the volume was not reprinted until 1952 and has never been translated into English—these preachers assured Sánchez's foundational influence on the collective imagination of Guadalupan devotees.

Some one hundred published Guadalupe sermons from 1661 to the end of colonial era in 1821 are extant. As the research of scholars such as Mayer has shown, together these sermons elaborate various themes that echo Sánchez's patristic-based analysis of Guadalupe such as God's providential guidance in Mexican history, Guadalupe's appearance as a foundational ecclesiological and salvific event, and the blessing and opportunity of contemplating Mary's countenance in the sacred *tilma*. Mayer concludes that, "taking Sánchez as the primary basis for their oratory," the preachers contended "with the appearance of Guadalupe, the New World was fully incorporated into the salvific promises" of God to redeem the world through Jesus Christ. These preachers also borrowed extensively from Sánchez's insights and imagery, such as his association of Moses, Mount Sinai, and the Ark of the Covenant with Juan Diego, Tepeyac, and the Guadalupe image. As David Brading insightfully concludes, "Nowhere was [Sánchez's] influence more obvious than in the application of Augustinian typology to the interpretation of the Mexican Virgin."[50]

Such typological interpretations of Guadalupe were less common during the nineteenth-century epoch of Mexico's independence, as public orations about Guadalupe tended to link her to visions of nationhood rather than of salvation history. By that time commentators had also forgotten the implicit acknowledgment in *Imagen de la Virgen María* that Guadalupan devotion evolved as a local tradition and only later was acclaimed as a defining event of Mexican history. The anachronistic projection of Guadalupe's current notoriety back into the early sixteenth century continues in many theological and other writings today. Nonetheless, a theological reading of *Imagen de la Virgen María* and its subsequent impact necessitates reexamining ongoing scriptural and patristic influences on the development of the devotion, art, preaching, and theological writings dedicated to Guadalupe. The most obvious indication of these influences is the consistent association of Guadalupe and the woman in Revelation 12, a correlation Sánchez borrowed from Augustine's contemporary Quodvultdeus. References linking Guadalupe and the famous woman of the Apocalypse extend from Sor Juana Inés de la Cruz's seventeenth-century sonnet to Guadalupe, which lauded her as "she whose proud foot made the dragon humbly bend his neck at Patmos," to Virgilio Elizondo's 1997 book *Guadalupe: Mother of the New Creation*, which cites the first two verses of Revelation 12 as an epigraph.[51] Numerous other writers, preachers, devotees, and artists have also connected Guadalupe to the biblical woman clothed with the sun, both as a means to place Guadalupe within the scriptural tradition and to explore her significance for Christian evangelization and faith in the Americas.

Though extensively focused on the *Nican mopohua*, the Nahuatl apparition account first published by Laso de la Vega, some of the most recent theological works on Guadalupe also attempt to recover key insights of Sánchez and explore their import for today. David Sánchez, for example, examines *Imagen de la Virgen María* as part of a broader cross-cultural study of interpreters who engaged Revelation 12 to subvert myths that undergird systems of domination and imperial rule. Josefrayn Sánchez-Perry compares Miguel Sánchez and his patristic theological approach to the use of typology in the early Christian debates about naming Mary "Theotokos" (God-Bearer or Mother of God), mutually illuminating the parameters and significance of these two key episodes in ecclesial and theological history. Michael Anthony Abril explores the importance of the apocalyptic in the apparition accounts and in Guadalupan theological writings, engaging in a mutually enriching dialogue between these sources and apocalyptic thought in our own time, particularly in the works of René Girard and Johann Baptist Metz. Abril succinctly states the contribution Sánchez's approach to scripture can make to such a dialogue, avowing that for Sánchez "the Bible is no mere book about the past; it speaks about the present, the future, and the theological character of time itself."[52]

Yet writers in modern times also criticize the Eurocentric limitations that enabled Sánchez to so expediently attribute the violent subjugation of Mexico to divine providence. As the biblical scholar Jean-Pierre Ruiz succinctly put it, "in arguing that the events of Tepeyac were a fulfillment

of scripture that confirmed the divine design involved in the Spanish conquest of Mexico, Sánchez simultaneously argued for the hermeneutical
sufficiency (and exclusive privilege) of European Christian categories
for comprehending and communicating religious experience in the
Americas."[53] Whether they are aware of Sánchez's work or not, theologians
today overwhelmingly eschew the Eurocentrism and colonialism that the
first Guadalupan theologian took for granted.

Indeed, taken as a whole, the claims of many theologians today present a reversed mirror image of major conclusions originally articulated
in *Imagen de la Virgen María* and popularized by subsequent preachers.
For example, various recent theological works claim that Our Lady of
Guadalupe didn't justify or abet the Spanish conquest but broke the
cycle of indigenous victimization and subjugation, that her apparitions
did not merely transplant European Christianity but incarnated the
Christian message in native idiom and imagery, and that her message
not only converted the indigenous peoples from practices such as human
sacrifice but also demanded that Spanish Catholics repent of their ethnocentrism and violence. To be sure, some present-day theologians presume their liberationist understandings were prevalent from the outset
of the Guadalupe tradition. They elide colonial theological publications
like that of Sánchez, which contradict such a presumption, as well as the
dearth of evidence that such understandings were widespread among
devotees. Nonetheless, Sánchez's modern theological successors draw
on his work in a fundamental way: they seek to address—often from
a liberationist perspective—the question Sánchez first posed about
Guadalupe's significance in shaping the lives of natives and newcomers
in the New World.

More broadly, Sánchez's theological successors have emulated his
Augustinian and patristic approach of engaging the scriptures. Just as
Augustine's *City of God* drew on Christian revelation in developing a response to the theological crisis of the collapsing Roman Empire, Sánchez's
Imagen de la Virgen María scrutinized the Christian biblical and theological heritage in formulating a response to the dilemma of rooting the faith
in a world previously unknown to Europeans. Like Sánchez, down to the
present theologians who write on Guadalupe seek to address the pressing
concerns of their world through the lens of the core gospel themes they unveil in the Guadalupe tradition. Consciously or not, these theologians extend Sánchez's theological project in their efforts to reveal the resonances
between the scriptures and the Guadalupan apparition narrative, image,

and devotional expressions. They uncover insights in these theological sources that Sánchez did not articulate, and in all probability would not have expected. Yet the writings of present-day theologians confirm *Imagen de la Virgen María*'s most enduring influence: Sánchez set a pattern of linking Our Lady of Guadalupe to theological investigations that assess the understanding and development of Christianity in the New World.

2

Evangelization

LUIS LASO DE LA VEGA'S *HUEI TLAMAHUIÇOLTICA* (1649)

LUIS LASO DE la Vega's *Huei tlamahuiçoltica*,[1] published the year after Miguel Sánchez's *Imagen de la Virgen María*, was the first treatise to focus on Guadalupe and the evangelization of natives, specifically the Nahuas of central Mexico. While the precise relationship between these two works is a debated topic, a comparison of their contents reveals their close correlation. Discrepancies such as the ordering of the main sections of the two volumes, the inclusion of twice as many Guadalupe miracle accounts in Laso de la Vega's treatise than in Sánchez's, and the number of times Guadalupe appeared to Juan Diego—five in Sánchez, four in Laso de la Vega—are minor as compared to the common thematic material contained in both works. Moreover, Laso de la Vega wrote a glowing commendation for inclusion in *Imagen de la Virgen María* in which he confessed that, though he had long venerated Guadalupe, "after I read the history of her miracle" in Sánchez's book "the desire to be totally hers has grown [even more] in my heart."[2]

Yet there are also noteworthy differences between the two works. While Sánchez's apparition account offers a relatively straightforward presentation of details, the *Nican mopohua* account in *Huei tlamahuiçoltica* employs an extensive use of poetic devices, diminutive forms, and the indigenous narrative style of accentuating dialogue. The *Nican mopohua* also accentuates Juan Diego's role. Indeed, from a literary perspective Our Lady of Guadalupe is the main character of Sánchez's apparition story, whereas the *Nican mopohua* gives heightened emphasis to Juan Diego's faith-filled response to her. Moreover, the theological elaboration and the numerous scriptural and patristic references found in *Imagen de la Virgen*

María are comparatively absent in *Huei tlamahuiçoltica*. Such differences demonstrate the most striking distinction between these two treatises. Sánchez sought to theologically examine Guadalupe and the evangelization of Mexico vis-à-vis the wider Christian tradition. Laso de la Vega's purpose was to promote Guadalupan devotion among Nahuatl-speaking residents and to animate them to follow the saintly example of Juan Diego in dedicating themselves to the Christian life.

Laso de la Vega was a Mexico City diocesan priest, though little is known about his life. He was enrolled in a course of study in canon law at the University of Mexico in 1623 and at some point completed his licentiate. In 1647 he was appointed to serve as vicar of the Guadalupe sanctuary. As vicar, Laso de la Vega oversaw the rebuilding of the original chapel on the site, as well as the construction of walls around the springs where many infirm drank water or bathed in search of healing. According to Francisco de Florencia, Laso de la Vega also had "beautiful" images of the Guadalupe apparitions painted on the walls of both facilities, including one of "the sovereign Queen of the Angels presenting Juan Diego with the flowers he was to take the bishop as a sign."[3] Subsequently Laso de la Vega was appointed to the Mexico City cathedral chapter. The full title of his publication was *Huei tlamahuiçoltica omonexiti in ilhuicac tlatocacihuapilli Santa Maria totlaçonantzin Guadalupe in nican huei altepenahuac Mexico itocayocan Tepeyacac* (By a great miracle appeared the heavenly queen, Saint Mary, our precious mother of Guadalupe, here near the great *altepetl* of Mexico, at a place called Tepeyac). In time its premier section, the *Nican mopohua* apparition account, had a significant impact on the Guadalupe tradition. But *Huei tlamahuiçoltica* began inauspiciously as a thirty-six-page tract with various typographical errors and inconsistencies in its text. It is Laso de la Vega's only known publication.

A number of theologians have examined the text of the *Nican mopohua* as a prime source for the Guadalupe tradition. But scholarly analyses of *Huei tlamahuiçoltica* as a whole are largely limited to short assessments in more general works on Guadalupe. Typically these works focus on the significance of *Huei tlamahuiçoltica* for larger historical debates about the origins of the Guadalupe tradition, as is exemplified in Stafford Poole's 1995 *Our Lady of Guadalupe*. Other studies, such as David Brading's 2001 *Mexican Phoenix*, focus primarily on a comparison of Laso de la Vega's publication to Sánchez's *Imagen de la Virgen María*.[4] A comprehensive analysis of *Huei tlamahuiçoltica* necessitates a theological examination of its full contents and its usefulness for pastoral outreach.

Like any such treatise, *Huei tlamahuiçoltica* both addresses and is limited by the circumstances of a particular pastoral situation, in this case the evangelization of the Nahuas in central Mexico. Laso de la Vega presented idealized portraits of Juan Diego and other native devotees in order to enhance Nahua conformity to Catholic norms and to colonial officials' expectations of proper native subjects. His writing is clearly rooted in the Eurocentric presumptions of his evangelizing predecessors, with the intent of persuading native peoples to abandon their purportedly idolatrous preconquest religion and embrace the Catholic faith wholeheartedly. Thus *Huei tlamahuiçoltica* must be understood within the context of the larger Spanish project to convert the natives into practitioners of the missionaries' ideals of faithful Catholics. At the same time, it must also be understood within the horizon of native response to these efforts, particularly the gradual development of indigenous devotion to Guadalupe over the century prior to Laso de la Vega's writing. Such a contextualized reading sheds light on core pastoral issues in Laso de la Vega's work that have enduring significance in the development of the Guadalupe tradition.

A Century of Unequal Religious Exchange

Notwithstanding the enthusiastic claims of some friars and other Spanish observers, the fundamental dynamic of native life in the wake of conquest was not mass conversions but demographic collapse. European diseases devastated native populations. In the case of central Mexico the most drastic contagion following the arrival of Europeans was a 1545–1548 epidemic, which wiped out at least 60 percent of Nahua residents. A subsequent 1576–1580 epidemic occasioned the low point of Nahua population, diminishing their numbers to scarcely 10 percent of what they had been on the eve of the conquest.[5] At first many Europeans perceived this destruction as just punishment for wanton sinfulness and idolatry, though by the end of the sixteenth century the high mortality rate provoked sorrow and questions about God's purpose. For Nahuas and other native peoples, addressing such rampant death was surely one of the core elements of whatever religious faith or rituals they practiced in the immediate aftermath of the Spanish takeover of their civilization.

Scholarly examinations of exchanges between Spaniards and native populations such as the Nahuas reveal that contact between diverse peoples, even those marked by conquest and unequal power relations, encompass processes of mutual accommodation. Thus contrary to the presumptions of some analysts, the native reception of Mary was not merely a superficial substitution of a Christian image for an indigenous feminine deity or deities. Mary is best understood as a sacred figure who emerged within the colonial milieu, not solely the ongoing presence of a preconquest goddess. Sabine MacCormack's study of Our Lady of Copacabana in colonial Peru (an image that later became the patron saint of Bolivia) illustrates this phenomenon. Copacabana is on a peninsula at the southeastern shore of Lake Titicaca close to an ancient cult site on the Island of the Sun, which for Incas was the birthplace of human history. MacCormack demonstrates that, in the emergence of devotions such as that to Our Lady of Copacabana, "At issue is not an unchanging, primordial—be it Andean—understanding of religion or cult, but a dynamic adaptive accommodation of practice and belief to religious, political, and social change" in colonial society.[6]

Similarly, interactions between the Nahuas and Spanish newcomers were the meeting ground of two forces in motion, inciting exchanges that varied across time, local circumstances, and the predilections of the particular natives and Spaniards involved. On the one hand, Spanish friars considered their faith and knowledge superior to that of the natives, whom they sometimes defended within the structures of colonial rule but nearly always perceived as spiritual children who required clerical tutelage. Missionaries alternatively argued that physical similarities between Nahua and Christian rites were due to natural reason, the work of the devil, or even the vestiges of pre-Columbian Christian evangelization in the region. Accordingly, friars viewed Nahua rituals on a continuum ranging from being a precursor of Christian sacraments to being a threat that could lead natives to misinterpret the sacraments in light of their own rituals and their meanings. In the face of these concerns, church as well as crown authorities issued numerous edicts intended to regulate matters such as natives' dramatic performances in ritual, song lyrics, access to devotional texts, and use of musical instruments and religious images. The attempt to control natives' bodies and external actions was predicated on the belief that doing so would transform their minds and hearts.

While the balance of institutional power clearly tilted toward Spanish authorities, the beliefs and practices of Nahuas and other natives inevitably shaped the reception of Spanish efforts to promote Catholicism. Scholars such as Lisa Sousa underscore the tensions and difficulties in communication between missionaries and the natives they sought to indoctrinate. Sousa demonstrates, for example, that well beyond the period of initial contact, natives and friars "continued to understand matters of marriage and sexuality in different terms." A number of natives resisted the friars' initial efforts to supplant the practice of serial monogamy and polygamy. Even when the Christian celebration of marriage became more normative, some natives continued to practice their own rituals, while others incorporated their understandings of marriage and at times native ritual practices into the new rites. Louise Burkhart confirms similar difficulties with regard to fundamental religious concepts such as sin and morality. Language, the creation of worship spaces, and the celebration of sacraments and other rituals were among the primary arenas in which natives introduced their beliefs about the cosmos and the drama of human life into the religious ambiance of colonial New Spain. Burkhart concludes "that the Nahuas, by selectively responding to the devotional options presented them by the friars, exerted considerable control over the creation of their church."[7]

The dynamics of unbalanced reciprocity were evident in the promotion of catechesis about Mary among the Nahuas during the century preceding Laso de la Vega's publication of *Huei tlamahuiçoltica*. Though natives' first introduction to Mary was "the conquistadors' emblematic use of Marian imagery in battle," subsequently their clerical instructors in the Catholic faith exerted considerable effort to shape native perceptions of Mary as the mother of God. In her study of Mary in Nahua colonial literature, Burkhart examines sermons and writings in which missionaries and their Nahua assistants expounded on Marian topics in the natives' language during the sixteenth and early seventeenth centuries. These works encompass Marian prayers, miracle narratives, and a range of topics such as Mary's role in the birth of Christ and as the sorrowing mother. *Huei tlamahuiçoltica* echoes the approach to Mary as mother and intercessor evident in a number of these texts, such as the oration in a 1607 sermon of Fray Juan de Mijangos for the feast of Mary's nativity: "You are the compassionate mother. May you help me and have compassion for me, may you speak for me before your precious child, our lord Jesus Christ . . . Therefore (oh precious noblewoman), by means of your honored advocacy, your help, we will obtain, we will be given heavenliness, utter joyfulness, glory." Burkhart concludes that "the most striking aspect" of these early Nahuatl-language texts on Mary "may be the sheer extent to which medieval European Marianism, expressed in narrative, liturgy, and prayer, found its way into Nahua hands." Four of the twelve required feast days for Christianized Nahuas were Marian feasts: Mary's Conception, Nativity, Annunciation, and Assumption. Mary also figured prominently in natives' devotion for celebrations of Christmas, Epiphany, and the Lord's Passion. Spanish friars promoted plentiful *cofradías*, many of them devoted to Mary, to foster Catholic faith and devotion. Nahuas participated in large numbers and engaged in practices such as singing Marian hymns and antiphons, observing Saturday as a day dedicated to Mary, wearing rosary beads, praying the beads, and reciting other Marian prayers as instructed.[8]

Yet Nahuas were not merely passive recipients of Spanish presentations of Mary. The role of Mary as celestial spokesperson illustrates that, intentionally or not, natives at times reinterpreted or even refashioned Christian precepts. In Nahuatl, Mary's intercessory role was often delineated with the phrase *tepan tlahtoa* (to speak for someone), the same phrase used to denote the function a lawyer performed for a client. The social context of the Spanish colonial world, which induced residents to obediently and patiently await the judgment of the court system rather than right perceived wrongs on their own, was reinforced with the teaching that the heavenly realm functioned in parallel fashion. Moreover, in numerous sermons and catechetical lessons, Mary was presented as a guide to a moral life on earth and an advocate for a favorable judgment in the afterlife. Nahua belief before the conquest focused on the manner of a person's death as the most determinative factor in their subsequent fate. Regardless of their moral conduct in their lives as a whole, for example, soldiers who died in battle or mothers who died in childbirth received the great reward of becoming companions of the sun. While the Nahuas had a developed moral code and emphasized harmonious relations, the notion that human behavior decided an outcome of heaven or hell in the next life was foreign to them. Mary's role in affecting their final judgment was an important means through which Spanish missioners introduced this novel concept. But as scholars such as Jorge Klor de Alva have shown, sixteenth-century Nahuas found it virtually impossible to fully grasp fundamental Christian teachings such as "the survival in an afterlife of a single, eternal soul, and the idea that that soul would be the object of rewards and punishments following from the moral quality of the individual's behavior during his or her lifetime."[9]

The choice of Nahua terms for Catholic concepts occurred in the midst of this wider process of linguistic and cultural accommodation, and of course shaped Nahua understanding of Marian and other Catholic beliefs. In his study of the Maya after the conquest, William Hanks deems this process "linguistic conversion," a "dynamic fusing of elements" through which "European and Christian meanings were converted into Maya [and other native] utterances." James Lockhart has charted how linguistic changes among Nahuatl speakers parallel three stages of change in Nahua life. First came a brief period of relatively little modification during the generation after the conquest, from 1519 to about 1540–1550. As the native population increasingly comprised new generations whose formative years transpired within colonial society, the following century was a time of increasing transformation reflected in the greater use of Spanish loan words, particularly nouns, but with minimal structural change in the Nahuatl language. Finally, from about 1640–1650 down to the present, widespread bilingualism led to even deeper transformations, including Nahuatl influences in the speaking of Spanish.[10]

A prime example of the complexity of Nahuatl-Spanish linguistic exchange is the Nahuatl word frequently applied to Mary herself, Tonantzin. The Franciscan missioner Bernardino de Sahagún decried Guadalupan veneration, stating it disguised the "idolatry" of indigenous devotees who in pre-Columbian times "had a temple dedicated to the mother of the gods, whom they called Tonantzin, which means Our Mother" on the hill of Tepeyac, the site of the Guadalupe chapel. He also reported that "there they performed many sacrifices in honor of this goddess." Thus he alleged that the natives continued to worship Tonantzin in the image of Guadalupe. Even though Burkhart demonstrates with multiple texts that Tonantzin was not a proper name but a common noun denoting "our mother" used to address the Virgin Mary under various titles beginning in the sixteenth century, to this day many take the statement of Sahagún at face value. Moreover, in preconquest usage Tonantzin was an honorific title that referred to various manifestations of the divine, as well as to natural phenomena such as mountains, earth, water, sun, and fire. Indeed the multiple names, functions, and personalities of Nahua celestial beings and the fluidity of the religious system they inhabited make dubious any attempt to associate a single Christian image with a single Nahua deity. Like the Spanish Catholics who had manifold names and images for Mary, the Nahuas had a highly multivalent view of the sacred. They also had little impulse to define a doctrinal understanding of each celestial being. Thus Nahuas did not formulate their understanding of Mary through simple substitution of a preconquest deity. Rather, they filtered Catholic teaching through the lens of a polyvalent indigenous religious system that had ongoing influence despite the asymmetrical power relations of colonial society.[11]

The same is true for the site of Tepeyac, which in the original Nahuatl "Tepeyacac" means "at the start of the hill." During preconquest and colonial times, before the former Lake Texcoco was drained and covered over in the creation of modern Mexico City, Tepeyac was a foothill of the Sierra de Guadalupe that jutted out into the lakeshore. It was not the domain of any single deity but rather was part of a series of ceremonial hilltop and mountain sites that Jeanette Peterson deems the "Tepeyac Sphere." Rituals performed in this sphere, which encircled the capital city of Tenochtitlan (Mexico City), buttressed imperial power and social hierarchy, offered prayers for communal needs such as rain and fertility, and celebrated events such as the winter solstice. Images of political rulers and sacred beings carved into the landscape marked imperial territory and revealed the Nahua perception that natural settings were themselves charged with divine presence. At least initially, then, many natives were drawn to Tepeyac due to its established power in a chain of sacred places, regardless of what Christian image was enshrined there.[12]

Nahua Guadalupan Devotion

Native devotion to Our Lady of Guadalupe emerged as part of an extensive array of religious practices and beliefs within which Guadalupe initially played a relatively minor role. Yet natives participated in the Guadalupe cult from the earliest stages of its evolution. The first uncontested primary sources that illuminate devotion to Guadalupe, the depositions from the 1556 controversy between Fray Francisco de Bustamante and the Mexico City archbishop Alonso de Montúfar, reveal that natives were already participating in the veneration of Guadalupe at Tepeyac. A lawyer related that he had seen both Spaniards and native peoples offer fervent devotion at the shrine. He and another witness stated they had observed Archbishop Montúfar call together "many Indians" gathered at the shrine to address them through an interpreter about the proper veneration of Mary. Another informant avowed that "men and women from all walks of life" venerated Guadalupe at Tepeyac. Though no natives were called upon to offer depositions in the official inquiry, the final witness noted that some natives had grown lukewarm in their devotion at the command of the Franciscans. But he also commented that "all kinds of people, noble citizens and Indians" continued to frequent the Guadalupe chapel.[13]

Like primary sources for early Spanish devotion to Guadalupe, various other documents provide glimpses of indigenous veneration. In 1576, the Mexico City archbishop Pedro Moya de Contreras and the Jesuit superior general Everard Mercurian requested that Pope Gregory XIII extend a plenary indulgence to those who visited and prayed at the Guadalupe chapel. The official decree for the indulgence noted that the "eminent devotion" associated with the Guadalupe shrine had deepened numerous natives' "faith in Christ." Sahagún's protestation of the Guadalupe cult included his testimony about widespread indigenous devotion, although his claims are probably exaggerated given his intent to thwart what he perceived as dangerous native enthusiasm. The 1563 will of Francisco Verdugo Quetzalmamalitzin, a Nahua lord from the town of Teotihuacan a short distance from Mexico City, bequeathed four pesos so the priest assigned to the Guadalupe chapel would offer Masses on his behalf after his death. His will went on to state, "To Our Lady the Blessed Virgin Mary, queen of heaven, I ask that she be my advocate before her precious son, the redeemer of the world." Similarly, the 1588 will of the noblewoman Catalina de Sena of Coyoacán (near Mexico City) offered four coins "to be devoted to our dear mother St. Mary there at Tepeacac." An entry in Juan Bautista's chronicle of events described a 1566 procession to Tepeyac in which Spanish dignitaries "and all of us Indians" participated.[14]

Indigenous involvement in festivities at Tepeyac on this and other occasions included practices linked to their native heritage such as celebratory drum beats and chants. In commemoration of a new viceroy's arrival in 1595, natives sanctified the plaza of the Guadalupe shrine with a performance of the *danza de los voladores* (dance of the flying ones), an acrobatic descent from a tall decorated pole of four plumed dancers held aloft only by a rope attached around their ankles. While specific details about ritual practices are lacking, other sources reveal that by the early seventeenth century devotees conducted separate fiesta seasons over successive weeks at Tepeyac, with native celebrations one week and that of Spaniards and mixed-race *castas* the other. Municipal records note that, while the Guadalupe image was away from Tepeyac at the Mexico City cathedral during the floods of 1629–1634, devotees who visited Tepeyac consisted overwhelmingly of "Indians from the mountains" who continued to pray at the sacred site even in the absence of its primary image. An anonymous author's 1634 poem recounted the return of the Guadalupe image after the flood abated. The poet attested that the general populace processed Guadalupe along part of the route back to Tepeyac, while the following day indigenous devotees held a separate procession to escort her image the rest of the way.[15]

Significantly, the 1634 native-led procession traversed territory with a majority indigenous population. Indeed, during the foundational period of the Guadalupe tradition everyone living near the Guadalupe shrine and its miraculous image was of native background, save for the resident chaplain. The Englishman Miles Philips passed by Tepeyac in 1573 and remarked on his observation that "about this Church [the Guadalupe chapel] there is not any town of Spaniards that is inhabited, but certain Indians do dwell there in houses of their own country building." An official visitation report of Franciscan houses in New Spain, which the order's commissary general Alonso Ponce conducted, stated that in July 1585 the party passed near Guadalupe, "a small town of Mexican [Nahua] Indians and in it, situated on a hill, an *ermita* [literally "hermitage"] or church of Our Lady of Guadalupe, where the Spaniards of Mexico [City] go to keep vigil and to have novenas." While this passage highlights the devotion of Spaniards who visited the shrine, it equally relates that native peoples were the only ones who actually lived around it. A 1570 report of the chaplain of the shrine, Antonio Freire, stated that about 100 unmarried and 150 married adult Indians lived there, and in the surrounding area there were about thirty or forty slaves and six Spaniard-owned sheep ranches.[16]

Documentation of these native residents' involvement in processions, festivities, and personal devotion at the shrine during the sixteenth century is not extant. This is not surprising, since Tepeyac was three miles outside the colonial city where ecclesiastical and civil authorities resided, and activities conducted apart from the watchful eye of authorities are less likely to be noticed or commented upon, particularly everyday occurrences among lower-status residents. Nonetheless, at least some natives living adjacent to the shrine no doubt joined the rising number of devotees who sought celestial aid from Guadalupe, especially amid increasing reports that she affected, in the words of Philips, "a number of miracles."[17]

The first official initiative to gather testimony about the Guadalupe tradition encompassed evidence of indigenous devotion as well as testimony that a native named Juan Diego had lived among those in the indigenous community around Tepeyac and prayed with his fellow devotees at the Guadalupe shrine. When the cathedral chapter of Mexico City sought papal promulgation of a Guadalupe feast day and proper office for all of New Spain, they conducted an inquiry into the Guadalupe tradition to bolster their case. Though ultimately unsuccessful in achieving the goal of papal recognition for their Guadalupan patroness, the 1665–1666 investigation provided testimonies from twenty witnesses. Twelve of them were Spaniards or *criollos* interviewed in Mexico City and eight were residents of Cuauhtitlan, the place traditionally considered Juan Diego's hometown. Seven of the Cuauhtitlan interviewees were Nahuas who gave their testimony through a Nahuatl–Spanish interpreter. The other was a *mestizo*, or mixed-race person of Spanish and indigenous descent. Although both Sánchez and Laso de la Vega published their volumes before the inquiry and clearly shaped its findings—Sánchez was in fact one of those interviewed—overall the witnesses encompassed a number of elderly informants who reportedly had a much longer lived experience of Guadalupan devotion than these two clergy authors.[18]

Nonetheless, caution must be exercised in assessing the value of the testimonies. The organizers of the inquiry were enthusiastic Guadalupan devotees and promoters of the effort to achieve papal recognition of the Guadalupe apparitions and cult. Their lengthy questions encompassed much of the information they wanted the witnesses to confirm, such as a narration of the apparition account, which the respondents were simply asked to verify.[19] Hence witnesses were influenced both by the information provided in the questions and by what they thought the officials interviewing them wanted to hear.

Consequently the most useful information from the inquiry is contained in statements that go beyond what the interviewers specified or implied in their questions. In this regard the fifth of the nine questions is particularly important. It addressed Juan Diego's life and virtues, a crucial consideration since the holiness of someone who had allegedly experienced an apparition is one sign—or countersign—of the apparition's validity. All the witnesses affirmed Juan Diego's integrity; in the words of the question posed, they stated he was indeed a "good Christian."[20] But the responses of the Mexico City witnesses tended to merely affirm a general tradition of Juan Diego's virtuous reputation, while those of the Cuauhtitlan witnesses offered various further details about Juan Diego not expounded in the questions. Multiple Cuauhtitlan witnesses attest, for instance, that an aged picture in a room at their local parish church depicted Juan Diego, his uncle Juan Bernardino, and the Franciscan missioner Fray Pedro de Gante. Another distinguishing feature of the Cuauhtitlan respondents, who according to the inquiry report ranged in age from seventy-eight to over one hundred and were nearly all older than the Mexico City interviewees, was that most of them recounted parents, grandparents, aunts, or neighbors who knew Juan Diego personally and told them about him.

The most unique feature of the Cuauhtitlan testimonies was statements about the veneration of Juan Diego. Marcos Pacheco recalled his aunt's frequent plea that "God would do to you [and your brothers] what he did to Juan Diego." Echoing an incidence conveyed in the books of Sánchez and Laso de la Vega and mentioned in various interviews from the official inquiry, Gabriel Suárez stated his parents told him Juan Diego resided and served at the Guadalupe chapel after the apparitions. But he also added further observations. Juan Diego was known among locals as "el Peregrino" (the Pilgrim) because of his frequent journeys to the Franciscan mission station at Tlatelolco to receive religious instruction. After he encountered Guadalupe and took up residence at Tepeyac, natives often visited him there "to ask that he intercede for them with the Most Holy Virgin to give them good seasons [harvests] in their maize fields."[21] The absence of references to existing Juan Diego devotion in other sources—including Sánchez, Laso de la Vega, and the Mexico City witnesses in the official inquiry—reveals that native witnesses spoke of a devotion to Juan Diego generated among their own communities, not one borrowed from Spanish or *criollo* informants.

On the whole our understanding of native involvement in the early stages of the Guadalupe tradition is relatively limited. Some scholars have overstated the extent of indigenous devotion with claims that Guadalupe's "early cult was overwhelmingly Indian" and that she "unif[ied] Indians in a single religious movement." Conversely, others have contended that native participation was negligible. Yet, given that Guadalupe's appeal was still confined to the local environs of Mexico City, as well as the comparatively modest evidence for Spanish practice of Guadalupan devotion during this same time period, it is clear that indigenous devotees participated in tandem with their Spanish counterparts. Even the sources Spaniards and other Europeans produced provide evidence of indigenous devotion, sometimes explicitly and in other instances only through a critical reading of their contents. Moreover, the natives' separate processions and feast-day celebrations reveal that their devotional expressions were at times distinct from those of Spaniards. As William Taylor concludes, in the early period although "it was not primarily an Indian devotion," in the vicinity of Tepeyac and Mexico City "clearly there were many Indian devotees of Our Lady of Guadalupe."[22]

Given the association of Tepeyac with pre-Columbian worship, the Nahua tendency to absorb rather than resist the sacred beings of their rivals, and the catastrophic effects of the conquest and European diseases on indigenous communities, it is not difficult to imagine that Guadalupe was a paradoxical figure for indigenous devotees. She was a powerful mother and intercessor, a brown-skinned woman like them who provided continuity with an ancient Nahua worship site. She worked miracles that alleviated their suffering. But she was also a force whom Spaniards engaged to enhance native peoples' acceptance of colonial rule and missionary efforts, a protagonist in the Spanish efforts to displace indigenous ways. From community to community—and even from person to person—natives adapted Spanish Catholic practices and the symbolic world they mediated to suit their own life situations. As one leading scholar of Mesoamerican religions, Davíd Carrasco, concludes, "In Guadalupe we see a curious and even furious cultural mixture. She is Indian and Spaniard. She is an Earth Mother and a Holy Mother. She is a comforter and a revolutionary."[23]

While the evidence is not conclusive, the existence of natives' devotion necessitates considering their possible influences on belief in Juan Diego's encounters with Guadalupe. It is not surprising, of course, that indigenous devotees were the first to venerate the unanticipated hero Juan Diego, both because he was one of their own and because most Spaniards and criollos did not tend to hold the natives in high regard. As a number of commentators have observed, at its core the apparition story is neither about criollo election nor about Spanish election, but about Guadalupe's providential choosing of an indigenous neophyte as her emissary. When coupled with the evidence for early native devotion to Juan Diego, his leading role in the apparition narrative intimates that natives participated in the development of a local devotion encompassing an oral tradition about a saintly indigenous neophyte. This conclusion leaves various questions unanswered, of course, not the least of which is a precise timeline for the origin and development of the apparition tradition. But it is consistent with Sánchez's claim that his source for the apparition story was in fact local informants and tradition. It is also consistent with the tendency for mutual accommodation between natives and Spaniards, a process that, as we shall see, is reflected in the Nahuatl-language apparition account published in Laso de la Vega's volume.

Huei tlamahuiçoltica

The friars' efforts to evangelize the natives faced growing obstacles by the end of the sixteenth century. Tensions with the increasing number of bishops in New Spain and between the missionary orders themselves sapped some of their energy. While initially the threat of native uprising was a constant preoccupation, such fears were considerably allayed as colonial rule was consolidated, weakening the impetus for crown officials to underwrite evangelization efforts. Meanwhile the quantity and apostolic reach of diocesan clergy were also on the rise. One important measure of these priests' effectiveness—and their suitability for more prestigious ecclesiastical posts—was their ability to increase indigenous and other parishioners' participation in liturgical and devotional life. As native population demographics gradually rebounded during the course of the seventeenth century, diocesan priests such as Laso de la Vega took on greater responsibility for the pastoral care of native peoples. Though priests still held suspect natives' knowledge and dedication to the faith, by then many natives had received baptism and other Catholic sacraments, especially in the regions surrounding central Mexico.

The publication of *Huei tlamahuiçoltica* corresponds with this later phase of evangelization efforts to consolidate and deepen the faith commitment of Nahuas and other natives. With some anomalies, *Huei tlamahuiçoltica* also corresponds to the second stage of Lockhart's periodization of the shifts in Nahuatl language and culture. The overall tendency for the use of loan words, for instance, mirrors ecclesiastical writing in Nahuatl of the period. Scores of Spanish nouns such as Dios (God), *lámpara* (lamp), *obispo* (bishop), and Santa María de Guadalupe were employed in the text, though generally used as necessary and not excessively. Such usages reflected the growing influence of Spanish vocabulary and concepts in Nahua life, an influence that priests such as Laso de la Vega sought to expand.[24]

Huei tlamahuiçoltica encompasses an author's preface, the *Nican mopohua* apparition narrative, a brief description of the Guadalupe image, the *Nican motecpana* ("here is an ordered account") relation of miracles attributed to Guadalupe's intercession, a short biographical sketch of Juan Diego, the *Nican tlantica* ("here ends [the story]") summarizing some history of Mary's influence in New Spain and exhorting the faithful to Guadalupan devotion, and an appended Guadalupan prayer loosely modeled on the Marian hymn of the "Salve Regina" ("Hail, Holy Queen"). Laso de la Vega's publication is a composite work, and scholars disagree about whether he was the sole author, collaborated with Nahua assistants, or outright reprinted some writings of others. In particular, historians have long debated the authorship and proper dating of the *Nican mopohua*. Proponents of a sixteenth-century original composition avow that the *Nican mopohua* reflects the style of Nahuatl from the early stages after the Spanish conquest, or even the elegant Nahuatl of a native speaker from that period. Moreover, as the Nahua specialist Miguel León-Portilla put it, the *Nican mopohua* evidences "frequent recourse to concepts of pre-Hispanic thought about the supreme divinity, death, the merits and destinies of human beings." Some attribute the document to the sixteenth-century Nahua intellectual Antonio Valeriano. Their opponents disagree and place the creation of the *Nican mopohua* in the seventeenth century after Valeriano's demise.[25]

Huei tlamahuiçoltica urges pastors and their indigenous charges to appreciate Guadalupe's great concern for the native peoples, see in her image a miraculous gift of her compassionate presence, and learn the Christian message in their native language. Its ultimate aim is to promote apostolic outreach that convinces Nahuas to abandon their former ways and embrace the devout practice of Spanish Catholicism in response to the love Guadalupe offers them. Father Baltasar González, a Jesuit fluent in Nahuatl who worked at the College of San Gregorio in Mexico City where he taught elite indigenous students, served as official ecclesiastical censor for the volume. He endorsed it for publication as a work that "will be very useful and advantageous for enlivening the devotion of the lukewarm and regenerating it in those who live in ignorance of the mysterious origin of this celestial portrait of the Queen of heaven."[26]

The catechetical purpose of *Huei tlamahuiçoltica* is highlighted in its preface, which is clearly of Laso de la Vega's authorship. It stated his desire that "the humble commoners see here and find out in their language all the charitable acts you [Guadalupe] have performed on their behalf," particularly "the very great miracle by which you have appeared to people and have given them your image which is here in your precious home in Tepeyacac" (55). In an apparent apologetic about his decision to write in the Nahuas' native tongue, Laso de la Vega directed himself to Mary the Mother of God, who does "not spurn the languages of different peoples when you summon them" (55). He also recounted that the marker above Jesus's head on the cross was written in three languages; cited the medieval Franciscan theologian Bonaventure as saying "the great, marvelous, exalted miracles of our Lord God are to be written in a variety of languages so that all the different peoples on earth will see and marvel at them" (57); and noted Mary's intercessory and encouraging presence at Pentecost, when the Holy Spirit enabled the disciples to be understood in diverse tongues. Calling on that same Spirit, Laso de la Vega prayed that he might "receive his tongues of fire in order to trace in the Nahuatl language the very great miracle by which you revealed yourself to the poor humble commoners and by which you also very miraculously gave them your image" (59).

Nican mopohua and Guadalupe Image

The *Nican mopohua* follows this brief preface. It is the centerpiece of *Huei tlamahuiçoltica*, encompassing 40 percent of its pages and serving as the primary reference point for the material that follows. The narration is suitable for use in public orations or proclamations and thus embodies the purposes Laso de la Vega articulated in the preface. Various commentators have noted similarities between this Guadalupe apparition account and European precedents such as the foundational narrative for Our Lady of Guadalupe of Extremadura, a major Spanish Marian image and shrine at the time of the conquest. These similarities include a personal encounter with Mary, the occurrence of the first apparition on a Saturday (a day Catholics dedicate to Mary), the importance of light in attracting the one who encounters her, the low social status of the one Mary approaches, the skepticism of authorities, miraculous signs that help them overcome their doubt, the erection of a church or shrine at the site, claims of ongoing miracles, and the growing fame of the site and its holy image. But these generic details are true of numerous European apparition accounts, not just Guadalupe of Extremadura. As William Christian has noted, in such accounts of miraculous occurrences "the repetition of individual items [narrative details] maintains a recognizable continuity in divine behavior." At the same time, "a different arrangement and occasionally a new motif distinguish the story of one sacred place from another." Thus it is more accurate to conclude that elements of the *Nican mopohua* resemble the broad genre of appearance stories in late Medieval and Renaissance Spain, not that they comprise a recapitulation of the Extremadura or some other specific Marian tradition. Moreover, the account of the fourteenth-century origin of the Extremadura Guadalupan devotion follows a common Iberian pattern of a Marian image hidden during Muslim occupation and later miraculously rediscovered—a tale more clearly emulated in the New World case of Our Lady of los Remedios—while the *Nican mopohua* presents Guadalupe of Mexico in the genre of an apparition. These differences reflect the higher number of recovered image narratives in Spain, as well as the comparatively low instances of such occurrences in New Spain, where enshrined holy images tended to emit divine presence in place independent of a miraculous rediscovery.[27]

Most importantly, the *Nican mopohua* draws both from European antecedents and the Nahua context of colonial Mexico. The location of the apparitions at Tepeyac and the centrality of Juan Diego and Juan Bernardino are two of the most obvious links to the native world. So too are Guadalupe's use of the Nahuatl language and her appearance as a woman with indigenous features, especially her "precious face" which was "courtly and somewhat dark" (89). According to the text, she introduces herself to Juan Diego as "the eternally consummate virgin Saint Mary, mother of the very true deity, God" (65), a description obviously resonant with the Catholic understanding of Mary. But she also identifies with the Nahua natives, deeming herself "the compassionate mother of you and of all you[r] people here in this land" (65). Similarly, the name she uses for God is both Spanish and Nahuatl—"Teotl Dios" (64)—a supreme being who spans the Nahua and Spanish worlds as "the giver of life, the creator of people, the ever present, the lord of heaven and earth" (65). Though it is not possible to specify who introduced such textual elements or the precise rationale for doing so, the presence of these elements is consistent with the process of mutual accommodation that marked native-Spanish interaction. Thus like much of Nahua Christianity, the *Nican mopohua* is not merely a transplanted European text or tradition. Rather, it is a faith expression that interweaves Nahua elements into a narrative structure drawn from European Catholic miraculous appearance accounts.

Emphasis on Juan Diego as a model of faithfulness—one that presumably Laso de la Vega and his fellow priests urged other natives to emulate—is a central motif of the *Nican mopohua*, as it is of *Huei tlamahuiçoltica* as a whole. Consistent with the claim that Guadalupe showed special favor to the Nahuas, from the outset the *Nican mopohua* states: "First she revealed herself to a humble commoner named Juan Diego" (61). Guadalupe's opening words to Juan Diego were "dear Juan, dear Juan Diego" (63), a tender greeting that resounded in her various exchanges with him throughout the narrative. The enchantment Laso de la Vega wanted devotees to feel in the presence of the Guadalupe image is modeled in the depiction of Juan Diego when his eyes first beheld the beauty of her countenance and its transformative effect on the landscape around her:

> When he came before her, he greatly marveled at how she completely surpassed everything in her total splendor. Her clothes were like the sun in the way they gleamed and shone. Her resplendence struck the stones and boulders by which she stood so that they

seemed like precious emeralds and jeweled bracelets. The ground sparkled like a rainbow, and the mesquite, the prickly pear cactus, and other various kinds of weeds that grow there seemed like green obsidian, and their foliage like fine turquoise. Their stalks, their thorns and spines gleamed like gold (63, 65).

The dramatic tension that drives the account centers on the skepticism of Bishop Juan de Zumárraga and his assistants and Juan Diego's corresponding perseverance despite self-doubt. On his first visit to the bishop's residence to relate Guadalupe's message and her desire that a temple be built in her honor, Juan Diego was kept waiting a lengthy time and in the end was dismissed with suspicion. Distraught, he returned immediately to Tepeyac to plead that Guadalupe "entrust one of the high nobles, who are recognized, respected, and honored, to carry and take your message, so that he will be believed. For I am a poor ordinary man" (69). In one of the most moving passages of the text, Guadalupe responded to him: "Be assured that my servants and messengers to whom I entrust it to carry my message and realize my wishes are not high ranking people. Rather it is highly necessary that you yourself be involved and take care of it. It is very much by your hand that my will and wish are to be carried out and accomplished" (71).

The following visit with the bishop was no more successful than the first, though the bishop "asked and interrogated him about very many things in order to be satisfied about where he saw her and what she was like" (73). Bishop Zumárraga was impressed with Juan Diego's confidence when the prelate requested that Guadalupe present him a sign to verify that she was the source of Juan Diego's messages. Nonetheless, the bishop sent some assistants to follow Juan Diego and report his activities. When they lost sight of him near Tepeyac, they became so angry that they told the bishop if he "should return, they would seize him on the spot and punish him severely, so that he would never lie and disturb people again" (75).

The climax of the story is Juan Diego's vindication in his final visit to the bishop's dwelling. His growing confidence surged when Guadalupe had him gather flowers that had grown out of season. The hostile reception he received again from the bishop's assistants turned to curiosity when they marveled at the flowers, though "all three times when they tried to step forward to take them [the flowers], they were entirely unsuccessful, because when they were about to grasp them, it was no longer real flowers that they saw but something seemingly painted, embroidered, or sewn on the cloak" (83). Ushered into the bishop's presence, Juan Diego recounted with joy his encounter with Guadalupe and the flowers she bid him gather in his cloak. When he dropped the flowers at the bishop's feet, her image appeared, and the bishop and his household "knelt down, they marveled greatly at it." Moreover, "the lord bishop, with tears and sorrow, implored and asked her forgiveness for not having immediately carried out her wish, her message" (85). Juan Diego and Juan Bernardino were received with great honor and were guests in the bishop's home until the Guadalupe chapel was completed and her image carried in procession from the Mexico City cathedral to Tepeyac.

Guadalupe's defense of the beleaguered Juan Diego—enabling him to diplomatically prevail even over the leading ecclesiastical figure in the colonies of New Spain—is but one instance of the *Nican mopohua*'s emphasis on her favor toward the native peoples. Above all, the account repeatedly underscores the celestial assistance Guadalupe desires to bestow on her sons and daughters. In her first encounter with Juan Diego, she asked that a temple be built for her at Tepeyac "where I will manifest, make known, and give to people all my love, compassion, aid, and protection . . . [and] listen to their weeping and their sorrows in order to remedy and heal all their various afflictions, miseries, and torments" (65, 67). Her words to Juan Diego in a later encounter when he was troubled about the illness of his uncle, Juan Bernardino, are the most quoted among present-day devotees: "Do not be concerned, do not fear the illness, or any other illness or calamity. Am I, your mother, not here? Are you not under my protective shade, my shadow?" (79).

In its narrative details and thrust, the *Nican mopohua* presents Juan Diego as an exemplar of a faithful believer's response to divine revelation and to Guadalupe's maternal care. He joyfully entered into a mystical encounter with Guadalupe and contemplated her beauty and presence. He spoke with her in deeply respectful yet intimate communion. He was quick to obey her requests and perseverant in overcoming the obstacles he confronted. He was humble and trusting. He honestly presented his concerns about his lowly status to her. His steadfastness in the Christian faith was evident when he discovered his uncle was in danger of death, as he quickly set out "to summon one of those beloved of our Lord, our friars, to go hear his confession and prepare him, for what we were born for is to come to await our duty of death" (77). As depicted in the *Nican mopohua*, from his first encounter with Guadalupe, their filial bond became his heart's treasure and overshadowed hesitancy and doubt.

Juan Diego's response to Guadalupe was mirrored in that of his indigenous contemporaries, who were also presented as models of dedication
that fellow natives and other believers should emulate. Juan Bernardino
testified before the bishop and his household that at the very moment
Guadalupe consoled Juan Diego about his illness she appeared to him and
he was cured. He confessed his trust in Guadalupe and attested "that he
really saw her in exactly the same way as she appeared to his nephew" (87).
More broadly, the final lines of the *Nican mopohua* avow that "there was a
movement in all the altepetls [communities] everywhere of people coming
to see and marvel at her precious image. They came to show their devotion
and pray to her; they marveled greatly at how it was by a divine miracle
that she had appeared, that absolutely no earthly person had painted her
precious image" (89).

A short physical description of the Guadalupe image follows. Located
immediately after the conclusion of the *Nican mopohua*, the intricacy of
this written sketch—encompassing details such as "her precious face,
which is perfectly wondrous" (89)—appears designed to entice devotees
to make pilgrimage to Tepeyac and behold and venerate her there. Seen
in this light, the primary purpose of the *Nican mopohua* as presented in
Huei tlamahuiçoltica is to foster among the faithful a deeper devotion to
Guadalupe's wondrous appearance, her maternal care, and her ongoing
presence in her miraculous image.

Nican motecpana

Like the *Nican mopohua*, the *Nican motecpana*, the other major section
of *Huei tlamahuiçoltica*, has parallels in Sánchez's *Imagen de la Virgen
María*. Both works are also similar to an earlier visual source, an engraving (c. 1613–1615) by the Flemish artist Samuel Stradanus depicting
eight scenes of miracles that devotees attributed to Guadalupe. These
eight scenes and six other miracles are presented in the *Nican motecpana*
(92–115), while Sánchez recounts seven miracles attributed to Guadalupe,
six of which are also narrated in the *Nican motecpana* and three depicted
in the Stradanus engraving. These three primary sources present the
earliest composite records of Guadalupe's interventions on behalf
of her faithful, most of them involving cures from various afflictions.
The collections parallel the far lengthier books of miracles used to promote holy sites in Europe. But unlike various earlier clerically authored
narratives of miracles in colonial Nahua manuscripts and publications,

those recounted in the *Nican motecpana* (as well as in Sánchez and the Stradanus engraving) were set in New Spain and were not direct adaptations or mere repetitions of events from the Old World. In this regard they resembled the *Nican mopohua* with its intermingling of Nahua and Spanish elements.[28]

Prints from the Stradanus engraving were distributed more than three decades before the publication of the Sánchez and Laso de la Vega volumes. Nonetheless, it is not clear if Stradanus is the original source. Peterson contends that "slight discrepancies between the Stradanus image and the Laso de la Vega written account argue for independent and perhaps multiple sources available to the Flemish artist and the creole authors working thirty years later." She notes, for example, that Stradanus depicts a nun healed in the spring waters at the Guadalupe shrine whom his caption identifies as "Catharina de niehta." The *Nican motecpana* narrates two accounts of women's cures at these healing waters, but does not give their full names nor identify either as a nun. According to Peterson, "Laso de la Vega would not have intentionally elided this kind of specificity as names and places (and rarely dates) anchor miracles in historical reality and would have been added if available."[29]

Whatever the original sources for the miracles recounted, it is important to bear in mind that Archbishop Juan Pérez de la Serna of Mexico City commissioned the Stradanus engraving and its prints to solicit donations for a new church edifice at Tepeyac. Thus it is not surprising that the beneficiaries depicted in the engraving are all Spaniards, with the possible exception of the child of Juan Pavón. The caption in the engraving presents Pavón as a sacristan, a service that natives often provided, leading Peterson to the plausible conclusion that he was of indigenous background. Of the four incidents Sánchez narrates that Stradanus did not depict, three exclusively involve native peoples as recipients of Guadalupe's care, and the fourth concerns the 1629–1634 Mexico City flood, when Guadalupe aided residents of all social backgrounds. In the *Nican motecpana*, four of the six incidents not depicted in Stradanus involve indigenous devotees, as might be expected since Laso de la Vega's book is aimed at fostering Catholic faith and life in native communities. Seen in this light, the two earliest narrative collections of Guadalupe miracles counteract the pronounced Spanish emphasis of the Stradanus engraving. Indeed, as Alison Fitchett Climenhaga has noted, the *Nican motecpana* no doubt "encourage[d] the demoralized, presenting devotion to Guadalupe as the solution to the pain of their physical and social condition."[30]

The first three miracles recounted in the *Nican motecpana* (which match the first three recounted in Sánchez's *Imagen de la Virgen María*) focus on Guadalupe's favor to the indigenous peoples, applying the lessons of Juan Diego to a wider indigenous audience. According to the account, when the newly constructed Guadalupe chapel was ready, a "grand" procession encompassing Spanish officials, "all the Mexica [Nahua] rulers and nobles," and "the people from other altepetls all around" (93) transferred the Guadalupe image the three miles from the Mexico City cathedral to enshrine it at Tepeyac. As figure 2.1 illustrates, unfortunately the exemplary collective response to this important occasion was disrupted along the way. A stray arrow from a mock skirmish, which residents of New Spain often conducted as an entertainment on such occasions, struck and killed one of the indigenous participants. His relatives placed him before Guadalupe and begged for her intercession, at which point he revived and his arrow wound was healed. Seeing this, "Absolutely everyone marveled greatly and praised the consummate Virgin, the heavenly Lady, Saint Mary of Guadalupe, for the way she was now carrying out the pledge she made to Juan Diego that she would always help and defend the local people

FIGURE 2.1. Workshop of José Juárez (attributed), *Traslado de la imagen de la Virgen de Guadalupe a la primera ermita y representación del primer milagro,* c. 1653. The first known painting of Guadalupe's first miracle portrays some richly dressed native leaders but primarily scantily clad warriors. Guadalupe's favor is bestowed on one of these warriors, with the presumption that her favor will uplift and "civilize" him according to Christian European standards. Courtesy Archivo del Museo de la Basílica de Guadalupe.

and all those who invoke her" (95). Moreover, "from that moment on this humble person remained at the precious home of the heavenly precious Lady; there he used to sweep her temple and home for her" (95). The clear parallel between Guadalupe's compassionate concern for Juan Diego and for his native brother who was slain with the arrow, as well as between the homage and service both offered to their mother Guadalupe in gratitude, revealed the need for all the natives to imitate Juan Diego in approaching Guadalupe and dedicating themselves to her.

The miracle accounts of the *Nican motecpana* reflected the religious sensibilities of seventeenth-century Catholicism in Spain and its New World territories. For example, the second account illuminated the Spanish Catholic tendency to view God as stern and distant, inciting appeals to Guadalupe and other Marian figures as compassionate mothers and intercessors. In the midst of the 1540s epidemic during which "our Lord the giver of life was reducing and depopulating the land" (95), Franciscan friars organized a procession to the shrine at Tepeyac. As the friars and natives made their way they beseeched "our Lord to have pity on his altepetl, that there be an end to his ire and wrath, in the very name and for the sake of his precious, revered mother, the consummate Virgin, our Queen, Saint Mary of Guadalupe" (95). They even employed the Spanish penitential practice of enlisting young children to flog themselves as they processed.[31] The narration implies that Guadalupe had a tempering effect on her son's perceived anger, as the epidemic soon subsided.

Such assertions reflected the Spanish Catholic tendency to view God as distant or even vengeful. Many priests and catechists urged devotees to approach God through an intermediary, especially Mary who as God's mother ostensibly has the most effective capacity to assuage divine wrath. Such a perspective has a long trajectory among Roman Catholics of various backgrounds, and was prevalent from the initial stages of evangelization in Mexico. As scholars such as Orlando Espín contend, in this context Mary "became a necessary religious symbol of compassion and care." Burkhart concurs that the Nahuas learned well the Spanish practice of approaching Guadalupe and other Marian representations as a "protector and advocate." Such an approach to Mary potentially mediated images of God as a stern father who lacks compassion and, indeed, of a dysfunctional celestial family in which one needs maternal intervention to cajole unpredictable paternal authority.[32]

A third miracle that benefited the indigenous illuminated the attitude of Spanish and *criollo* clergy such as Laso de la Vega toward the indigenous peoples and their faith. The beneficiary was Juan de Tovar, the caretaker of the image of Our Lady of los Remedios. According to the *Nican motecpana*, because Juan "knew how the heavenly Lady [of Guadalupe] had healed Juan Bernardino" (97), he had his loved ones carry him to the Guadalupe sanctuary, where he was cured. In the process of narrating these events, the account states that Guadalupe "cherished, aided, and defended the local people" (97) in the wake of the Spaniards' arrival. Yet at the same time the *Nican motecpana* concurred with the Spanish colonial enterprise in presuming that Guadalupe abetted Spanish efforts to displace native religion since, because of her compassion, the natives "despised and abhorred the idolatry in which they had been wandering about in confusion on the earth, in the night and darkness in which the demon had made them live" (97). The Guadalupan pedagogy that Laso de la Vega expounded is clear: in his view Guadalupe allied herself with the Spanish enterprise, bestowing her favor on the natives as a means to allure them to "entirely give themselves and adhere to the faith" (97) that Mary of Guadalupe and Catholic missioners propagated among them.

Unlike Sánchez, who compared Guadalupe and Remedios to the scriptural figures of Naomi and Ruth and stated they are complementary, Laso de la Vega tended to accentuate Guadalupe's prominence. In a subsequent section *Huei tlamahuiçoltica* reminded readers "that the heavenly precious Lady, the only precious mother of God's precious child, is a single thing" (119) and thus her various manifestations "everywhere in the world" (119) are all the same Mary the mother of God. But the text also reiterated that Remedios was an image the Spaniards brought from their homeland, while Guadalupe appeared in Mexico and "set up her residence here at Tepeyacac and by a great miracle gave people her image, which no earthly human artist made or colored" (121). Thus Guadalupe was distinctive in that she was both native to Mexico and her image was a gift from heaven to the people there. Consciously or not, in attempting to maximize the appeal of Guadalupe to the Nahuas, *Huei tlamahuiçoltica* intimated that her primacy over Remedios and other images provided a rationale for natives to sense their own divine election.

Parallel to Juan Diego's vindication before the bishop and his assistants, the emphasis on Guadalupe's care for the natives was particularly evident in an account of how she miraculously counteracted the decrees of Spanish authorities. According to this narrative, in 1558 Francisco Quetzalmamalitzin of Teotihuacan led his people in protest of a decision to replace the Franciscan friars with Augustinians in their local community.

When royal officials sought to punish them, the natives "went about hiding in various places, because they were being sought everywhere" (111). In this hour of need Quetzalmamalitzin turned to Guadalupe, who convinced the viceroy and members of the *royal audiencia* (royal tribunal) to rescind the mandate to remove the Franciscans and to desist from punishing the natives who had opposed their decrees. Of course even while Guadalupe sided with native subjects, the narrative still confirmed the ascendancy of Christianity, as she assisted natives to voluntarily retain their Franciscan evangelizers.

Collectively, the fourteen miracles enumerated in the *Nican motecpana* range from petitioners being saved from a horse accident and falling lamp to healings of headaches, dropsy, and severe swelling of the feet and neck. Like the eight miraculous scenes of the Stradanus engraving shown in figure 2.2, these miracles were recounted as independent units and with relatively little interpretive analysis of their deeper significance. The briefest of the miracle accounts illustrates their suitability for proc-lamation as illustrations in sermons or other orations, as well as their basic pattern of affliction, supplication, and celestial aid, with expressions of thanks and grateful commitment to Guadalupe added in various instances (though not the one cited here of the aforementioned child of Juan Pavón):

> A sacristan named Juan Pavón, who took care of the churchly home of the heavenly Lady, our precious mother of Guadalupe, had a small child, and it contracted a swelling of the neck. It was gravely ill and about to die; it was no longer able to breathe. He took it before her and anointed it with the oil that burns in her lamp. At that very moment it was healed, favored by the heavenly Lady (111).

The intended effect of such testimonies—individually and taken as a whole—is to draw the faithful to Guadalupe and to her home at Tepeyac. One passage described the spring at Tepeyac that "is effective with all dif-ferent kinds of illnesses for those who in good faith drink it or bathe in it" (105). The wonders recounted in the *Nican motecpana* are merely a sam-pling of the "innumerable" (105, 113) miracles affected through Guadalupe's intercession. They were related in order to attract the devout and those in need so that in seeking Guadalupe's aid they might also strengthen their Catholic faith.

FIGURE 2.2. Samuel Stradanus, *Virgen de Guadalupe con escenas de ocho milagros*, c. 1615. The visual witness to miraculous favors expanded devotion to Guadalupe and other celestial patrons. Guadalupe is depicted in the center of this engraving to underscore she is the source of the eight wonders on the side panels, including the healing of Juan Pavón's child in the seventh panel (the second one from the bottom on the right-hand side). Courtesy Archivo del Museo de la Basílica de Guadalupe.

Juan Diego, *Nican tlantica*, and Guadalupan Prayer

The next section of *Huei tlamahuiçoltica* is a short treatment of Juan Diego's life. In *Imagen de la Virgen María*, Sánchez had interspersed details about Juan Diego and presented various analogies between Juan Diego and biblical figures. For example, he asserts that Moses's theophany on Mount Sinai and reception of the Ten Commandments prefigured Juan

Diego's ascent of the hill of Tepeyac to encounter Guadalupe and receive her miraculous image as a new Ark of the Covenant.[33] But Laso de la Vega published the earliest sustained synopsis of Juan Diego's life, which he posed as a prototype of the ideal Nahua response to the many marvels of Guadalupe.

It is not clear if Laso de la Vega intended to do so, but his hagiographic sketch portrayed Juan Diego as a model Franciscan lay brother or lay person living a consecrated life. After his encounters with Guadalupe, Juan Diego "dedicated himself entirely to the heavenly Lady as his patron" (113). He served as caretaker of the Guadalupe image and site, where he spent the remainder of his days in prayer, fasting, penance, and solitude and with frequent confession and communion. His relation to Guadalupe was so strong that "whatever he would ask her for, when he prayed to the heavenly Lady, she would grant it all" (115). The account even claimed that, though married to a woman named María Lucía who died two years before the apparitions, Juan Diego remained a chaste virgin throughout his life in response to a sermon of Fray Toribio de Benavente, one of the original Franciscan "twelve apostles" to Mexico who was also known as Motolinía ("the poor one"). *Huei tlamahuiçoltica*'s description of Juan Diego's death related a comforting vision of Guadalupe in which she welcomed him into the joy of heaven, a favor the account stated she had earlier bestowed on his uncle Juan Bernardino. The text also stated that both uncle and nephew were buried within the Guadalupe chapel. Laso de la Vega's catechetical purpose in *Huei tlamahuiçoltica* was acutely manifest in the concluding invocation of his exposition about Juan Diego's saintly life: "May it be her [Guadalupe's] wish that we too may serve her and abandon all the worldly things that lead us astray, so that we too may attain the eternal riches of heaven" (115).

The final section of *Huei tlamahuiçoltica*, the *Nican tlantica*, situated Guadalupe within the wider context of Mary in the Catholic world. Echoing an antiphon from matins of the Little Office of the Blessed Virgin Mary,[34] Laso de la Vega reminded his readers that Mary has "destroyed and annihilated all idolatry and perverse belief over the entire earth" (125). Guadalupe fulfilled this Marian mission among the natives of New Spain. She elected to reveal herself to Juan Diego, Juan Bernardino, and their fellow natives; won their hearts with her healing love; gave them her miraculous image as an enduring presence; and led her indigenous daughters and sons to dispel "the images of the demon" and "revere and believe in our Lord Jesus Christ" (123). Thus "not only did the heavenly Queen, our precious mother of Guadalupe, come here to reveal herself in order to aid the humble commoners in their earthly afflictions, she wanted even more to give them her light and aid so that they would recognize the one true deity, God, and through him see and know the heavenly life" (123).

Laso de la Vega confessed that many of the wonders Guadalupe worked have regrettably been forgotten with time, but he contended that enough was known and recounted in his treatise to make her maternal predilection and salvific desire for the natives abundantly apparent. The apostolic duty of pastors such as Laso de la Vega was to ensure natives fully appreciate "that it was for their very sake that their Queen condescended to house herself there" (121) at Tepeyac. Above all, pastors were to make the designs of Guadalupe known to native (and other) believers so they might "awaken and open their eyes to see . . . [what] the heavenly precious Lady did for their sake, in order to consider what they need to do to return and pay back her love . . . with all our heart here on earth until that time when by her aid we will see her with our eyes in her fortunate dwelling place" (125).

The final page of *Huei tlamahuiçoltica* presented a "prayer to be directed to the heavenly Queen, our precious mother of Guadalupe" (127). In the original publication it was set off from the main body of the text on a single page, suggesting it was an appendix intended as a prayer for devotees to memorize and recite. Indeed, the oration summarized the main themes of the treatise and served as a concise catechetical tool for imparting and interiorizing its core contents. The prayer opens with a Trinitarian invocation, calling on Mary to rejoice as "the precious daughter of God the Father . . . the precious mother of God's precious child . . . the precious spouse of God the Holy Spirit" (127). Successive further invocations laud her for miraculously revealing herself to the native peoples and giving them her image so they could present their supplications to her. Then the prayer turns to petition, asking for her assistance in our troubles, her light to guide us on the heavenly path, and her help in receiving from God forgiveness for our sins. Echoing an earlier reference about God whose "ire and wrath" (95) ostensibly lacks the compassionate qualities Guadalupe was said to embody, the prayer text also asks her intercession to "appease the heart of your precious child; may all his wrath and anger subside" (127). Finally, reinforcing various statements in *Huei tlamahuiçoltica* about our ultimate destiny as humans, the prayer (and the treatise itself) concludes: "And then at the time of our death please remove and put to flight our foe, who leads us astray, so that happily and peacefully our souls may go to lie entirely in your hands, so that they may go appear in the presence of God, their creator. Amen." (127)

Laso de la Vega and Guadalupan Evangelization

The immediate impact of Laso de la Vega's *Huei tlamahuiçoltica* on evangelization efforts among Nahuatl-speaking natives is difficult to assess. Like most other tracts of its era, *Huei tlamahuiçoltica* undoubtedly had a relatively limited publication run. The fact that it was written in Nahuatl further reduced its reading audience. Certainly Guadalupan devotion spread among indigenous and other devotees subsequent to Laso de la Vega's publication, though the extent of *Huei tlamahuiçoltica*'s influence on these developments is not clear. Priests sent to rural parishes with indigenous congregants after receiving their seminary training in Mexico City facilitated the expansion of the geographic range and density of Guadalupan devotion, but the impact of these clergy increased most dramatically more than a century after the publication of Laso de la Vega's treatise.[35] Moreover, the full text of *Huei tlamahuiçoltica* was not reprinted until 1926, when the Mexican historian and Nahua specialist Primo Feliciano Velázquez published an annotated version with a Spanish translation.[36] The subsequent influence of *Huei tlamahuiçoltica*, particularly the *Nican mopohua*, is easier to chart than the significance of the treatise in Laso de la Vega's own era.

Yet *Huei tlamahuiçoltica* articulated pastoral concerns prevalent in Laso de la Vega's time that had an enduring influence. It was the first work to highlight what many subsequent clergy have deemed the most pressing challenge of Guadalupan pastoral ministry: the need to link the favors Guadalupe bestows on her devout with her call to deeper faith and apostolic service. The approach of *Huei tlamahuiçoltica* to this challenge is consistent with many ensuing efforts in Guadalupan pastoral outreach. For Laso de la Vega, the content of Guadalupan catechesis was straightforward and its promotion a crucial pastoral priority. He admonished his fellow leaders to entice indigenous peoples with the beauty of Guadalupe and to teach them about Guadalupe's providential election of Juan Diego and of them as her favored sons and daughters. Their favor was indicated in Juan Diego's vindication before Bishop Zumárraga, as well as in the *Nican motecpana*'s exposition of a remarkable incident in which Guadalupe defended the natives of Teotihuacan over against the viceroy and other Spanish officials. Moreover, their favor was underscored in the Mexican Guadalupe's precedence over the Spanish Our Lady of Remedios, an inference rooted in a bold claim repeated in various passages of *Huei tlamahuiçoltica*: without Spanish intermediary, the mother of God herself had descended from heaven to evangelize the natives through Juan Diego. Laso de la Vega beseeched his readers to impress these mysteries of celestial election on the hearts of Guadalupe's faithful and to beckon them to lay their burdens before her. Most importantly, pastors were then to lead the faithful to seek the ways of heaven out of gratitude for the boundless love of Guadalupe and her son, Jesus Christ.

The ongoing influence of the pastoral challenge Laso de la Vega addressed is evident in the efforts of present-day pastoral leaders such as the Mexican American priest Allan Figueroa Deck. In a homily for the Guadalupe feast, Deck observed that the relation between Guadalupe and her faithful "is sometimes simply that of a loving mother who literally lavishes care and concern on her needy children." He contended that this is only half the meaning of Guadalupe, since "the story of Tepeyac . . . graphically portrays the central role of love and service in our Christian lives." Exhorting his listeners to put into action their gratitude for the gift of God's love offered through their mother Guadalupe, Deck concluded: "Seized and saturated by such love, what will be our response to others, especially those most in need?" His admonishment extends to the present Laso de la Vega's approach of engaging devotees' dedication to Guadalupe as a means to enhance their faith commitment.[37]

Laso de la Vega's presentation of Juan Bernardino and especially Juan Diego as models of saintliness is another significant contribution of *Huei tlamahuiçoltica* that subsequent pastors and devotees have emulated. Indeed, the first known initiative to gather indigenous testimony about Guadalupe indicated native veneration of Juan Diego. While it is not clear if *Huei tlamahuiçoltica* had a direct link with witnesses for the 1665–1666 Guadalupan inquiry, their testimony was consistent with Laso de la Vega's pastoral counsel that Juan Diego be presented as an exemplar of Christian life. Though systematic treatments of his life did not emerge until the twentieth century, subsequent writers and preachers followed Laso de la Vega in expounding the evangelical virtues of Juan Diego.

The most conspicuous contribution of Laso de la Vega's treatise is his publication of the *Nican mopohua*, which over time became commonly acclaimed as the foundational text for the Guadalupe tradition and the guiding narrative for the widespread worship practice of dramatic proclamations and reenactments of the apparitions. Thus *Huei tlamahuiçoltica* promoted both the dissemination and the pastoral engagement of Guadalupe's encounter with Juan Diego. The focus on the *Nican mopohua* in present-day Guadalupan theologies continues the work Laso de la Vega began. It is an ongoing attempt to articulate the theological and catechetical significance of a sacred narrative that gradually grew in stature among millions of devotees. Like Laso de la Vega, a number of today's commentators observe that at its core the *Nican mopohua* relates Guadalupe's call that Juan Diego be her messenger. Many note the significance of Guadalupe communicating with Juan Diego in the Nahuatl language and cultural idiom, an observation based in large part on Laso de la Vega's Nahuatl-language publication. Various writers reflect on the dramatic reversals effected in the apparition narrative, such as Juan Diego's transformation from a sense of his inferiority to the dignity of serving as Guadalupe's emissary, the bishop's changing attitude toward Juan Diego from initial suspicion to confidence, and the shifting geographic focus from the bishop's residence in the capital city to the indigenous settlement around Tepeyac, a place on the peripheries of society where in the end the bishop and his entourage accompanied Juan Diego and Juan Bernardino to build the temple that Guadalupe requested. These present-day writers also mirror Laso de la Vega in exhorting Guadalupe's devotees to live a gospel-based life out of wonder and gratitude for the gift of Guadalupe.

Huei tlamahuiçoltica is rooted in the presumption that God and Mary of Guadalupe are already present and active in everyday human life. The pastoral task is to increase awareness of this abiding presence and saving action, and above all to inspire Christian conversion borne of thankfulness for the splendid gratuity of divine love. Human limitations can diminish such a lofty pastoral vision, as is evident in Laso de la Vega's Eurocentric presumption that Guadalupe was an ally in eradicating the natives' former way of life, as well as his notion that the Jesus of the Christian tradition is a vengeful God. Nonetheless, Laso de la Vega's attempt to ground his pastoral vision in the concrete realities of local life—the sacred site of Tepeyac, the encounter with Guadalupe, the witness of Juan Diego, and testimonies of celestial aid—illuminates an approach to evangelization that has continued to shape the Guadalupe tradition down to the present.

PART II

An Evolving Tradition

3

Divine Providence

SERMONS IN COLONIAL SOCIETY

MIGUEL SÁNCHEZ AND Luis Laso de la Vega presumed in their mid-seventeenth century writings that divine providence guided Spanish evangelization and colonization in the New World. Subsequently numerous preachers reinforced and explored this notion in sermons, a form of public discourse that had a significant impact on church and society. Bartolomé Felipe de Ita y Parra was the most prolific of the published Guadalupan preachers during the colonial era and arguably the most influential. Four of his twenty-two extant published sermons were centered on Guadalupe. Each corresponded to a significant moment in the life of New Spain and its capital city: the celebration of the two hundredth anniversary of the Guadalupe apparitions in 1731, the final service for a 1737 novena held at Tepeyac to plead for Guadalupe's aid during a severe epidemic, and two sermons linked with the campaign to declare Guadalupe the patroness of New Spain, one while the campaign was still underway and a second to mark devotees' public declaration of Guadalupe as their patroness in 1746. Ita y Parra's sermons illuminated the theology of divine providence at the heart of colonial Guadalupan sermons and devotion—indeed, at the core of colonial Catholicism and society.

Current access to the contents of colonial preaching is primarily through sermons that were published and have survived down to the present. Carlos Herrejón Peredo cites approximately two thousand such publications in New Spain from the first known published sermon in 1577 until the end of the colonial era in 1821. Of these he found 36 percent were focused on the Virgin Mary and more than one hundred specifically on Our Lady of Guadalupe.[1] It is important to bear in mind, however, that the

corpus of published sermons comprises but a fraction of the sacred oratory from the colonial period. The publication of a sermon was contingent
on funding, which came from sources such as private patrons, a *cofradía*
that had sponsored a religious feast and its sermon, or a preacher's religious order. Funders' proclivities influenced the choice of which sermons
would be published, if not the contents of the texts themselves. Published
sermons were largely directed at elite readers who were literate and could
afford them. Consequently the published versions tended to include more
references to classical sources and even untranslated Latin passages, since
readers were often expected to have reading knowledge of that language.
A number of published sermons also addressed disputed questions and
employed literary discourses that presumably were not typical of oral,
unpublished sermons given to neophytes and ordinary parishioners.
Sermonarios, or books of sample sermons that busy pastors could consult
or use, offer some sense of the messages everyday congregations may have
heard, though there are relatively few colonial Guadalupe sermons in these
sources and no comprehensive evidence about who employed them and
in what contexts.[2] For all these reasons, it is necessary to recognize that
textual analysis of the available published sermons does not provide an
all-inclusive perspective on sacred oratory in New Spain. Nonetheless, the
pervasive influence of that oratory underscores the significance of extant
sermons for understanding church, society, and Guadalupan theologies
during the colonial era.

Studies of the colonial sermons have tended to elaborate their collective
thematic content.[3] A number of recurring themes and images stem from
Sánchez's foundational *Imagen de la Virgen María*, such as the correlation
between Guadalupe and the woman of Revelation 12, the fulfillment of biblical prophecy in the Guadalupe event, and Guadalupe's decisive role in the
New World spread of Christianity. At the same time, colonial-era preachers
also proposed various new hypotheses about Guadalupe. Some postulated
in Neoplatonic terms that Guadalupe's image authentically depicted the
divine concept of Mary, a thesis articulated in the first known published
Guadalupan sermon,[4] José Vidal de Figueroa's 1661 oration *Teórica de la
prodigiosa imagen de la Virgen Santa María de Guadalupe de México* (Theory
of the prodigious image of the Holy Virgin Mary of Guadalupe of Mexico).
Jesuit preachers were the primary advocates of another theological innovation: just as the transubstantiation of bread and wine into the body and
blood of Christ occurred in the Mass, so too Mary was sacramentally present in the perpetual miracle of the Guadalupe image. An often-repeated

assertion was that Christ evangelized the Old World through the apostles' preaching of the word of God, while Mary of Guadalupe effected the evangelization of the New World through her miraculous image, a visual means of communication highly suited to the indigenous psyche.[5]

Of course, sermons are speech events, dynamic interactions between a speaker and hearers. They occur within a time and space marked off as sacred, an ambiance that amplifies the authority of both the preacher and the message. In New Spain the central place of sermons in heavily sensory ritual environments further enhanced this authoritative aura. Thus it is not surprising that the art of preaching was an essential component of clerical training. The Franciscan friar Martín de Velasco's *Arte de sermones para hacerlos y predicarlos* (The art of creating and preaching sermons) illuminates the approach to preaching taught in New Spain. The typical structure of colonial Guadalupan sermons is consistent with the recommendations in Velasco's treatise: a dedication and greeting, an introduction that states the basic thesis of the oration, the body of the sermon expounding on its central theme, and a final salutation that exhorts the hearers to enact the message received. Like other sermon manuals, *Arte de sermones* emphasized careful attention to bodily expressions in preaching such as gestures, posture, and voice fluctuation. New Spain preachers learned from mentors such as Velasco their understanding of the sermon as "a complete artifice, which Christian rhetoric arranges to persuade (teach, delight, and move) hearers to the love of virtues [and] the abhorrence of vices."[6]

The exuberant and grandiose baroque artistic style reflected in Velasco's manual gave form to preaching during the seventeenth and eighteenth centuries. It appealed to hearers' emotions with vivid images and anecdotes as opposed to sheer logic and rational argument. At the same time, the reforms of the Council of Trent (1545–1563) shaped the content of sermons, prompting preachers to promote uniformity in adherence to Catholic doctrine, practices, and morality. Preachers tended to presume that Catholic principles were intrinsically linked to the social, cultural, and political realities of Spain and its colonies. Obedience in faith entailed conformity to societal norms and expectations. Along with images, church architecture, rituals, drama, and catechetical materials and lessons, preaching fostered the acculturation of indigenous neophytes and the promotion of group cohesion in colonial society. When linked to the promotion of the intimate bonds devotees developed with patron saints such as Guadalupe, sermons had an even greater potential to sanctify the status quo of colonial society in listeners' imaginations. As Alicia Mayer has maintained, "Through the pulpit, ideas were conveyed that, taken together . . . constituted a true ideological system" intended to encompass all aspects of life in New Spain.[7]

Ita y Parra was a native of Puebla who received his education from the Jesuits, gained renown for his eloquence, and rose to prominence as a diocesan priest in the inner circles of Mexico City. A number of his published sermons solemnized important occasions in the life of New Spain and its capital city, such as the celebrations for the canonizations of Saint Aloysius Gonzaga and Saint John of the Cross, funerals for prominent figures such as Archbishop José Pérez de Lanciego y Eguiluz, and the Mexico City commemoration of the deceased Spanish monarch Felipe V. Ita y Parra held a number of distinguished ecclesiastical appointments, including his long service as a canon of the Mexico City cathedral chapter and eventually as treasurer of that body. Like various other canons, he also taught theology at the Royal and Pontifical University in Mexico City.

Even before Ita y Parra's distinguished career, initiatives of civic and ecclesiastical leaders as well as grassroots devotees expanded the circle of Guadalupe's faithful beyond the vicinity of Mexico City and Tepeyac. But the decades in which Ita y Parra delivered his Guadalupan orations were critical in the historical development of devotion to her. The period culminated in an unprecedented 1754 papal endorsement of Guadalupe that further enlarged her cult and catapulted devotion to her over that of all other sacred images in New Spain. Ita y Parra's sermons accompanied and fostered Guadalupe's ascendency. Understanding the trajectory of Guadalupan devotion sheds light on the theology of divine providence that Ita y Parra and his contemporaries advanced in their preaching.

Patroness of New Spain

Guadalupan devotion was largely concentrated in Mexico City and the environs until the mid-seventeenth century. Devotees' growing acclaim for Guadalupe's miraculous assistance helped spur interest in her beyond the capital district. An even greater catalyst for Guadalupe's widening geographic renown was Sánchez's publication of the first theological work on Guadalupe in 1648 and Mateo de la Cruz's abbreviated version of his treatise a dozen years later. Though ultimately unsuccessful, the 1665–1666 initiative of the Mexico City cathedral chapter to secure papal promulgation of a Guadalupe feast day and proper office illuminated the mounting efforts to spread her cult. Invocations of Guadalupe's aid became more frequent and geographically dispersed, as is evident in the expedition that brought the first Spanish subjects as far north as present-day San Antonio, Texas, in 1691. Domingo Terán de los Ríos, the military leader of the group, echoed the title of Francisco de Florencia's *La estrella del norte de México* published three years earlier by acclaiming "the powerful Virgin of Guadalupe" as the "polestar and guide" of his expedition.[8] Ecclesial institutions dedicated to Guadalupe also expanded, first and foremost toward the north, beginning in 1654 with leaders in San Luis Potosí who collaborated to "build a house for she who housed our God and Lord . . . the true effigy of the queen of angels." Subsequent institutions dedicated to Guadalupe included a chapel at the indigenous community in Zacoalco, Jalisco, in 1658; a Franciscan mission in what is now Ciudad Juárez (across the river from El Paso, Texas) in 1659; a church completed at Querétaro in 1680; and in 1707 at Zacatecas a Franciscan *colegio*, one of the missionary training centers where friars prepared for apostolic work among the indigenous peoples of northern New Spain. Devotees far from Tepeyac, many of whom had never seen the *tilma* original, perceived miraculous properties in copies of the Guadalupe image, as was evident in testimonies that a painted image at San Francisco Conchos, Chihuahua, perspired three times in 1695.[9]

Sermons evidenced the extensive veneration of Mary, which was unparalleled among any cult to a saint in New Spain and was crucial for the growth and expanding range of devotion to Mary under her specific title of Guadalupe. The first published Guadalupan sermons that are extant span the last four decades of the seventeenth century. They marked Guadalupe celebrations in various locales of the capital city, such as the Mexico City cathedral and the religious houses of the Franciscans, the Augustinians, the Mercedarians, and women religious dedicated to Saint Catherine of Sienna. Other published sermons delivered in cities such as Querétaro, Zacatecas, and Puebla reflected the growing devotion outside Mexico City.[10]

Similarly, the increase in artistic depictions during the seventeenth century revealed the expanding geographical range of Guadalupan devotion, as well as the evolving theological reflection on her image and message. Painting titles such as *Virgen de Guadalupe coronada por la santísima Trinidad* (Virgin of Guadalupe crowned by the holy Trinity) and *La Virgen de Guadalupe intercede por la salvación de un alma y Cristo la redime* (The Virgin of Guadalupe intercedes for the salvation of a soul and Christ redeems him), both anonymous works dated to the seventeenth century, underscored the theological attempts to link Guadalupe to core tenets of salvation history and the Christian faith. The first known painting that depicted native peoples as beneficiaries and devotees of Guadalupe was the 1653 work *El primer milagro* (The first miracle), attributed to the Mexico City workshop of José Juárez. It portrayed the healing accounts published in Sánchez and Laso de la Vega a few years previously, presenting in elaborate detail the scene of a native brought back to life through Guadalupe's intercession after a stray arrow had slain him during a mock skirmish that was part of the first Guadalupe procession (see p. 69). Natives are seen both as attackers in loincloth and as aristocratic participants in communal devotion. As Jeanette Peterson has shown, this important work reflected the colonial theological and pastoral imaginary of two competing—even contradictory—perspectives on the different groups of native peoples: "the savage Chichimec, a bellicose barbarian redeemed only through grace, and the civil, noble Aztec, marked by his demeanor, his dress, and his equal footing with the upper echelons of Hispanic society." Significantly, whatever their state in life, such depictions presumed all natives were subjects of the Christian project of evangelization.[11]

By the 1650s, painted images of Guadalupe were extant in San Luis Potosí, Querétaro, Antequera, Zacatecas, and Saltillo. While the exuberant claim of Florencia in 1688 that Guadalupe's image was now in "every church, chapel, house, and hut" of New Spain is overstated, during the second half of the seventeenth century prints, ex-votos, and paintings of Guadalupe appeared in an increasing number of places both in the viceroyalty and beyond. Indeed, the first dated painting of Guadalupe with accompanying apparition scenes to Juan Diego, a 1656 piece from the workshop of José Juárez, helped instigate transatlantic propagation of her cult. The patron was Francisca Ruiz de Valdivieso, a lady-in-waiting for the wife of a viceroy of New Spain. Described as a "humble slave" of Guadalupe in the painting's central inscription, Ruiz de Valdivieso transported the work back home with her to Agreda, Spain. There it adorned the local Conceptionist convent of Abbess Sor María de Agreda, whose mystical travels to the Americas became legendary.[12]

Still, greater Mexico City remained the epicenter of the devotion. Beginning in the early seventeenth century the archbishop and cathedral chapter of Mexico City oversaw the administration of the Tepeyac shrine. Many of these ecclesiastical leaders also promoted Guadalupan devotion. With their support, rituals and prayer offerings at Tepeyac gradually amplified. The first recorded instance of the apparitions being ritually enacted at the shrine was on the evening of December 11, 1676. An annual observance on December 12 was customary by the 1690s, though apparently the principal celebration at that time was the more long-standing annual two-week fiesta in November, one week for Spanish and mixed-race *casta* devotees and the other for natives. The number of devotees who touched and kissed the Guadalupe image was sufficient to cause growing concern for its durability; in 1677 Archbishop Payo Enríquez de Rivera y Manrique decreed that the glass case protecting the *tilma* should no longer be opened in order to curtail such expressions of veneration.[13]

Patrons financed projects to further promote devotion. A chapel dedicated in 1667 marked the location on the hill where according to tradition Guadalupe appeared to Juan Diego. Two years later a Mexico City devotee, Teresa de Aguirre, provided an endowment for an annual December 12 fiesta at this new chapel. Archbishop Rivera y Manrique funded the 1675–1676 construction of a grand highway that linked the Guadalupe basilica with the main plaza in Mexico City and was lined with fifteen chapels dedicated to the fifteen mysteries of the rosary. The improvement of the road added further decorum to the century-old practice of Mexico City officials meeting viceroys, archbishops, and other dignitaries at Tepeyac and ceremoniously ushering them into the city.[14]

The sale of Guadalupe images and the collection of alms to support her cult were further indicators of her growing popularity. An entrepreneur named Joseph Ferrer claimed that beginning in the 1620s he created and sold Guadalupe *medidas*—ribbons embossed with her name and image—which he vended both at the Guadalupe shrine and in Mexico City. His business was sufficiently brisk that he reportedly paid the vicar of the shrine an annual commission of one hundred pesos along with fifty pesos' worth of *medidas*. A 1679 dispute pitted members of a Guadalupe *cofradía* at Tepeyac, which indigenous devotees had founded the year before, against predominantly Spanish devotees in Mexico City. Authorities of the ecclesiastical court ruled in favor of the Mexico City faction. The court decision limited the Tepeyac devotees to solicitations solely from their fellow natives in the capital, leaving to their Spanish counterparts the alms of the more lucrative benefactors. This vehement dispute evidenced Guadalupe's increasing appeal to Mexico City donors.[15]

The most ambitious communal project to boost Guadalupan devotion was a new shrine completed at Tepeyac in 1709. It replaced the previous church structure dedicated in 1622 and added an impressive sacred edifice to the existing facilities at Tepeyac, which by then encompassed the hill chapel, a parish church for local indigenous peoples, and a structure that covered the holy well and its healing springs. On April 30, 1709, a formidable procession encompassing church and crown officials, religious orders, *cofradías*, the municipal council, and university professors joined numerous fellow devotees in transferring the Guadalupe image from its temporary quarters in the natives' parish church to its new sanctuary. Following the customs of Spanish public ritual, the procession included floats and symbolic mannequins, such as gigantic figures each some fifteen feet tall that depicted aristocratic couples from the continents of Africa, America, Asia, and Europe. This massive representation of the four parts of the world was an unmistakable assertion of the universality of both Catholicism and of Spanish imperial rule, as well as the unbounded patronage of the Blessed Virgin Mary. A novena of daily sermons and Masses from May 1 to 9 followed this spectacle. One sermon survives in published form, that of the Jesuit Juan de Goicoechea, *La maravilla immarcescible y milagro continuado de María Santísima Señora Nuestra en su prodigiosa imagen de Guadalupe de México* (The unfading marvel and continuous miracle of Our Holy Mother Mary in her prodigious image of Guadalupe of Mexico). Goicoechea lauded the most magnificent shrine built on the Tepeyac site to date. But he also noted that, as formidable as it was, the building would one day pass away, while the "continuous miracle" of Guadalupe's sacramental presence on the *tilma* would perpetually endure. The imposing edifice and ceremonials, along with the workers and benefactors who enabled the new shrine to be built in a mere fourteen years at the costly sum of nearly half a million pesos, comprised the most visible indication to date of Guadalupe as a central and sanctifying presence in New Spain.[16]

Rising Guadalupan devotion must be understood within the wider context of an expanding devotional culture shaped by the human needs and religious sensibilities of a diverse population. A variety of religious expressions marked the lives of residents at all levels of the Spanish caste system, which, though not rigidly deterministic, generally placed peninsular Spaniards at the top of the social hierarchy, *criollos* at the next level, blacks and Native Americans at the bottom, and the ever-increasing numbers of *castas*, or mixtures of all these groups, in between. While *castas* were often the most vulnerable residents of colonial society, life was tenuous among all social groups. Common ailments such as a ruptured appendix could be fatal. Infant mortality rates were high. Many residents did not enjoy the privilege of what today is called food security. For the average person in New Spain, survival for another day was cause for heartfelt gratitude. New Spain residents shared the conviction that all was in the hands of God: relief from epidemics, protection from enemies, the well-being of the monarch and the kingdom, rain, drought, harvest, and personal security and prosperity. Inhabitants from all strata of society expressed and addressed this conviction through an array of spiritual responses to the realities of daily life.

Thus Guadalupe's advance occurred in tandem with the genesis of new holy images and growing devotion to established traditions. Cornelius Conover's examination of Mexico City municipal council records reveals that, during the seventeenth century, city council members named seven new heavenly protectors for Mexico City, though Guadalupe was not one of them. Over the same century, devotees processed the image of Our Lady of los Remedios from her shrine in Naucalpan to the capital on at least seventeen occasions. Conversely, they invoked Guadalupe in this fashion solely during the floods of 1629–1634. A Guadalupe chapel in the Mexico City cathedral was dedicated in 1671, but this was but one of more than thirty invocations of Mary or other saints chosen as patrons of new or refurbished religious buildings, chapels, or altars in Mexico City from 1650 to 1690. To be sure, in assessing Guadalupe's place within the religious life of Mexico City, Conover fails to fully accredit the growing importance of the nearby Guadalupe shrine and the significant devotional traffic between the capital city and Tepeyac. Nonetheless, he demonstrates that in Mexico City, Guadalupe was but one important figure among an array of celestial patrons.[17]

Conover also argues convincingly that the preponderance of European figures among these celestial patrons calls into question the assertion of various scholars that by this point *criollo* patriotism was the driving force of religious devotion in New Spain's capital (and beyond). The variety of saints venerated in the personal piety of Mexico City *cofradía* members adds further credence to this assertion. Moreover, while *criollo* patriotism was certainly evident in sources such as some artistic works and published sermons, the desire for Guadalupe's protection cut across caste groups. Indeed, various peninsular Spaniards—viceroys, bishops, priests, magistrates, and other dignitaries—advanced Guadalupan devotion in significant ways. In his examination of the Guadalupe image, William Taylor concurs that "its popularity in the colonial period had more to do with its miraculous properties (defined in the sixteenth and seventeenth centuries) than with a precocious providential nationalism."[18]

The patterns of growing Guadalupan devotion within a robust devotional culture persisted over the first decades of the eighteenth century. Ceremonies to mark the completion of the new shrine in 1709 and the celebrations to mark the bicentennial of the Guadalupe apparitions in 1731 were two high points of Guadalupan devotion. Other noteworthy celebrations in Mexico City marked occasions in the years surrounding the bicentennial. In 1729 devotees commemorated the 198th anniversary of the apparitions and the centennial of the outbreak of the great flood that Guadalupe had abated in her first renowned public miracle. Five years later they feted the centennial of the relief Guadalupe provided from the flood. By this time most Mexico City churches had annual celebrations on December 12 to honor Guadalupe. Yet even as Guadalupe's acclaim grew, other saintly figures continued to receive noteworthy attention. Published sermons for Saint Francis and Saint Peter outnumbered those dedicated to Guadalupe. Mexico City municipal council members fostered devotion to a variety of saints and Marian images. Their most noticeable initiative within official ecclesial circles was to promote devotional privileges for Saint Gertrude, who had been declared patroness of the West Indies at the request of King Felipe IV of Spain. In 1716 city council members won papal approval to embellish the liturgical designation for Saint Gertrude's feast. Then they asked the pope to give her feast an even higher liturgical designation and extend this designation to celebrations throughout New Spain.[19]

The multifaceted devotional world of New Spain was strikingly evident during the disastrous *matlazahuatl* epidemic of 1736–1737, which claimed an estimated 192,000 lives, more than 40,000 in Mexico City alone. As was often the case, this plague was particularly devastating for the natives. *Escudo de armas de México* (Shield of arms of Mexico), Cayetano de Cabrera y Quintero's celebratory account of Guadalupe's eventual release of the population from the scourge of the epidemic, illuminated the social disorder the plague caused. Though Cabrera y Quintero's derogatory attitudes toward native peoples may have led him to exaggerate, his account claimed that some natives angry at the suffering in their communities threw corpses into the Mexico City aqueducts. Allegedly they also mixed victims' blood in bread, which they then sold on the plaza to spread the contagion. One native woman clarified the motive for such acts when she reportedly pled in the Guadalupe sanctuary: "Don't allow that we all die, dear Mother. But if the Indians must die, Lady, let the Spaniards die also."[20]

Yet Guadalupe was not the first heavenly protector—nor the first Marian figure—devotees called upon to quell the epidemic. In tandem with an array of public health initiatives, Mexico City residents followed the customary Spanish Catholic practice of successively appealing to heavenly intercessors with processions through the streets, novenas, and other prayers until one of their patrons provided relief. Cabrera y Quintero recounts that devotees turned first to Our Lady of Loreto, then to Our Lady of los Remedios. When supplications to these Marian guardians did not produce the desired effect, the city council of Mexico City implored Guadalupe's aid. But Archbishop Juan Antonio de Vizarrón y Eguiarreta, an ardent Guadalupe devotee, refused the council's request to have her image brought to the cathedral as had been done during the flood of the previous century. He insisted that, since Guadalupe had chosen Tepeyac as the site where she would appear, her faithful should make pilgrimage to her shrine and organize a novena there rather than bring her image into the city. The epidemic still continued to rage after this novena, and even after the city council pledged to accept Guadalupe as their patroness and to sponsor an annual novena to her. According to Cabrera y Quintero, the council and other devotees invoked as many as thirty saints and Marian invocations in their effort to combat the epidemic. Eventually the city council returned to Guadalupe and joined with the cathedral chapter in adopting her as a patroness of Mexico City and promising to promote her designation as the patroness of New Spain. On May 24, 1737, a citywide procession through streets lined with numerous images of Guadalupe united devotees of all social classes to celebrate the ecclesiastical and civic officials' solemn oath to Guadalupe. Over the following weeks, a number of city councils and cathedral chapters in the viceroyalty opened proceedings to join their Mexico City counterparts and declare Guadalupe their patroness. Finally the epidemic abated. The December 1737 issue of the Mexico City *Gaceta de México* credited Guadalupe with the diminution of the plague, a testament to Guadalupe's assistance visually underscored in figure 3.1, the frontispiece of Cabrera y Quintero's *Escudo de armas.*[21]

Over the next eighteen months the leaders of at least fifteen cities and towns joined Mexico City in taking an oath to Guadalupe as patroness of New Spain. But subsequently the effort to complete the process across the viceroyalty stalled. The master of ceremonies for the cathedral in Puebla, a rival municipality of Mexico City, even published a 1738 pamphlet in which he questioned the validity of liturgical rites for the December 12 Guadalupe feast absent formal Vatican approval of the Guadalupe tradition. Cabrera y

FIGURE 3.1. José de Ibarra (artist) and Baltasar Troncoso y Sotomayor (engraver), *La Virgen de Guadalupe escudo de salud contra la epidemia del Matlazahuatl de 1736–1738*, frontispiece of Cayetano de Cabrera y Quintero, *Escudo de armas de México . . .* (Mexico City: Viuda de D. Joseph Bernardo de Hogal, 1746). A small band of prominent Mexico City residents, including the author Cabrera y Quintero whose face is illumined as he gazes piously at Guadalupe, are shown offering the supplication that led Guadalupe to dispel the devastating epidemic that surrounds them. Photo courtesy of the Marian Library, University of Dayton.

Quintero offered an array of arguments in response to this objection in his 1741 tract *El patronato disputado* (The patronage disputed). He contended that ecclesial and civic leaders had a right to declare their own celestial patrons, especially in this instance when their choice was the Virgin Mary herself, not some unknown saint. But still the matter remained unresolved.

Subsequently it was a foreigner, the Milanese nobleman Lorenzo Boturini Benaduci, who first secured Vatican permission to crown Guadalupe as the patroness of New Spain. When Boturini arrived in the viceroyalty and began fundraising efforts for his project in 1742, he was arrested for entering the jurisdiction without a license and infringing on the royal patronage that required all ecclesiastical matters be cleared with the Spanish Council of the Indies. Archbishop Vizarrón y Eguiarreta and Viceroy Pedro Cebrián oversaw an investigation of the initiative of Boturini, who was deported.[22]

Finally, Vizarrón y Eguiarreta provided the catalyst to complete the now decade-old *patronato* initiative—that is, the effort to declare Guadalupe the patroness of New Spain. He decreed in 1746 that city councils across New Spain officially designate Guadalupe as their patroness. His authority, in combination with the support of Mexico City officials and the capital's centrality as a trend-setting city for other municipalities, led city councils and cathedral chapters across New Spain to comply with his directive that same year. Three years later, donors enabled church leaders to realize a goal four decades in the making when they endowed a chapter of canons for the Guadalupe shrine at Tepeyac, further enhancing its ecclesiastical prestige. The burgeoning initiative reached its ultimate aim in 1754 when Pope Benedict XIV declared Guadalupe the patroness of New Spain and sanctioned her December 12 feast in the papal bull *Non fecit taliter omni nationi* (God has not done thus for any other nation), a title taken from the words of Psalms 147:20. Celebrations of this papal recognition throughout the viceroyalty advanced Guadalupe's evolution from a celestial protector in the Mexico City vicinity to a patroness with a far more ample sphere of influence.

Thereafter the geographic range and density of Guadalupan devotion grew even further, though it was by no means universal. Not surprisingly, the intensity of the devotion varied from community to community. In some cases native peoples even objected to their pastor's mandate that they celebrate the Guadalupe feast, such as in 1757 when indigenous residents of the Zacualpan jurisdiction of the state of Mexico complained that their clerics introduced the annual celebration in order to impose its cost on the community and increase their own incomes. Moreover, at least twenty other shrines with holy images had regional followings at the close of the eighteenth century. Indeed, various shrines such as those to Nuestra Señora de San Juan de los Lagos in Jalisco and el Señor de Chalma southwest of Mexico City continue to attract numerous devotees today.

Marian images first introduced in New Spain during the mid-eighteenth century also attracted considerable numbers of devotees in tandem with Guadalupe's ascent, such as Nuestra Señora de la Luz (Our Lady of Light) and Nuestra Señora del Refugio (Our Lady of Refuge). Nonetheless, Guadalupe's prominence within Mexico's constellation of holy images and sites was well established and continued to increase.[23]

A sign and cause of the widening devotion was petitioners' supplication for Guadalupe's help with an ever-growing variety of needs. They increasingly solicited her protection not just from illness, floods, and epidemics but from other maladies as well, such as drought, failed crops, fire, earthquakes, and enemy attacks. The number of published sermons also grew; about one third of the extant Guadalupe sermons published during the colonial era appeared in print during the decade following the announcement of the papal promulgation of Guadalupe as New Spain's patroness. Royal officials granted licenses more frequently for alms collectors soliciting funds for the Tepeyac shrine, including a viceroyalty-wide license issued as early as 1756. Later in the century when requests to collect alms beyond immediate parish boundaries were regularly denied, officials continued to grant such licenses for the Guadalupe shrine and image. With the augmented financial support, construction projects at Tepeyac further evidenced Guadalupe's growing renown. These included a new high altar chapel, a convent for Capuchin nuns, and the Capilla de Pocito (Chapel of the Well), which marked the traditional site where Guadalupe met Juan Diego when he was in route to get a priest to attend to his uncle Juan Bernardino. Increased veneration of Guadalupe was also evident in the substantial growth of her presence in numerous institutions and devotional expressions: diocesan shrines, parish churches, home altars, prints and paintings of her image, devotional literature, the dedication of academic theses to her, place names, Guadalupan *cofradías*, novenas, miracle accounts, and baptismal names, as Guadalupe became the most popular given name in the viceroyalty for the first time. As Taylor has avowed, "by just about any measure a historian can summon, the devotion seems to have grown as never before after 1754."[24]

Señora de los Tiempos

Ita y Parra delivered and published his four Guadalupan sermons during the period when the successful campaign for Guadalupe's papal recognition germinated. On three of these occasions he preached on the

Guadalupe feast. At that time the gospel text proclaimed on the feast was the genealogy of Jesus in Matthew's gospel, which situates Mary at the pinnacle of the "family record of Jesus Christ" (Matthew 1:1).[25] Yet like his colonial contemporaries, Ita y Parra drew liberally on a range of texts from the scriptures, as well as the fathers of the church and fellow theologians of his own epoch. His purpose was to probe Guadalupe's significance in God's redemptive plan, and his overarching framework was a theology of divine providence he and his fellow preachers saw operative in world history and in colonial society. For clergy such as Ita y Parra, an essential component of the preaching task was to delineate how current human events, historical references, astrological occurrences, holy images, and even suffering were all signposts of the mysterious ways of God working in the world. Christian scriptures, sacraments, and theology comprised the hermeneutical lens through which those signposts could be interpreted.

Ita y Parra imparted his four orations at the Guadalupe shrine of Tepeyac before congregations that encompassed dignitaries from Mexico City such as the viceroy, judicial officials, the archbishop, and members of tribunals, religious orders, and the city council. He delivered the first of his sermons, *La imagen de Guadalupe, Señora de los tiempos* (The image of Guadalupe, Lady of the ages), at the December 12, 1731, celebration of the "two centuries of her miraculous apparition."[26] Ita y Parra preached at the climactic event of extended festivities that included a grand procession from the center of the capital city to the Guadalupe shrine. As the title of his sermon states, his primary thesis was that Mary is the "Lady of the Ages, [the] Queen of the Centuries" (1). His evidence to support this claim spanned Mary of Guadalupe's presence from the beginning of time to beyond the end of the world. If Sánchez and other predecessors had situated Guadalupe within the biblical narrative of salvation history, Ita y Parra widened his frame to its ultimate breadth: Guadalupe is best understood within the history of the cosmos—indeed, within the history of eternity, an assertion that artists such as those who created figure 3.2 subsequently reinforced. Ita y Parra's purpose was to convince his hearers they were not merely marking the bicentennial of a prestigious event but savoring a timeless manifestation of divine grace that reveals God's eternal plan and the eternal destiny of human beings.

First Ita y Parra lauded Mary's past wonders. Since the dawn of time, all creation eagerly awaited her coming. And since her birth, every year and every single day have been enriched with her miracles. The genealogies of Jesus Christ in the gospels of Matthew and Luke reveal that she is his

FIGURE 3.2. Cayetano Zampinos (sketch artist) and Antonio Baratti (engraver), *El alma de la Virgen es Guadalupana*, frontispiece of Francisco Javier Lazcano, *Opusculum theophilosophicum de principatu, seu antelatione Marianæ gratiæ: Illud S. Joannis Damasceni oratione prima de nativitate Virginis Mariæ circa principium explanans effatum* . . . (Venice: Ex typographia Andreæ Poletti, 1755). This sketch accentuates Guadalupe's eternal existence. Mary is surrounded by the Holy Trinity, flanked by Saint John Damascene and Saint John the Evangelist, and positioned above her parents Saint Anne and Saint Joachim. The Guadalupe image is depicted behind a traditional image of Mary of Nazareth with the Latin inscription *Anima Virginis prima creata*, indicating that Guadalupe was the soul of Mary before the creation of the world. Reproduced from the original held by the Department of Special Collections of the Hesburgh Libraries of Notre Dame.

mother, a descendant of the chosen people of Israel and a culminating figure in the human story that began with Adam and Eve. In a word, citing the convention of his time regarding the span of the earth's existence, Ita y Parra claimed that the fifty centuries from the world's creation to the birth of Mary (and her son, Jesus Christ) was a time of preparation for the human race to receive Mary with gratitude. Ita y Parra acknowledged that these beliefs about Mary's place in salvation history had been previously explicated. He repeated them in order to expound a new thesis: what is true of Mary generally is also true in the particular case of Our Lady of Guadalupe.

Thus Ita y Parra insisted that the best way to honor the two hundredth anniversary of Guadalupe's appearance was to consider her place in the history of the cosmos. He explicated three cosmological signs in the Guadalupan image on the *tilma*: the stars, the sun, and the moon. The forty-six stars on Guadalupe's mantle are a symbolic number he associated with the genealogy in Luke's gospel, which spans back to Adam (as opposed to Matthew's genealogy, which begins with Abraham). Citing the early church theologians Augustine, Bede, and Cyprian as the sources for his argument, Ita y Parra posited that the four letters of Adam's name in Greek correspond to the first letters of the four parts of the world as delineated in ancient Greece: Arctos, Dysis, Anatole, and Mesembria. Furthermore, the numerical values of the name Adam in Greek—one for each letter *a*, four for *d*, and forty for *m*—add up to forty-six. Thus the forty-six stars link the Guadalupe image to human origins as well as to the human race throughout the earth that is called to recognize her as their own.[27] The one hundred sunrays that envelop her and the twelve rays on her crown symbolize her timeless presence, with the one hundred representing all the years in a century and the twelve all the months in a year. Finally, Ita y Parra observed that astrologers divide years into cycles of the sun and the moon. The lights from these two sources are separate, one to brighten the day and the other the night. Indeed they split time into segments of day and night. Yet in the Guadalupe image these two celestial bodies and their corresponding time frames are brought into unity, with sunrays emanating from her and the moon under her feet. Moreover, in our world the moon is not a dependable illumination, since at times in its cycle the night is dark. But Guadalupe stands on the moon and tames its "inconstancy" (8). Hence Guadalupe illumines all of humanity and all times past, present, and future. In Ita y Parra's words, the conjoining of the heavenly lights—stars, sun, and moon—make Guadalupe a "beautiful image [that] gathers in itself all times, unites all years, encompasses all centuries" (12).

Ita y Parra marshaled biblical evidence to support this reading of the image on the *tilma* and the marvelous way Guadalupe presented her image to the inhabitants of New Spain. He quoted Song of Songs 6:10, a text that asks, "Who is this that comes forth like the dawn, as beautiful as the moon, as resplendent as the sun?" (8). He answered that this biblical text "is a literal portrayal of our image and her miraculous apparition," a scriptural reference that shows Guadalupe is indeed the "Lady of the Ages" (8) who "descend[ed] from the majestic throne of her glory, to the humble valleys of our despised lands" that she might become the "mother of these her new children" (10). Ten years after the conquest she appeared to Juan Diego, the "Jacob of our Indies," who, like the patriarch Jacob of Genesis, received "a blessing for his peoples" (10–11). Echoing Sánchez's frequently repeated interpretation of Revelation 12, Ita y Parra affirmed that the purpose of Guadalupe's visit from on high was to defeat the dragon of idolatry that had plagued the natives. In all of this, he attested, the words of the prophet Isaiah were fulfilled: "Behold, I am about to create new heavens and a new earth" (12; Isaiah 65:17).

Guadalupe's visitation to the New World was a recurring event that endured into the present through the sacred *tilma*, which Ita y Parra deemed a "continuous apparition" (14) of her abiding presence. Citing his predecessor Vidal de Figueroa, and asserting the conviction expressed in paintings such as figure 3.3 that the Guadalupe image was divinely created, Ita y Parra further lauded the *tilma* as a "perfect likeness" of Mary "decreed in eternity" (15). All the wonders of the world—the jasper of Greece, the marble of Italy, the bronze of Germany, the ramparts of Babylonia, the bulwarks of Nineveh, the pantheons of Rome, the pyramids of Egypt— will one day be reduced to dust. Yet despite the corruptible material of which it was made and the destructive climate in which it was kept, the *tilma* had retained its color and beauty for two centuries. Its durability reflected its origins, since it was "miraculously forged in the office of the Omnipotent" and its "painter was the Guardian Angel of this vast empire of the Indies" (5). Like the pillar of cloud and the pillar of fire that led the Israelites through the desert on their way to the Promised Land, Ita y Parra acclaimed the *tilma* as "a permanent column . . . to guide the residents of the Indies [Indianos] to heaven" (13).

Moreover, Ita y Parra boldly proclaimed that the future of the *tilma* and Guadalupe's influence were endless. Addressing himself to the Blessed

FIGURE 3.3. Anonymous, *El Padre Eterno pintando a la Virgen de Guadalupe*, 18th century. Artistic works such as this painting make the bold claim that the *tilma* is a divine creation. God the Father paints the Guadalupe image in company with Jesus and the Holy Spirit depicted as a dove. The citation of Psalm 147:20, *non fecit taliter omni nationi* (God has not done thus for any other nation), proclaims the singular election of Guadalupe's Mexican children as the beneficiaries of so great a gift. Courtesy Archivo del Museo de la Basílica de Guadalupe.

Sacrament that was publicly exposed in the Guadalupe sanctuary for the occasion, Ita y Parra posited that the consecrated host Catholics believe is the very body and real presence of Christ would endure even after the end of the world. He supported this claim with the writings of the church fathers John Damascene, Athanasius, and Jerome, as well as the works of the seventeenth-century Spanish Jesuit theologian and mystic Juan

Eusebio Nieremberg. Ita y Parra further avowed that, as John Chrysostom contended, the cross on which Christ was crucified will also last beyond the end of time. Though he cited no theological authorities, he added that the original copies of the four gospels will eternally exist as well, suggesting that all these holy objects would be enshrined together on an altar in heaven. Alluding to the Guadalupe *tilma* before which he preached, he concluded that "in an altar formed like this by God, how could his love be complete, if he does not enshrine as well the image of his mother?" (17).

The conclusion of the sermon urged Ita y Parra's hearers to respond in faith to the eternal gift of Guadalupe. She came among the native peoples when they were still in the darkness of sin. Yet, like all peoples, the natives were capable of receiving the light, and they did so: Guadalupe's "sacred image was the marvelous instrument of their conversion" (19). Similarly, devotees of that time were called to be her worthy sons and daughters. Since Mexico City was under the "shadow of her patronage" (19), its residents needed to be converted from their vices and offenses and, fulfilling the words of Sirach 24:11, transform their municipality into the "holy city" where Mary of Guadalupe would "abide" (19–20). Finally, speaking in the name of King Felipe V, Archbishop Vizarrón y Eguiarreta, and other dignitaries and devotees, Ita y Parra avowed to Guadalupe that "this great multitude humbly adores you" and implored that all "weep for their sins" (22) so that, through the gift of grace, they might honor Mary and her son, Jesus Christ, in the eternal glory of heaven.

Madre de la Salud

The idyllic perspective presented in his *Señora de los tiempos* sermon was tested in Ita y Parra's next distinguished occasion to preach at Tepeyac: the February 7, 1737, closing service for the Guadalupe novena prayed there during the 1736–1737 *matlazahuatl* epidemic. Earlier sermons on Our Lady of los Remedios help illuminate the significance of that Guadalupan oration. In a sermon delivered in 1730 during a novena to ask for protection of a flotilla that had embarked for Spain, Ita y Parra had expressed utter confidence that turning to Remedios was an unfailing step in securing protection. Like the Israelites of old, whom God saved from the slavery of Egypt even before they knew to ask for divine intervention, Ita y Parra praised God who is "so swift in favoring us that before our supplication reaches his ears, grace has already proceeded from the throne of his mercy." Similarly, recognizing the constant protection of Remedios, Ita y Parra insisted to his hearers that he "should not pray to ask her for the safe conveyance of the flotilla, but rather proclaim gratitude to her that it had already arrived." Ita y Parra contended that the only real danger for the fleet was not storms at sea or attacks of enemies but sinfulness that could provoke divine wrath. Yet despite their failings the people of New Spain had nothing to fear because their mother Mary, "the sole remedy (Remedio) of our America," alleviates the punishment that human sins justly merit.[28]

The situation of the devastating epidemic seven years later prompted Ita y Parra to heighten his emphasis on the human causality of calamity, as is indicated in the title of his culminating sermon for a 1737 Remedios novena preached in the cathedral of Mexico City: *Los pecados única causa de las pestes* (Sins: The sole cause of plagues). Unlike his earlier Remedios sermon, he did not profess that prayers are answered before they are uttered but initiated his oration with a solemn supplication: "We implore today the remedies of Mary [Our] Lady, or to Mary [Our] Lady of the Remedies, so that Mexico be healed of the epidemic." He rejected explanations that rooted the plague in the stars, bad sanitation, contaminated food or drink, or other natural causes. Instead he stated flatly that the "cause of the plague . . . is solely the punishing hand of God [who is] irritated at our offenses."[29]

Ita y Parra employed various biblical precedents to support his position, most strikingly a plague that took seventy thousand lives during the time of King David (2 Samuel 24). God visited this pestilence on the people as a reprimand for a census David had ordered, an action judged as offensive since the people of Israel belonged to God and thus God alone should know their exact number. Seeing his people suffer for the sin he had committed, David offered a sacrifice of atonement and begged the Lord to direct the punishment at him and his kindred. Ita y Parra applauded David's actions and reminded his congregation, which encompassed New Spain's principal civil and ecclesiastical leaders, that the native peoples had suffered far more from the epidemic than the congregants had. Hence, imitating David, they should atone for their sins, for their own sake and for that of the viceroyalty. According to Ita y Parra, the procession of the Remedios image to the Mexico City cathedral paralleled the Israelites' appeals to the divine presence in the Ark of the Covenant, but even the presence of so great an intercessor as the mother of God would not be efficacious if sincere repentance and conversion did not accompany her devotees' prayers. The preacher told his hearers that, as in the days of David, God afflicts some in order to incite the community to change its sinful ways, but God is merciful and does not want to destroy all. At the same time, Ita y Parra avowed that suffering is an unpredictable force and that the only certainty in this life is everyone will die. He openly admitted that at the conclusion of the Remedios novena devotees' "prayers have not ceased, but neither has the epidemic ceased, indeed it is becoming more intense." Thus he implored his hearers that "if we want to save ourselves like David, we have to do penance like David." He finished his sermon with a heartfelt plea to Remedios that she intercede for the healing of body and soul, asking her rhetorically what would become of her altars, churches, images, and devotions in New Spain if she allowed the continued affliction of the viceroyalty's inhabitants.[30]

As the epidemic continued to rage, the opening words of Ita y Parra's sermon less than three weeks later at Tepeyac, *La madre de la salud: La milagrosa imagen de Guadalupe* (The Mother of health: The miraculous image of Guadalupe), indicated that he perceived it as a continuation of his earlier Remedios oration: "This is the second time in but a few short days, and before the same assembly, that I address the same matter." He went on to remind his listeners that in his previous sermon he had "painted the sad spectacle of the epidemic we are enduring" and implored "the protection of the miraculous image of los Remedios."[31] Now he led them in their prayers before the "holy prodigious image of Guadalupe, [who is] also mother of our desired health in the present contagion" (2). The interrelation between the two sermons was implicitly acknowledged when censors in Madrid officially authorized their publication in a single decree.[32] Moreover, the Guadalupe sermon encompassed an extended analysis of the collaborative roles of Remedios and Guadalupe in confronting the plague. Indeed, the sermon is structured around two "uncertainties" (3) that Ita y Parra posed. The first was why devotees processed Remedios from her sanctuary to the capital for her novena, while the residents of the capital journeyed to Tepeyac for the Guadalupe novena. More fundamentally, the second was why, given Remedios's numerous past miracles, the populace "had not experienced any relief" after asking her aid, while Guadalupe "heals us" (13).

Ita y Parra was well aware that a practical explanation resolved his first uncertainty: the Guadalupe novena occurred at Tepeyac because Archbishop Vizarrón y Eguiarreta mandated prayers to her be offered at the site of her apparitions. For pedagogical reasons, however, in his sermon Ita y Parra posed the issue of the pilgrim Remedios and the stationary Guadalupe as a theological dilemma. Drawing on a distinction between

Remedios and Guadalupe established in the works of Sánchez and Laso de la Vega, Ita y Parra noted that Remedios originated in Europe and thus "does not have her own place" in New Spain but rather "all of America, to which she came, is her house, her temple" (4). Conversely, the Guadalupe image "was born here" (4). Therefore, just as subjects travel to their ruler's palace to ask for aid, Guadalupe's faithful travel to her home at Tepeyac to offer their supplications. In biblical imagery, Ita y Parra posited that the Ark of the Covenant typifies Remedios, while Guadalupe personifies the burning bush through which Moses encountered God on Mount Horeb. Like the ark, the Remedios image was crafted by human hands and borne from place to place to accompany the people in their struggles. Like the burning bush, Guadalupe appeared unexpectedly as a luminous presence on a mountaintop that devotees continue to ascend to meet her. While Remedios signifies celestial accompaniment in the vagaries of life, Guadalupe signifies the sudden, gratuitous eruption of divine presence.[33]

The Guadalupe image and shrine confirmed for Ita y Parra that she is the burning bush. Referencing the rays of the sun that surround her in the *tilma* image, he avowed that she is "embraced by fire" (6). Yet, like the burning bush that the fire did not consume, two passing centuries have not deteriorated the sacred *tilma*. Similarly, in the present epidemic "for the four winds surrounding villages are infested with the contagion, some almost devastated, [but] in Guadalupe's enclosure [at Tepeyac], there is not a single infirmed person!" (12). Ita y Parra went on to cite a historical precedent for his claim also expounded in the works of Sánchez and Laso de la Vega—namely, the intervention of Guadalupe to quell a 1540s epidemic that afflicted numerous native peoples. Thus he concluded that Guadalupe is the burning bush and Tepeyac is the Mount Horeb of the New World, since the flames of epidemics consumed surrounding communities, but not those on the holy ground of Guadalupe's shrine.

Most importantly for Ita y Parra, Guadalupe the burning bush soothes the wrath of a just God who sends down fire "to punish our offenses" (6). Accordingly, when God comes to demolish the wicked thorns, Mary appears as the "rose among the thorns" who "appeases God's anger with her beauty" (7). Ita y Parra cited a father of the early church, Peter Chrysologus, for his contention that the thorns represent "Israelite ingrates and sinners" (6) who are obliterated in the fires of God. However, as an analysis of this sermon by the present-day theologian Michael Griffin shows, the Guadalupan preacher made three important theological moves to modify the thorn-sinner correlation. First, while the Chrysologus citation implies that God will destroy sinners, Ita y Parra contended that God will destroy our sins. Second, drawing on another early Christian thinker, Bishop Theodotus, Ita y Parra replaced the language of punishment—which he himself had already employed—with the concept of purification. Finally, he further extended his argument with the bold assertion that, for the sake of the roses, God will spare even the thorns, including those of "this sinful Babylon of Mexico" (9). Indeed, in the same way the roses distract attention from the repugnance of the thorns, Mary's beauty overshadows the revulsion of sinners. In Ita y Parra's words, Mary is the most graced of humans in whose womb God "humanized" (8). The union between God and humanity in Mary incites divine mercy such that "although [God] dwells among sinners, he does not punish them, but purifies them; does not consume them, but benefits them" (8). Griffin concludes that the identification of Guadalupe as the burning bush "allows Ita y Parra to place the puzzling juxtaposition of destructive force and abiding presence within a context of hope."[34]

Ita y Parra then proceeded to his second "uncertainty." He noted how to date almsgiving, the expansion of hospital facilities, and the provision of medicine, nutrition, and warmth had not liberated the populace from the epidemic's deadly effects. But he was most incredulous that, unlike numerous past instances in which Our Lady of los Remedios had been processed from her shrine to the Mexico City cathedral, devotees' plea for her aid had seemingly gone unanswered. Ita y Parra posed his dilemma pointedly: "Why has Mexico not experienced any relief" after "invoking the protection of the image of los Remedios, [who is] powerful to address whatever necessity arises?" (13) Given the rising *criollo* spirit that various analysts have emphasized, one might surmise that Ita y Parra would engage such a question as an opportunity to show Guadalupe's primacy over Remedios. In fact he does just the opposite, arguing for a complementarity between the two Marian images, and even defending Remedios despite the ongoing scourge after a novena of prayers sought her intercession. Ita y Parra's answer: "In secret (believe me) the image of los Remedios heals us; but in public the image of Guadalupe gives us health" (14).

Echoing yet other claims first published in the works of Sánchez and Laso de la Vega, Ita y Parra explicated the healing story of Don Juan, the early caretaker of the Remedios image, and echoed Sánchez's comparison of the collaborative relationship between Remedios and Guadalupe with the biblical figures of Ruth and Naomi. But Ita y Parra also added some new twists. He noted that, like Remedios, the foreigner Ruth operated in private when she declared that Naomi's people will be her own, while the native Naomi publicly acclaimed their kinship relation. Ita y Parra also elaborated on earlier accounts of Don Juan's grave illness, avowing that his ailment was a punishment from God after he moved the Remedios image from his house to a hermitage, apparently because in doing so he had disrespectfully thrown Remedios out of his home. Guadalupe defended the honor of the foreigner Remedios but also effected Don Juan's cure, underscoring her status as a native inhabitant with dominion in these lands, as well as her particular concern for the native peoples. Similarly, though the two images of Mary were the "same Lady" (16), the healing from the contagion was made public in Guadalupe because "the Indians are the infirmed, the special children of Guadalupe, in that they are under her particular loving jurisdiction" (17). Guadalupe's favor of the indige-nous peoples is further evidenced in the chosen site of her appearance, Tepeyac, where she replaced "the venomous serpent of idolatry, which on this mountain the Gentiles [natives] blindly adored" (6). Most importantly, in her apparitions Guadalupe requested that the "blessed and beloved Indian Juan Diego . . . build me a temple, in which I will show myself a merciful mother to you and yours" (10–11). Thus, according to Ita y Parra, Our Lady of los Remedios accepted that Guadalupe receive the public ac-claim for abating the epidemic in order to "incite, with the prodigy, their [the natives'] lukewarm faith" and increase "her cult and veneration" (16) among them.

Madre de la salud did not explain away the horror of *matlazahuatl*. Rather, it explored the scourge in light of Christian faith. Citing Saint Paul (Romans 1:20), Ita y Parra contended that "the invisible things of God are known through those that are visible" and "the most hidden mysteries of Providence are traced through its deeds" (14). Thus plague and any other malady must be understood in light of the broader context of salvation history. Ita y Parra in fact bracketed his sermon between the original sin in that history and the present situation of New Spain: he began with the reminder that "in Adam human nature was infected with death" (2) and ended with an admonition to faith and prayer that would secure for "all our Indies abundance in their grains, fertility in their fields, prosperity in their times, medicine in their infirmities, health in their living, grace in their souls, and glory in Eternity" (18). The intervening material of the oration—from the frank admission that intercession had not yet alleviated the epidemic to reflections on the burning bush and the Guadalupan evangelization of the native peoples—probed the unfathomable but trustworthy ways of God. As Griffin adeptly put it, Ita y Parra narrated the *matlazahuatl* event as if it were one more episode of the scriptures, boldly asserting that despite collective suffering the divine "Lord of history" was "the main protagonist" of the story and the eternal salvation of souls its ultimate plot line.[35] Thus redemption was not manifest solely or even primarily in divine rescue from the *matlazahuatl* but rather in the divine-human partnership of grace that overshadowed this single occurrence in the unfolding of salvation history.

Promoting the Patronato

At the end of his *Madre de la salud* sermon Ita y Parra urged that "both [Mexico City] councils, ecclesiastical and secular, swear an oath to this holy image [of Guadalupe] as their universal patron for the entire kingdom" (17) of New Spain and that her feast be celebrated on December 12 throughout the viceroyalty. Other Mexico City authorities supported Ita y Parra's plea, though Archbishop Vizarrón y Eguiarreta decreed they only had the jurisdiction to declare Guadalupe patroness of the capital city. The approval of civic and ecclesiastical councils from throughout the viceroyalty would be necessary to declare her New Spain's general patroness. On April 27, 1737, Ita y Parra was one of two ecclesiastical leaders who joined with their civil counterparts to solemnly declare Guadalupe the patroness of Mexico City, a pledge their fellow capital city leaders and the general populace confirmed in the aforementioned citywide Guadalupe procession the following month. Ita y Parra's final two published Guadalupan sermons contributed to the subsequent campaign Mexico City leaders spearheaded to extend approbation of the Guadalupan *patronato*.

The occasion for both sermons was the Guadalupe feast-day celebration at Tepeyac. As the *patronato* initiative slowly proceeded, in 1743 Ita y Parra delivered the first of the orations, *La imagen de Guadalupe, imagen del patrocinio* (The image of Guadalupe, image of patronage). He underscored his bold intent in the very first lines of the oration: to demonstrate "that this sovereign image in its prodigious apparition of Guadalupe is the only and the most fitting image of [celestial] patronage" for New Spain. Then he reminded his audience that "patronage" is the "help a powerful person offers one in need; it is favoring that person under the shade [of their protection]."[36]

Such gratuitous protection, he contended, was clearly demonstrated in the history of New Spain through the appearance of Guadalupe to Juan Diego, inaugurating a relationship in which "Mary is the one who protects, and the Indian is the one protected" (2). Ita y Parra then went on to acclaim the favor Guadalupe bestowed on the indigenous peoples. He observed that, for natives such as Juan Diego, their cloak was their source of warmth, their bed, their only article of clothing. The *tilma* that Juan Diego used for these purposes was the canvas Guadalupe designated for her celestial portrait. But she replaced it with a new source of sustenance, as she now "assists [the people of the Indies] perpetually without ever ceasing to shelter them" (13). Ita y Parra avowed that in the epoch before they received "the light of the gospel" the indigenous were "barbaric in their customs and idolatrous in their worship" (25). But Guadalupe, the "loving Mary of the Indies," transformed them with her miraculous image, through which those who "don't know how to read [the scriptures] are content with seeing" (29) in her beauty the message of salvation.

Extending his focus from the "*indios*" (Indians) to "Indianos" (all the residents of the Indies), Ita y Parra dedicated the bulk of his sermon to deepening his hearers' appreciation of how splendid a gift Guadalupe is for all the inhabitants of New Spain, enhancing the ever-widening exaltation of Guadalupe's providential care illustrated in artistic works such as figure 3.4. Ita y Parra compared Guadalupe to the prophet Elijah, whose disciple Elisha asked for a double portion of his master's spirit (2 Kings 2:9–15). As Elijah ascended to the heavens in a whirlwind on a chariot of fire, his mantle fell to the ground and Elisha picked it up. Ita y Parra noted that "in [leaving Elisha] the cape he gave him his spirit" (9). Similarly, since "the one who gives the cape gives their spirit" (10), Guadalupe imparts herself in the image imprinted on the *tilma*. Just as Elijah gave his patronage to Elisha, in her miraculous image Guadalupe offered her patronage to the peoples of the Indies.

The marvel of Guadalupe's patronage is most revealed in the light of Christ's incarnation, the great mystery through which God became flesh, taking on "the cape of human nature" (7). Ita y Parra was careful to note the theologically orthodox position that only Christ became incarnate, but he hastened to add that there is nothing "more comparable to the incarnate Word than the appearance of Mary of Guadalupe" (8) on Juan Diego's *tilma*. Christ did not merely assume our human nature; he redeemed it on our behalf. Similarly, Guadalupe received the *tilma* from Juan Diego and returned it to her children of the Indies in an enhanced state: stamped with

FIGURE 3.4. Anonymous, *El patrocinio de Nuestra Señora de Guadalupe,* c. 1746. Juan Diego presents his *tilma* to regal women representing both native peoples and those of Spanish descent as a pledge of Guadalupe's unfailing patronage to the residents of New Spain. Courtesy Archivo del Museo de la Basílica de Guadalupe.

her image and her very presence as a pledge of her love and protection. While all the faithful are children of Mary, "only the people of the Indies obtain the rarest happiness that, conceiving them, but not giving birth to them, [Mary] always has them with her" (17). In other words, Guadalupe's presence on the *tilma* is analogous to God's incarnate presence with humanity in Jesus Christ: the people of New Spain are those providentially chosen not only to be Mary's children but, like a child in the womb, to permanently have her tangible presence in their midst. Moreover, just as in the incarnation God raised the dignity of sinful humans higher than that of the angels, in Guadalupe "the most inferior of the world" (27) are made "superior to other nations" (28). Standing in the sanctuary at Tepeyac before the Guadalupe image, Ita y Parra addressed the final lines of his oration to "Most Blessed Mary," who honored New Spain with "this cloak on which you stamped the figure of your patronage, extending it over all your servants, who are your faithful" (30–31).

The exuberant proclamation of New Spain's celestial election was somewhat tempered three years later in Ita y Parra's final published Guadalupe sermon, *El círculo del amor formado por la América Septentrional jurando a María Santísima en su imagen de Guadalupe* (The circle of love formed by Northern America pledging itself to Most Holy Mary in her image of Guadalupe). While he prominently cited Florencia and his correlation of Psalm 147:20 to the Guadalupe event—*non fecit taliter omni nationi*[37]—he also dedicated the sermon to Fernando VI, "King of Spain and Emperor of the Indies."[38] Two months after that sermon, Ita y Parra preached for yet another significant event, a commemoration at the Mexico City cathedral in honor of the king's deceased predecessor and father, Felipe V. On that occasion Ita y Parra vowed his loyalty to the new king and implored that he "engrave in the banner of his kingdom this sacred image of the Mexican Guadalupe" so that "your military will be ever victorious."[39] Clearly the preacher did not see any inherent contradiction between loyalty to the crown and theological claims about Mary of Guadalupe's special favor to the inhabitants of New Spain. Indeed, as Taylor has observed, preachers such as Ita y Parra avowed that Guadalupe simultaneously "sanctified both an American identity and the authority of the colonial system."[40]

Ita y Parra's *Círculo del amor* sermon coincided with the 1746 oath to accept Guadalupe as the universal patroness of New Spain. As he had done nine years earlier, he was among the ecclesiastical dignitaries who represented Mexico City in taking this solemn oath, this time after securing commitments from town councils and ecclesiastical chapters throughout the viceroyalty. The Mexico City contingent swore their oath on December 4. Ita y Parra's sermon the following week explicated its meaning. He stated that a *patronato* is a twofold covenant between a guardian and the beneficiaries who honor him or her for the protection received. In the case of New Spain, in her miraculous appearance Mary of Guadalupe first gave herself to the nation. Now her devotees pledged themselves to her as their universal patroness. Ita y Parra reminded his listeners that in his 1743 sermon for the Guadalupe feast he "demonstrated the first" (12) element of the Guadalupan *patronato*. His purpose in the current sermon was to persuade them to fulfill the second: to publicly acknowledge her as their "general patroness" and to make themselves truly "her children" (12) by offering the gift of their lives in gratitude for her patronage.

Echoing and expanding on themes from his earlier sermons, Ita y Parra reminded his listeners that the "true God" was present in the consecrated Eucharist, "this sovereign host, this sacred placenta" (6) exposed in the sanctuary for the Guadalupe feast. Similarly, the "Queen of Heaven" (6) adorned with the stars, the sun, and the moon was in their midst through the *tilma*, which "truly is a work of heaven" (7) and a lasting sign that "Most Blessed Mary chose for her own inheritance" (8) the peoples of America. Her arrival among them resembled Christ's incarnation but has elicited a more universal response than has Christianity in other parts of the world: "The image of the Word [Jesus Christ] appears in the bush, his fire burns in it, but it is not consumed with the fire. The image of Mary burns in America when she appears in Guadalupe, and all of America burns, and all pledge [themselves to her], may [our hearts] be inflamed forever" (18).

Ita y Parra's core innovation and central theme in *Círculo del amor* was his extended explanation of the sermon's title. He noted that the genealogy in the gospel of Matthew begins and ends with Christ. The first words of Matthew, "A family record of Jesus Christ" (1:1) culminate in the subsequent pronouncement "It was of her [Mary] that Jesus who is called the Messiah was born" (1:16). In Ita y Parra's reading of this text, the first verse indicates that "in the beginning Christ gave himself to Mary" when he "made himself her son" (11). Similarly, in the final verse "Mary gave herself to Christ" (11) when she became his mother. The mutual self-giving of son and mother reveal "the mysterious circle formed in the gospel," (11) a circle of love between Jesus and Mary that illumines the wider circle of love between God and humanity. To enter that circle we must imitate Mary, whose life was "all for Christ" (11). Indeed, we must become like Christ himself. Citing Augustine, Ita y Parra declared Christ was "God [who] became human, so that humans could become more Godlike" (14).

Ita y Parra cited various further examples to show that covenantal love permeates the biblical tradition. David and Jonathan exemplify the mutual bond between human friends in that, "not having anything else to give, [they] commit their souls, both promising their total dedication to the other" (21, 1 Samuel 18:1–5). Abraham's pact with God is a model of divine initiative and human response, as God called him and promised to bless him with abundant descendants who would possess the land, and Abraham in turn pledged his faith and obedience to God (cf. Genesis 12:1–8, 15:5–7, 22:15–18). Jesus himself established the relation between Mary and Christian believers at the foot of the cross. Ita y Parra reminded his hearers that just before Jesus died he commended his mother and the disciple John to one another with the words "there is your son" and "there is your mother" (John 19:26–27).

The people of New Spain now found themselves in the same place as the disciple John. Through the appearance of Our Lady of Guadalupe, Mary became their mother as she had for John at her son's command. Through her encounters with Juan Diego, Guadalupe had tenderly pledged her love and protection to the people of the Indies. Now it was up to them to enter into this heavenly circle of love through their actions. Ita y Parra explained that "it is one thing for Mary to be our mother, it is another for us to be her children" (24). Thus he exhorted his hearers to embrace "now the glory that comes to those who make themselves children of Mary in declaring their consent to the [*patronato*] oath" (29). He further explicated that Mary is the natural mother of the faithful, since from the cross Christ offered her to all through the apostle John. But the people of the Indies are doubly her children, since they are also the children she adopted through her encounters with Juan Diego, children who now publicly consented to her adoption through their *patronato* oath.

Ita y Parra reminded his listeners that the incarnate Word "was born, died, and prayed for all" (34). Yet the scriptures also refer to God at least twenty-seven times as "the God of Jacob" (35), revealing God's special relation with those who, like Jacob, are called and respond to divine love with a vow of devotion and obedience. As the populace of Mexico City and New Spain enacted a similar vow to Guadalupe, Ita y Parra underscored the heavenly favors they would continue to receive, the Christian fidelity to which they had pledged themselves, and the circle of love they had entered through their acceptance of the Guadalupan *patronato*.

Divine Providence and Colonial Society

The most prolific years for colonial-era published Guadalupe sermons were 1756–1758, as news of Pope Benedict XIV's 1754 official declaration of Guadalupe as patroness of New Spain spread through the viceroyalty. At least eight sermons were published annually during these years, nearly all of them at celebrations that proclaimed and confirmed the pope's declaration. One of the first orators to preach for this momentous occasion was Juan José de Eguiara y Eguren, a professor of theology and a canon at the Mexico City cathedral, where he delivered his sermon in 1756. Eguiara y Eguren's panegyric, *María Santísima pintándose milagrosamente en su bellísima imagen de Guadalupe de México, saluda a la Nueva España y se constituye su patrona* (Most Holy Mary painting herself miraculously in her most beautiful image of Guadalupe of Mexico, greets New Spain and becomes its patroness), illustrated the influence of the new Vatican-designated scripture readings for the Guadalupe feast. The sermon also epitomized the claims of many preachers regarding Guadalupe's role in colonial society.[41]

Expounding on the prescribed reading of Mary's visit to her kinswoman Elizabeth (Luke 1:39–45), Eguiara y Eguren echoed the conviction first articulated in Sánchez that "the future event of Guadalupe was prophesied and foreseen" in the scriptures, in this case through Mary's "past journey, visit, and salutation."[42] As Mary's greeting to Elizabeth brought her kinswoman peace, so too her salute to the New World with the gift of her image and her protection had for 225 years wrought numerous conversions to Christ, temporal blessings, healings, and continuous peace. And just as Elizabeth expressed her joy that Mary had come to her, so too the faithful of the New World responded to Guadalupe through their prayers, processions, writings, orations, dedication of churches and altars, and now through offering the Mass, divine office, and official title—patroness of New Spain—that Benedict XIV providentially designated to her. In effect, Eguiara y Eguren posited an intrinsic link between the gospel vision of God's peaceful reign and the social world of New Spain as evidenced in its pervasive Guadalupan devotion, with nary a mention of any deficiencies in church or society in the viceroyalty during the more than two centuries since the Guadalupe event.

Eguiara y Eguren's discourse reflected the major limitation of colonial sermons: a triumphalism that associated New Spain with the most harmonious social relations depicted in the scriptures. No doubt the significant presence of civic and ecclesiastical elites who heard such sermons conditioned preachers to accentuate this correlation. The sermons of Ita y Parra and Eguiara y Eguren were concurrent with Guadalupe's rise in prominence as the celestial overseer of colonial society, accentuating perceptions of her role as sanctifier of existing structures. Seen in this light, the orations of colonial preachers were a form of social control, eschewing individual liberty and bolstering conformity with communal norms. A marked emphasis on the concept of sin and personal responsibility as evidenced in orations such as Ita y Parra's *Los pecados única causa de las pestes* sermon reinforced the drive for conformity. The sense of compliance could be so pervasive that residents presumed one's state in life reflected a divine plan in which stratified Spanish society mirrored the hierarchical ordering of the heavenly dominion.

In fact, Ita y Parra's first published Guadalupe sermon, *La imagen de Guadalupe, Señora de los tiempos*, even presented Guadalupe as a guardian of a cosmic order decreed before creation and destined to last for all eternity. Though the intent of such a marvelous claim was to affect awe at the providential designs of God, it also buttressed a static ideal for the current order of the world. By God's design the earthly world imitated the celestial realm: the world was ordered in such a way that natural occurrences and human events all conformed to a higher reason and purpose. Such a vision tended to downplay the idea that Christians should change the world in light of the gospel message. Rather, it reinforced the notion that the primary vocation of the Catholic was to maintain faith and personal equilibrium amid the joys, pains, and hardships of life as it is.

Given the tenuousness of human existence in colonial New Spain, the sense that forces beyond human control affected daily life is not surprising. Yet the theology of divine providence underlying colonial sermons did not lead all preachers to propose a blindly fatalistic or rigidly deterministic view of the world. Nor were sermons merely an instrument of group cohesion. Deeply held convictions of a divine plan and ordering of the universe were tempered by human experiences that led preachers to maintain that penitence and faithfulness could alter situations in life. Fervent prayer and the performance of ritual duties could also influence life outcomes, but faith was not a simplistic calculation of a cause-and-effect relationship between intercession and heavenly assistance. Indeed, supplication for needs such as an end to the 1736–1737 *matlazahuatl* epidemic was not always answered in the time and manner desired.

Ita y Parra's sermons for the novenas imploring Remedios and Guadalupe to alleviate the plague clearly underscored such complexities of divine providence and intercessory prayer. His frank admission of the epidemic's destructive intractability disavowed facile claims that Guadalupe's celebrated intervention somehow expunged or justified the affliction. Rather, he insisted that human sin caused much suffering in the world and called on his hearers to purify their intercessory pleas with repentance. He also posited that the divine equation of providence was both just and beyond human comprehension. Most emphatically, he confessed that human tragedy and suffering were part of a larger, inscrutable narrative of redemption. Salvation was glimpsed in the signs of providence and acts of human solidarity in this world, but only fully known in the world to come. In the shifting terrain between belief in a divinely established plan and the possibilities of human initiative and divine intervention, New Spain preachers such as Ita y Parra fostered and refined a theology of divine providence adaptable to shifting communal needs and the vicissitudes of daily existence.

Ultimately, the theology of divine providence was not rooted in a concept but in the relations between celestial beings and their devotees. Residents of New Spain followed the established Spanish practice of developing, as William Christian has documented, "a unique [ritual] calendar built up from the settlement's own sacred history." From the vast array of feast days, saints, and Marian images in the Catholic tradition, devotees honored heavenly intercessors deemed to have a particular interest in their community. The theology of divine providence associated with naming patron saints asserted that celestial beings and God's assistance were not distant but, as Ana María Díaz-Stevens demonstrated in her study of Puerto Rican Catholics, "constantly manifested in daily occurrences." Like the intermediaries who were so often necessary to deal successfully with local magistrates and crown officials, patron saints linked their devotees to the power of divine succor. In Ita y Parra's words, their celestial patronage exemplified the "help a powerful person offers one in need." Though local celestial patrons varied from place to place, the process of designating them bolstered the theology of divine providence throughout the Spanish dominions.[43]

Guadalupe's rise to prominence in the viceroyalty and the sermons that helped facilitate her ascendancy must be understood within this broader context. Far from perceiving the emergence of their Guadalupan patroness as mere historical coincidence, New Spain preachers espoused the Spanish Catholic belief that God's providence provided this blessed protector to accompany them and assist them in their struggles. Such gratuitous patronage necessitated a response, a reciprocal relationship that Ita y Parra implored his hearers to enact in his *Círculo del amor* sermon. Like the examples of divine-human interaction throughout the scriptures, particularly the endless circle of love between Jesus and Mary, the *patronato* oath required that New Spain devotees make return for the special favor bestowed on them through Our Lady of Guadalupe.

Devotees from all strata of society embraced the theology of divine providence as the prime lens through which they confronted fortune and fate. Artists depicted the intercessory power of heavenly patrons in works such as a painting of Guadalupe arbitrating the salvation of a sinner. Municipal councils, *cofradías*, and individual devotees honored scores of patron saints. In times of crisis such as the *matlazahuatl* epidemic, the desperate populace serially invoked multiple protectors. The ways they engaged their patrons as they faced such travails illuminated their theological ruminations about providence. For example, Cabrera y Quintero's observations about native responses to their disproportionate suffering from *matlazahuatl* revealed that they turned to Guadalupe for help even as they questioned why their communities bore the greatest brunt of disease and death. Thus native response to the *matlazahuatl* disclosed in collective behavior a communal acknowledgment of their plight and their faith, implicitly addressing the tension between theological ideal and lived reality in the understanding of providence. Natives' response also accentuated their personal relationship with Guadalupe, a guardian from the heavens who deigned to dwell with them on earth, listen to their cries, and take up their concerns as her own. Likewise, devotees' desire to touch and kiss the Guadalupe image on the *tilma*—a practice so prevalent church authorities closed the glass case that protected it—underscored their deep sense that their loving mother Guadalupe was intimately present to them. Saint devotions culminated in public *patronato* oaths and their attendant community-wide celebrations, which ratified the bond between the celestial agents of divine providence and the people chosen to be their loyal beneficiaries.

Guadalupe sermons were a crucial component of this devotional world. Like Laso de la Vega, Ita y Parra and his contemporaries sought to unveil Guadalupe's presence and action in the distinct circumstances of their congregants' lives, calling their hearers to respond in faith. Like Sánchez, the preachers sought understanding of God's salvific plan in the New World through engagement of classical Christian sources. A sermon of Augustine illustrates the ongoing scriptural and patristic influences on Guadalupan theologies. Preaching on Christ's feeding of the multitudes, Augustine reproached his hearers for marveling that the Lord could feed thousands with only five loaves and two fish while at the same time faltering in their amazement at the God "who multiplies the seeds that grow in the earth, so as that a few grains are sown and whole barns are filled."[44] Augustine's critique was directed at those who understand the miraculous solely as something inexplicable or, in the parlance of our own times, as something that science cannot explain. New Spain preachers adopted Augustine's perspective: they contended that, while unfathomable outbursts of divine mercy produce widespread awe, those trained with the eyes of faith can also perceive the abundant and no less miraculous workings of providence in quotidian life.

Colonial Guadalupe sermons urged generations of Catholic faithful to embody this understanding of divine providence. Though these sermons encouraged congregants to accept and justify the social status quo, they also fortified believers with a providential vision and celestial patrons who helped them appraise and alter their life situations. The potency of New Spain residents' belief in divine providence was later compellingly evident during the struggle for Mexican independence. Far from contesting the centrality of divine providence, nineteenth-century insurgent leaders declared Guadalupe the patroness of their cause and contended providence itself had ordained the dawn of the Mexican nation.

4

Covenant

GUADALUPE AND THE MEXICAN NATION

THE MOST SHOCKING Guadalupe sermon ever proclaimed was the feast-day oration at the Guadalupe shrine by the Dominican friar Servando Teresa de Mier in 1794. Nothing in the opening of his presentation foreshadowed the novel thesis he was about to present. Echoing what were by then common claims about Guadalupe, he asked rhetorically, "Is not this [New Spain] the chosen people, the privileged nation, and the cherished offspring of Mary signaled to all the world with the glorious insignia of her special protection?" He went on to confirm that "the joy of America in the annual festivities for Mary of Guadalupe has very solid motives in the wonders of her glorious apparitions." Mier also cataloged a number of the devotional practices enacted throughout the various regions and classes of colonial society for her feast: decorative altars and streets, Marian banners, displayed copies of the Guadalupe image, songs, prayers, votive offerings, native dances, processions, concerts, and special events of pious societies, artisans, and government bodies. He summarized the well-known claim of Guadalupe's unparalleled role in the evangelization of the native peoples. Then he reiterated the long-standing association of the Ark of the Covenant with Guadalupe. He concluded his introductory remarks with an admonition: "Let us always be mindful of the covenant that [Guadalupe] celebrated with us, and the temple she ordered us to build her as a recompense for her protection in all the centuries to come."[1]

But then Mier's discourse took a startling turn as he announced his primary objective: to disclose "the true and marvelous history of our Most Holy Mother of Guadalupe according to her genuine tradition now free from equivocations" (738). He explicated his version of this history in four propositions that he based on archaeological evidence of ancient Mexico, early colonial chroniclers, and the works of previous authors, especially Luis Becerra Tanco. First, the Guadalupe image was not on the *tilma* of Juan Diego but on the cape of Saint Thomas the Apostle, who had evangelized the natives during the apostolic age. Second, Christian natives had venerated the Guadalupe image and built her a temple some 1,750 years earlier. Third, the natives' faith faltered and they sought to damage the Guadalupe image, so Saint Thomas was compelled to hide it. When Guadalupe appeared to Juan Diego ten years after the Spanish conquest, she told him where the image was concealed and it was that ancient image that he presented to Bishop Juan de Zumárraga. Finally, the image was no less remarkable when one considered its origins in this fashion, since the Virgin Mary had personally imprinted her likeness on Saint Thomas's cape during her life on earth.

The response to Mier's hypotheses was severe. The Mexico City archbishop Alonso Núñez de Haro y Peralta condemned his sermon, sentenced him to exile in Spain, and prohibited preachers from speaking against the standard Guadalupe apparition tradition.[2] Nonetheless, Mier's sermon reflects several important transitions in the Guadalupe tradition as the colonial era reached its final stages and Mexico became an independent nation in 1821. One transition was the increasing focus on the historical origins of belief in the Guadalupe apparitions,[3] though most Mexican clergy and their parishioners continued to uphold the traditional apparition account as a dogmatic tenet of Mexican Catholicism, if not of Mexican nationality itself. Another development was the ongoing spread of Guadalupan devotion across all sectors of society. Mier's description of the depth of the devotion in local communities reveals the continuing evolution of Guadalupe's rise to prominence in the half century since her celebrated intervention in the 1736–1737 *matlazahuatl* epidemic and her subsequent declaration as the patroness of New Spain. By the time of the struggle for independence, the Guadalupe image had been the most celebrated symbol in the viceroyalty for several generations. Subsequently the winning of independence and the public homage that Mexico's first leaders offered Guadalupe sealed her status as the national emblem.

Theological writings continued to be largely confined to published sermons. In concert with Guadalupe's recognition as the national symbol of the Mexican nation, a number of preachers echoed Mier's statement about Guadalupe enacting a covenant with her chosen Mexican people, in various ways calling on their hearers to offer what Mier called "recompense for her protection" (738). Nineteenth-century preachers offered their visions of the Guadalupan foundation for national history and patrimony, extending claims about Guadalupe's formative role in colonial society that predecessors such as Bartolomé Felipe de Ita y Parra had expounded. Like those colonial predecessors, independence-era orators tended to expediently presume that Guadalupe sanctioned the political and social order they espoused. At the same time, they differed from their colonial counterparts in several respects. Whereas colonial preachers tended to examine the Guadalupe event as part of salvation history, after independence most preachers examined it within the narrower scope of Mexican history. Consequently the nineteenth-century preachers gave noteworthy emphasis to the Guadalupe apparition account as the foremost source of divine revelation within Mexican history, while offering far less attention to the fathers of the church than did Miguel Sánchez and colonial preachers. As preachers sought to employ Guadalupe's symbolic potency to promote their moral vision for Mexican citizens and society, many also adopted a more didactic oratorical approach that rivaled the baroque style so prevalent through the mid-eighteenth century. The 1771 Fourth Mexican Provincial Council, the first such meeting of Mexican bishops since 1585, had already decreed a more straightforward approach to sermons with greater emphasis on Catholics' internalizing their faith and enacting it in daily life. As Carlos Herrejón Peredo has shown, these trends continued into the nineteenth century.[4]

Consciously or not, the growing attention to personal virtue upheld the value of religious faith in an age of heightened rationalism. As scholars such as Pamela Voekel have noted, clergy and other religious reformers played as significant a role as their secular counterparts in seeking to advance an alternative to baroque communitarian Catholicism. Religious reformers contended that interior piety and individual morality were the hallmarks of authentic Christians and were crucial characteristics for leaders in all spheres of communal life. Thus they contested elaborate public rituals and the notion that divine providence sanctioned stratified colonial society. In Voekel's words, while for most of its history New Spain "was an ancien régime society whose fixed hierarchies operated with God's approval," by the final decades of the eighteenth century religious reformers "promoted a nominally egalitarian theology that attacked the spiritual vacuity of baroque display, the dominant language of Old Regime social hierarchies." In its place reformers sought "to recreate new social distinctions on a different foundation"—namely, the foundation of individual virtue, achievement, and leadership ability.[5]

Yet reformers often exaggerated the distinction between the external religious practices of the baroque and the "enlightened" internal religion they advocated, disregarding the long history of dynamic interplay between interiority and ritual expression in Christianity. As Michelle Molina has shown, the reformers' discourse tended to "overlook the possibility that the 'modern' practices [they] claimed to be introducing grew out of spiritual practices that belonged squarely within the Baroque Catholicism that the reformers disavowed." Moreover, by no means did the admonitions of elite reformers eradicate baroque influences, nor did they change the practices of all devotees, many of whom continued to express their piety publicly. Local communities' vigorous defense of their religious patrons and traditions convinced clergy, even would-be reformers, to focus their efforts on modifying rather than significantly transforming or abolishing established customs. Those who instigated more radical reform frequently met staunch communal resistance, if not outright rebellion. The result was often a tacit agreement in which officials accepted local practices so long as devotees maintained a sense of ritual decorum, provided financial support, and respected the authority of ecclesiastical and colonial rule. In the end, as William Taylor concludes, the success of efforts to curtail the baroque and promote a more interiorized piety "pale in comparison to the many signs of vitality, official encouragement, mounting wealth, and popularity of image shrines, or the frequent news of miracles in the late colonial period."[6] Following independence the juxtaposition of vibrant devotional culture, reform-minded criticisms of that culture, and initiatives to refashion it shaped leaders' competing attempts to enlist Guadalupe in their nationalist visions.

The association of Guadalupe and devotion to her with the Mexican nation influenced the shifting theological emphasis of Guadalupan sermons. Colonial devotees and preachers had introduced the notion of covenant, as is evident in the collective proclamation of the *patronato* oath and in Ita y Parra's *Círculo del amor* sermon. But Ita y Parra and his fellow preachers underscored even more the wonders of divine providence they saw guiding the destiny of New Spain, its social structures, and its inhabitants. Conversely, preachers in an independent Mexico accentuated the various instances and understandings of covenant in the scriptures, especially in the Old Testament, usurping the biblical prerogative of Israel for their own nation. The fluid concept of biblical covenant encompassed belief in unconditional divine loyalty to God's chosen people. But it also stressed the reciprocal responsibilities of those people as a condition for continued divine favor. Just as Moses enjoined the people of Israel to fulfill their covenant with God through obedience to the law given at Mount Sinai, Mexican preachers commanded their flocks to fulfill the Guadalupan covenant through their adherence to the precepts the orators claimed were inherent in the Guadalupe event. Furthermore, while church and state officials in New Spain worked in relative collaboration, the increasing separation of church and state in Mexico led many clergy to criticize or even oppose political leaders. Indeed, clergy turned to Guadalupe as a bulwark in their efforts to combat what they perceived as an increasing moral decay that transgressed the Guadalupan national covenant.

Extending a trend well underway during the eighteenth century, diocesan clergy replaced their religious order counterparts in preaching an overwhelming majority of published sermons. Given that diocesan priests tend to originate from the local diocese they serve, as opposed to the greater international membership of religious orders, this trend helped facilitate the narrower focus on the Guadalupan covenant with the Mexican nation. No single figure was predominant among nineteenth-century Guadalupan preachers. Individually published sermons are extant in various archives. One 1890 volume is a compilation of more than two dozen Guadalupan sermons, nearly all of them preached during the nineteenth century. Sixteen of the month-long series of sermons given for the 1895 Guadalupe coronation ceremony at Tepeyac are in another collection. Save for one exception, every preacher in these two publications has only one sermon attributed to him.[7] Collectively the sermons reveal the new trajectory of Guadalupan theology. Preachers built on the foundational conviction of colonial orators and devotees that Guadalupe offered not just a message but an invitation to enter into loving relationship. They developed the notion of a covenant relationship between Guadalupe and the Mexican nation within the context of the struggle for independence, the tribulations of the early Mexican republic, and the momentous occasion of the Guadalupe coronation. Devotee adulation of Guadalupe as the national emblem of Mexico reinforced the clergy's efforts to engage her as the conscience of the nation.

National Symbol

The noteworthy growth of Guadalupan devotion following her papal designation as the patroness of New Spain in 1754 advanced even further in
the half century leading up to Mexican independence. One factor in this
ongoing expansion was more vigorous clerical efforts to foster the devotion among natives. The Franciscan Juan de Mendoza had given the first
known sermon that accentuated Guadalupe's identity as an indigenous
woman in 1672. The next such iteration of this claim was not until 1741,
when the Jesuit Nicolás de Segura proclaimed that "this most benign
Mother appeared with the avowed intention of resembling in every way
the natives of the country, valuing the Indians so highly that she seems
to have affected their appearance in every way." Thereafter the association
became more and more frequent as preachers sought to entice natives'
devotion by encouraging their ethnic identification with Guadalupe and
with Juan Diego. One elderly pastor, for instance, counseled his younger
counterparts to deploy these two saintly figures as evangelizing agents
among their indigenous parishioners:

> With our image of Guadalupe [the Indians] live exceedingly proud,
> and with good reason: any kind of copy of the image furnished
> to them is gratefully received and kept; and when they hear that
> that most fortunate Indian, Juan Diego, was worthy of receiving
> the apparitions of Our Lady when he was on his way to catechism
> lessons, they become very emotional and are moved to venerate her.

In 1779, the college of canons at the Guadalupe shrine received funding
for six members who had expertise in native languages—Mazahua, Otomí,
and four in Nahuatl—presumably to celebrate sacraments and enrich the
faith of visiting pilgrims from the growing variety of native groups who
venerated Guadalupe. Meanwhile many priests endeavored to propagate
Guadalupe's cult among native peoples beyond the immediate confines
of Mexico City and Tepeyac. The Jesuit priest Ignacio de Paredes's 1759
collection of sermons and instructional lectures supported this initiative.
It included a short history of the apparitions explicitly intended for the catechesis of natives.[8]

Artists complemented these ministerial efforts. A number of them
depicted the four apparition scenes to Juan Diego in the corners of
Guadalupe paintings, a practice extant since at least the mid-1650s but

much more prevalent by the latter half of the eighteenth century. A few artists produced the first stand-alone portraits of Juan Diego himself, most famously the renowned painter Miguel Cabrera. Cabrera's 1751 work *Verdadero retrato del venerable Juan Diego* (True portrait of the venerable Juan Diego) shows the pilgrim with staff and hat in hand surrounded by the birds whose singing first drew him to ascend Tepeyac, where Guadalupe is seen in the background (see figure 4.1). Such saintly depictions had obvious resonance with priests' presentation of Juan Diego as an exemplar for their indigenous charges.

FIGURE 4.1. Miguel Cabrera, *Verdadero retrato del venerable Juan Diego*, 1751. Portraits such as this personified Juan Diego as a saintly model to be emulated. Courtesy Archivo del Museo de la Basílica de Guadalupe.

Natives in many locales responded favorably to clerical initiatives, especially in central Mexico among those who spoke Nahua and Otomí. Indigenous devotees also fostered veneration of Guadalupe and Juan Diego in their own ways. Their pleas to Guadalupe became more frequent in official records such as legal disputes and wills. Likewise, Guadalupe became more frequent as a baptismal name in their communities, along with an increasing number of images, chapels, and altars dedicated to her. Father Julián Cirilo de Castillo, a priest of native background, endeavored to create a college for indigenous priests at Tepeyac during the late 1750s and 1760s. Though ultimately unsuccessful in this effort, he did secure approval to establish the institution at Tlaxcala. A sodality of native devotees established in 1784 took on the task of caring for the original sixteenth-century chapel at Tepeyac and constructing a lodge for indigenous visitors. Five years later a petition from residents of Tolpetlac sought approbation to build a chapel on the site where they claimed Guadalupe cured Juan Diego's uncle, Juan Bernardino. And in 1803 a woman from Cuauhtitlán, traditionally thought to be Juan Diego's hometown, discovered a document purported to be the 1559 will of Juan Diego's aunt, Gregoria María. The woman led an effort to build a chapel on a site she identified as the location of Juan Diego's house. An Italian Franciscan who lived in Mexico City during the 1760s marveled at the numerous devotees who processed from the city to Tepeyac, many praying the rosary as they walked the route. He summed up the ongoing increase of indigenous devotion at the Guadalupe shrine, noting that "the concourse of Indian folk, especially, is so immense that it is a source of wonderment."[9]

Indigenous veneration of Guadalupe during the decades leading up to Mexican independence in 1821 revealed two broader, interrelated devotional patterns: the tendency of both royalists and insurgents to call on Guadalupe for assistance, and the ongoing strength of local religious traditions. When Father Miguel Hidalgo y Costilla issued his *grito* (cry) for independence from the small town of Dolores, near Guanajuato, on September 16, 1810, he famously called on Our Lady of Guadalupe for support and adopted her image as the banner for the insurrectionary movement. Popular sentiment and even some historians hold that Hidalgo's appeal to Guadalupe galvanized natives with other residents in a spontaneous mass movement of independence. Yet throughout the insurgency years the Guadalupe shrine at Tepeyac was in royalist territory. Consequently public orations there proclaimed Guadalupe's support of the crown, even as native (and no doubt other) sympathizers of both warring factions continued to worship at the site. The ambiguity of Guadalupan devotion was also evident in the actions of indigenous groups such as the Zacapoaxtlas in Puebla, who named Guadalupe their patroness in defending the royalist cause, credited her with their re-peated victories over Hidalgo's forces, and then sought permission to build a sanctuary in her honor in gratitude for her assistance in battle. The Zacapoaxtlas were not the only indigenous group who defended the royalist cause, and native volunteers for the armies of Hidalgo and his successors were not as abundant as is commonly presumed. Even the substantial numbers who did join the insurrectionists often displayed more local than nationalist concern in their actions. When Father Hidalgo commanded the indigenous community of Juchipila in Zacatecas not to plunder the wealth of a local Spanish official—an order their parish priest reiterated to them in person—they disobeyed, claiming that Guadalupe had authorized their action. Apparently their desire to settle local polit-ical scores overrode Hidalgo's intent to respect private property as he sought to gain allies for a national independence movement.[10]

Bourbon reforms also contributed to the prominence of Guadalupan devotion during the period leading up to Mexican independence. José de Galvéz's official inspection tour of New Spain, conducted from 1765 to 1771, initiated these modernizing reforms in earnest within the viceroyalty. The Bourbon focus on economic productivity included attempts to reduce offi-cially mandated feast days, both their number and their scale, as a means to decrease the quantity of work holidays and the funds expended on communal festivities. These new regulations had an immediate effect on communal ritual calendars. In Mexico City, for example, due to Galvéz's decrees public officials participated officially in fewer feast days, the city council sponsored such occasions less frequently, and the financial sup-port the council provided also decreased. Indeed, in an unprecedented new trend, from the 1771 conclusion of Galvéz's inspection until the end of the colonial era a half century later the city council in the capital did not add a single new patron saint nor attend any new feast days as a corporate body. On the ecclesiastical front, at the 1771 Mexican Provincial Council bishops also reduced the number of feasts with required Mass attendance for Catholics. These developments coincided with Guadalupe's rising im-portance as the viceroyalty's patroness, in effect diminishing the array and relative prominence of competing saint-day celebrations. Thus an unin-tended consequence of the Bourbon reforms in New Spain was to further amplify Guadalupe's devotional stature.[11]

The Bourbon reforms also heightened *criollo* resentment of peninsular Spaniards' power in New Spain, as increased appointment of *peninsulares* to prestigious ecclesiastical and government posts reversed a trend of *criollo* advancement.[12] Frustration at their secondary status was an important factor in the eventual decision of many *criollos* to embrace the movement for Mexican independence, as well as the association of the native Guadalupe with that movement. Various insurgent leaders were *criollos* and Guadalupan devotees, including Father Hidalgo himself. A decade after his proclamation of Mexican independence another *criollo* headed the effort that finally established the new nation. The military commander Agustín Iturbide, who had thwarted insurgent efforts for a decade, switched sides in 1820 after Spain established a constitutional monarchy that limited the powers of the Spanish king. Iturbide united church officials, military personnel, landowners, and the general populace around his Plan of Iguala and its three guarantees: the establishment of Roman Catholicism as the national religion, independence from Spain, and unity without distinction between the American- and European-born. With this broad support, Iturbide marched his army ceremoniously into Mexico City, where officials declared Mexico's independence on September 28, 1821. Iturbide was named president of the provisional government and then in July 1822 became emperor of the new nation. To solidify his rule, he established an Imperial Order of Guadalupe, with himself as its grand master.

Iturbide's deployment of Guadalupe to validate his ascendancy reveals that, while Guadalupe was certainly the most prominent extant emblem available to represent evolving sentiments of nationhood, it is also true that the process of achieving and consolidating independence further advanced her acclaim. Shifting scenes of conflict during the war for independence resulted in geographic mobility that brought residents from isolated areas into more sustained contact with Guadalupan devotion. Moreover, many of the eventually victorious insurgents who succeeded Hidalgo followed his lead in invoking Guadalupe as their protector in combat. None was more vociferous in his public displays of devotion than the *mestizo* priest José María Morelos. His battle flag bore the blue and white colors traditionally associated with Mary, he conspicuously attributed his military victories to Guadalupe, and his soldiers used her name as a countersign. Then in 1828, Mexico's first constitutional president, who had changed his name from Manuel Félix Fernández to Guadalupe Victoria during the war of independence, presided over the ceremony to rename the settlement around the Guadalupe shrine at Tepeyac. Long known as Guadalupe, he rechristened the place Guadalupe Hidalgo, solidifying the link between Guadalupe and the celebrated father of Mexican independence.[13]

Guadalupe's strong association with independence and the newfound nation emerged despite an ambiguous church response to Mexico's split from Spain. On the one hand, some Spanish clerics refused to serve in an independent Mexico, most notoriously the archbishop of Mexico City, who resigned his post. Moreover, the right the pope had previously given the Spanish monarch to name bishops did not automatically pass to the new nation, and Vatican officials stalled the process of naming Mexican bishops while the matter remained unresolved. On the other hand, immediately following independence Catholicism was still the established religion. Delegates who had assembled to create the new government even went together to the Mexico City cathedral for Mass before opening their proceedings, foreshadowing a continuing practice in the young republic of celebrating public events with church services. The Mexican Congress also declared Guadalupe's feast day a national holiday. Jean Louis Berlandier, a French immigrant who arrived in 1826, summed up Guadalupe's status well. He described her as "the most venerated saint in Mexico, especially since independence" and testified that her image was so popular that it was "found not only in churches but even in establishments alien to the faith."[14]

The 1831 celebration of the tercentennial of the Guadalupe apparitions illuminates the combined efforts from all sectors of Mexican society to honor their national patroness. Members of the Junta Guadalupana committee that organized the commemoration included the directors of national agencies, senators, governors, municipal officials, judges, military officers, professors, canons of the Mexico City cathedral, heads of religious orders, and priests. All these groups participated in the four days of celebration in Mexico City, along with *cofradías* and various musical ensembles. The festivities included church services, floats depicting the Guadalupan apparitions, fireworks, and processions through streets local residents adorned with altars and flags. Since the canons of the Guadalupe shrine denied the request to bring the Guadalupe *tilma* into the city, devotees processed to Tepeyac for the culminating ritual. Father José María Gastañeta, a priest whom Spanish authorities had imprisoned and then sent into exile during the war of independence, gave the concluding sermon at Tepeyac. According to the Junta Guadalupana report, in his emotional oration as he linked Guadalupe to Mexican independence Gastañeta "did not lose from sight the vicissitudes of the 1810 revolution of which he was a victim."[15]

The collaborative church-state relations on display during the tercentennial were not lasting. Building on earlier Bourbon reform efforts to limit the social power of the church, Vice President Valentín Gómez Farías oversaw the institution of Mexico's first anticlerical measures after he assumed office in 1833. His reforms encompassed the secularization of the educational system that Catholic clergy had previously directed. Subsequently liberal political leaders such as Gómez Farías battled their conservative counterparts on a number of fronts, including the role of the church in society. The liberal victory in the War of the Reform (1858–1861) enabled the enactment of even more stringent measures under President Benito Juárez, including the confiscation of church property, the suppression of religious orders, and the forced exile of Catholic bishops who had publicly supported the opposing side in the war. Though he retained the Guadalupe feast as a holiday when he decreed a reduction in the number of national religious feasts, Juárez also confiscated funds, sacred vessels, and other valuable adornments from the shrine at Tepeyac. In 1869 Catholic leaders issued an alarming report that for the first time since its establishment in the mid-eighteenth century the shrine's college of canons might need to be disbanded due to a lack of funds.[16]

Yet veneration of Guadalupe remained strong. As the sheets of tin on which they were typically drawn became widely available at a low cost during the nineteenth century, ex-voto paintings that depicted a favor asked or received from heavenly benefactors such as Guadalupe multiplied among devotees of all classes. So too did printed images of Guadalupe, devotional books, and pamphlets. Pilgrimages to Tepeyac, which residents of Mexico City and the environs had undertaken since the inception of the shrine, expanded in frequency and in distances traveled, abetted by the advent of railroads. At the same time, in numerous local communities an active laity expanded their leadership in devotional celebrations. Women's leadership in such communal devotion was more visible than ever. Terry Rugeley has documented, for example, the growth of women's participation in cofradías over the course of the nineteenth century in the Yucatán Peninsula of southeast Mexico. Women became the overwhelming majority in cofradías that previously had been predominantly male, and some of these devotional societies even had exclusively female membership. The opportunity these organizations offered women to "exercise creativity and leadership" outside their homes facilitated the "pronounced tendency toward feminization" in the organizations and their pious expressions. Women's increasingly public religious leadership was not unique to the Yucatán and contributed to the devotional cultures of holy figures such as Guadalupe.[17]

Despite the loss of valuable assets, devotion at the Guadalupe shrine also continued to elicit praise. Perhaps the most famous nineteenth-century panegyric of Tepeyac as the national sanctuary came from the pen of the novelist and journalist Ignacio Manuel Altamirano, an ardent youthful supporter of anticlerical measures who subsequently dedicated himself to literary pursuits in which he portrayed Mexican Catholic traditions such as Guadalupe with great respect and admiration. His 1884 book *Paisajes y leyendas, tradiciones y costumbres de México* (Landscapes and legends, traditions and customs of Mexico) included a lengthy section titled "La fiesta de Guadalupe." Altamirano recounted with fervor the Guadalupan devotion on display in locales throughout the nation and especially at Tepeyac, where he noted vast crowds congregated every day, with even greater numbers on the twelfth of each month, and more than ever on her December 12 feast day. He also forcefully articulated the growing sentiment that Guadalupe not only liberated Mexico from Spain but that her feast day was the sole occasion when the Mexican nation was free from social divisiveness. Ultimately neither government leaders nor patriotic sentiment bonded the diverse population and political factions of Mexican society. Rather, Altamirano contended, "in the ultimate extreme, in cases of desperation, the cult of the Mexican Virgin is the only bond that unites them." He further marveled at the way Mexicans of all castes and political persuasions gathered in "equality before the Virgin." His concluding statement about Guadalupe's centrality in Mexico was frequently quoted among preachers, journalists, and other commentators well into the twentieth century: "The day that the cult of the Indian Virgin [of Guadalupe] disappears, the Mexican nationality will also disappear."[18]

Catholic clergy embraced Guadalupe's rise as the Mexican national symbol and articulated their vision of the kind of nation Guadalupe directed her sons and daughters to fashion. Nowhere was that vision more evident than the imposing Guadalupe coronation ceremonies of 1895. The practice of canonical coronation, which requires official papal authorization, increased in popularity amid a rising wave of pious devotion during the nineteenth century. Devotees celebrated coronations in a number of nations and dioceses, including the renowned crowning of Our Lady of Lourdes in 1876. In the same way that the Lourdes devotion became a focal point for the renewed vigor of the Catholic Church in France, the Guadalupe coronation was a symbolically climactic moment in a revival of the Mexican Catholic Church. Porfirio Díaz began his long tenure as president in 1876 and made a tacit arrangement with Catholic bishops that allowed the church some latitude to function alongside his regime. Lay leaders helped reinvigorate the church's public works, particularly the Ladies of Charity, the most prominent Mexican Catholic women's organization that by the early twentieth century operated thirty-two hospitals, twenty schools, and seventeen orphanages. The first Catholic social encyclical, Pope Leo XIII's 1891 *Rerum Novarum* (On capital and labor), also inspired Mexican Catholic bishops and priests to support Catholic worker circles. Church leaders' intent to form cooperative alternatives to more radical labor organizing efforts aligned their workers' initiatives with government interests and helped recuperate the institutional status of the church. Various other factors contributed to the ecclesiastical revival and to the Guadalupe coronation: the Vatican contacts that Mexican prelates had established while in European exile, the consequent Vatican creation of new Mexican dioceses and archdioceses, and the patronage of a small group of elite Mexican Catholic laity who helped finance Catholic publications and projects, including major renovations of the Guadalupe sanctuary as well as the coronation events.[19]

The catalyst of the coronation venture was José Antonio Plancarte y Labastida, whose foundational leadership was rewarded with his consecration as a bishop and his installation as the abbot of the Guadalupe shrine college of canons the year of the coronation ceremony. Dioceses and parishes throughout the country organized local celebrations to honor the occasion. Próspero María Alarcón, the archbishop of Mexico City, joined with his fellow bishops to open the official proceedings with a ceremony to consecrate the refurbished Guadalupe shrine and its altars. Daily coronation celebrations at the shrine followed during the entire month of October, affording bishops and dioceses throughout the country the opportunity to lead worship on an assigned day. Religious orders, diocesan clergy, *cofradías*, and other pious societies also had their own designated days to offer Mass and devotions. Twenty-two Mexican bishops, fourteen more from the United States, and one each from Québec, Havana, and Panama congregated for the solemn coronation itself. On the afternoon of October 11 Archbishop Alarcón led sung pontifical vespers, along with litanies and other prayers. The next morning he officiated at the coronation ceremony, blessing the bejeweled crown, which he and his fellow prelates processed to the Guadalupe image. Priests, elite devotees, and as many members of the general public as could fit into the remaining seats and standing spaces filled the Tepeyac shrine. Bishops officiated at two pontifical Masses, one before and one after the coronation. The honor of leading the climactic moment, the placing of the crown on the Guadalupe image, was reserved for Archbishop Alarcón and his fellow prelate, the Michoacán archbishop José Ignacio Árciga.[20]

Though President Díaz never rescinded the anticlerical statutes his predecessors had promulgated, such pomp and his informal peace with Catholic officials elicited accusations of government and episcopal collusion to appease the Mexican masses through devotional pageantry. One editorialist, who tellingly wrote from San Antonio where he had exiled himself from Porfirian Mexico, asked rhetorically about the numerous pilgrims who journeyed to Mexico City for the coronation ceremonies: "But what does all this prove? Only that there are fanatics who spend on pipes and flutes significant sums of money that could serve the poor and the public good." He also urged his compatriots to forget "superstitious practices" and foster "honorable sentiments of human dignity and justice." His critique echoed that of nineteenth-century liberals who insisted they were not anti-Catholic but wanted to purify Catholicism from what they saw as clericalism and excess and restore it to what they contended was its more pristine apostolic origins.[21]

At the same time, many lay enthusiasts supported the bishops' initiatives. Journalists vied with one another in composing reports that widely disseminated news of the coronation. A number of musicians composed original songs to laud their mother and patroness. On October 18 literary figures convened a vigil to honor Guadalupe with discourses and poems.[22] Yet exclusive clerical control was a marked feature of the official coronation events, particularly in comparison to previous grand occasions such as the 1831 tercentennial and the *patronato* declarations of the mid-eighteenth century. While lay and civic leaders had prominent roles in organizing those earlier commemorations, at the coronation ceremony the laity were passive participants at a clerically orchestrated ritual. Moreover, the official *Album de la coronación de la Sma. Virgen de Guadalupe* does not even mention the participation of civic officials. Liberal attacks on the Catholic hierarchy and the Romanization that the prelates had experienced during their Vatican exile no doubt influenced the clerics' decision to assume control of official Guadalupan ceremonies. In crowning Guadalupe, the bishops sought to assert their authority as the primary caretakers and interpreters of the image that over the course of the preceding century had clearly become the uncontested national symbol of Mexico.

Independence

The 1801 sermon for the Guadalupe feast at Tepeyac of Father Joseph Ignacio Heredia y Sarmiento, professor of rhetoric at the Pontifical College Seminary of Mexico City, illustrates the patriotic sentiment associated with Guadalupe as the nineteenth century dawned. Preaching on the officially designated gospel passage of the visitation (Luke 1:39–45), Heredia y Sarmiento directed his hearers' attention to the line that states John the Baptist leapt for joy within his mother Elizabeth's womb when she heard Mary's greeting. He emphasized that "the arrival of Mary in the mountains of Judea and her visit to Elizabeth made the Baptist advantageously great over other men." The thesis of his oration was that, in parallel fashion, "the arrival and apparition of this same Lady on these mountains of Tepeyac constitute Americans [peoples of the New World and specifically of New Spain] on such a high level of glory that they appear among other nations as the special and very distinguished favored ones of Mary."[23]

Heredia y Sarmiento's lengthy sermon repeatedly underscored his core thesis with rhetorical flourish. He referred to his native land as "blessed America" (46) and the "most joyful subject of her [Mary of Guadalupe's] most particular favors" (24). His catalog of Guadalupe's benefits spanned the purportedly rapid spread of Christianity among native peoples following her appearances to Juan Diego to her constant protection ever since, during times of drought, flood, epidemic, war, and all other manner of calamity. Heredia y Sarmiento summarized her benevolence with a citation of the by then pervasive claim based on Psalm 147:20—*non fecit taliter omni nationi* (59)—and expanded on that text with bold comparisons such as his people were "a thousand times fortunate" (61) and had received in Guadalupe "a blessing that the other parts of the world will always envy" (50). Because of her, he and his compatriots had become "a Catholic nation to which the Most High God makes himself present, near, intimate" (52), a nation that enjoys "the greatness and happiness with which the insignia of Guadalupe exalts our nation over the rest of the others" (38).

Heredia y Sarmiento's oratory reflected a growing trend that would continue throughout the nineteenth century and beyond: a more expansive engagement of the Guadalupe apparition narrative as a relatively independent source of divine revelation. Sánchez structured a major section of his theological analyses around the apparition narrative and Luis Laso de la Vega published a Nahuatl version of it. But Sánchez and preachers such as Ita y Parra explicated the apparitions as a pious tradition best interpreted through the lens of biblical typology and classical Christian sources. While Heredia y Sarmiento followed his predecessors in his reliance on such sources, particularly the Lucan text that his sermon expounded, in one central passage he cited at length the revelation of Guadalupe to the New World through her words to Juan Diego:

> My son, let nothing afflict you, nor fear illness, nor another grievous misfortune . . . Am I not here, who is your Mother? Are you not under my shade and protection? What necessity do you have of anything else? I will show myself a merciful Mother with your people, with my devotees, and with those who seek me as a remedy for their necessities . . . I will hear their tears and their prayers to give them consolation and relief (42).[24]

One of the longest quotations of the apparition narrative in any published Guadalupan sermon to that point, Heredia y Sarmiento exclaimed that these words were "the secure pledge of our joy!" (42) and confidently deemed them "effective promises through which the Lady obliges to us without limit or reservation the benefits of her power, the protection of her arm, the riches of her mercy, and the blessings of her sweetness" (42). His claims illustrate preachers' increasing inclination to focus on the New World Guadalupan event as a self-authenticating revelation of unconditional love for the people of those lands.

As had Ita y Parra and other preachers before him, Heredia y Sarmiento concluded his sermon with a call to faithfulness in gratitude for so great a heavenly patroness. He asked rhetorically: "What would it [the visitation of the mother of God] have benefited the Baptist . . . if afterward he himself had not heroically maintained and advanced his holiness?" (65) While Heredia y Sarmiento acknowledged that "none of us [alone] can be all that John [the Baptist] was," he contended that "all of us together with a proper distribution of his virtues among ourselves" (67) can collectively make return to Mary of Guadalupe for her benevolence. This generalized plea to holiness notwithstanding, the overwhelming emphasis in Heredia y Sarmiento's sermon was not on the Christian obligations of his hearers but instead on their singular divine election as the chosen sons and daughters of Our Lady of Guadalupe.

When insurgents drew on such sentiments to help foment rebellion, loyalists countered that their posturing constituted nothing less than apostasy. The historian Jorge Cañizares-Esguerra has demonstrated that warring factions in locales across the Spanish Americas displayed remarkable ingenuity in orations that "anchored their world in the Old Testament and interpreted the present as episodes prefigured in the biblical past." In the same way that earlier writers and preachers had presumed the conquest of the New World fulfilled biblical prophecy and divine providence safeguarded the Spanish enterprise in the New World, both those struggling for and against independence displayed hermeneutical savvy in their capacity to find biblical precedent and justification for their cause. With the advent of armed hostilities, what was strikingly new was that both sides encompassed Catholics who revered the same sources of revelation. The wars of independence in the Spanish colonies were not only military and political contests, but rhetorical clashes of biblical interpretation as well.[25]

Guadalupan preachers engaged in these same debates regarding Guadalupe's response to agitation for independence in New Spain. Father José de la Canal, a Spanish church historian and the assistant general for the provinces of Spain and the Indies of his Augustinian order, prayed with his Madrid congregation on the Guadalupe feast in 1819 that she would "restrain the arm of the avenger God that threatens the Americas." Displaying an imperialist view of both past and present, Canal reminded his hearers of "the prodigious feats of our forefathers in America, especially the propagation of the Gospel in those most vast regions." He compared Guadalupe's exploits to those of Mary in her image of Nuestra Señora del Pilar (Our Lady of the Pillar), whose "apparition to the apostle James in the immortal Zaragoza [Spain]" is acclaimed as the first Marian appearance in history and as a pivotal event in the early Christian evangelization of Spain. Like Spain in the Old World, through Guadalupe her colonies owed to Mary "the singular favor that Heaven dispensed to New Spain, which so greatly contributed to its spiritual conquest." Conversely, Canal denounced insurgents who "exaggerate with hypocritical hearts and tongues their slavery and our dominion." Condemning their "fratricidal furor" which sought to "bathe with Spanish blood the lands that Mary [of Guadalupe] visited, that Mary sanctified, that Mary chose," he asked rhetorically "Oh tender mother, will you look with indifference upon the devastation of your inheritance?" Ultimately, Canal claimed insurgents had defied the will of God: "Ungrateful and denaturalized children, is this how you repay the benefits of God, and thank those who brought Mary among you? Sacrileges, and you dare to stamp her [Guadalupe's] image on your rebellious flags?"[26]

Three years later, another Guadalupan preacher with a similarly unequivocal view pointed to a completely opposite effect of celestial aid. After Iturbide's ascent to power, the Order of Guadalupe he established held its first annual function in December 1822. The preacher chosen for the occasion was an outspoken supporter of the new regime, Father Manuel de Bárcena, archdeacon of the Valladolid (later renamed Morelia to honor the insurgency leader Morelos) cathedral in Michoacán. Bárcena was a Spanish-born royalist who had advocated for an independent Mexican empire out of disgust at antagonistic church-state relations under the Spanish Cortes, the new governing body in his native land. In his sermon he echoed Canal's pro-Spain oration in his avowal that it was "thanks to divine providence" that "in America God replaced the loss [of so many to Protestantism in Europe] with a great excess" of fervent new converts to the Catholic faith. But he attributed to those same forces of providence Mexico's recently won independence: "Believe me compatriots: if we have conquered our sovereignty, if we have triumphed over our enemies, if the country of Anahuac [Mexico] breathes liberty, we owe it all to the Virgin of Tepeyac."[27]

Bárcena opened his sermon paraphrasing the biblical canticles of Zechariah and Simeon from the infancy narrative of Luke's gospel (1:68, 2:29–30): "Blessed be the God of Israel, who has conserved my life until this joyful day [of Mexican independence]" (3). He exclaimed that "Anahuac has never seen a day like this" (3). His text for the sermon came from the Genesis account of the Great Flood, when God promised through Noah that no inundation would ever again destroy the world, placing a rainbow in the sky and avowing "this is the sign of the covenant between me and you" (3, citing Genesis 9:12). The implication of this text for the present occasion was unmistakable: through Our Lady of Guadalupe a similar heavenly promise had been made to guide and protect the Mexican nation.

Bárcena went on to speak of the three "principal favors" (5) bestowed on Mexico through Guadalupe, which he identified with Iturbide's three guarantees in the establishment of the nation. According to Bárcena, the first, "Holy Religion, the foremost gift that the heavens can give to the earth, we owe most especially to the Virgin of Guadalupe" (5). Her influence on the evangelization of Mexico was so pervasive that "in more than fifteen centuries history had not seen an epoch so glorious for our holy Religion" (6). Similarly, just as Guadalupe was the architect of Mexicans' faith, the most essential of all "spiritual goods," she was also the source of their independence, the greatest among a people's "temporal goods" (7). Indeed, in Bárcena's view it was Iturbide's dedication of his independence initiatives to Guadalupe that enabled him to achieve in six months and "without the cost of blood" (7) what had not been obtained in eleven years of violent warfare. This rapid change of fortune stemmed from Guadalupe's generous bestowal of Iturbide's third guarantee, union. Bárcena noted that during the decade of armed conflict both insurgents and royalists "invoked the Virgin, but in vain because the Queen and Mother of Mercy could not be the patroness of persecutions" (8). In the end it was Guadalupe who "inspired union" (8) among the Mexican people and consequently brought them to independence and peace.

Gratitude for Guadalupe's favors should invoke a fervent response from her devotees. In Bárcena's words, "Mary is not like men: they demand gift for gift, benefit for benefit; but our heavenly patroness only asks us that we conserve and defend the gifts that she herself gave us, the three guarantees" (9). Their first obligation was not only to live the Catholic faith, but also to "propagate and defend it against its enemies" (9). Bárcena urged his hearers to firmly resolve that "the one who is not an apostolic Christian [Roman Catholic] is not a citizen of ours; he is not a Mexican" (9). Secondly, they should preserve their independence through the promotion of civic virtue and patriotism, seeking the "common good" (12) of the nation above egotistical desires. From the ancient times of Athens and Rome, Bárcena contended, "history confirms that vices, and not conquerors, have been the cause of the destruction of nations" (11–12). Finally, commenting that the cause of independence faltered until Iturbide united diverse factions under the Plan of Iguala, Bárcena urged his compatriots to recognize that "origin, language, blood, and religion unite us" (13) and to guide their fellow Mexicans to live in harmony as one people and nation.

Bárcena concluded with an exhortation to Iturbide and the other prominent leaders in his congregation, insisting to these members of the Imperial Order of Guadalupe that "we are more especially obligated: the insignias that we wear on our chests incessantly remind us of this duty: Religion, Independence, Union" (14). Just as the three colors of the Mexican flag represent the three guarantees, Bárcena continued, and in ancient times the rainbow signaled God's promise to Noah, their insignias express "the pact we have celebrated with the Guadalupana: this is the sign of the covenant between me and you" (14, citing Genesis 9:12). Effectively, Bárcena extended the theology of divine providence that had been propagated by New Spain preachers such as Ita y Parra into an avowal of a covenant between Guadalupe and the newfound Mexican nation. His deployment of Old Testament models of covenant became one of the most distinctive features of Guadalupan oratory in the century following Mexican independence.

Tribulations

Preachers frequently examined Guadalupe's role in the ongoing development of the nation. In the face of tribulations such as the 1846–1848 war in which the United States conquered half of Mexico's territory, preachers echoed and refashioned the thesis of predecessors such as Bárcena about the Guadalupan covenant with the Mexican people. Consciously or not, in addressing the thorny question of how so blessed a nation as Mexico could face the catastrophes that beset them, they also echoed earlier orations such as Ita y Parra's Remedios and Guadalupe sermons during the 1736–1737 *matlazahuatl* epidemic. Like their predecessors, nineteenth-century preachers posited that sin could lead to calamity but, at the same time, avowed that suffering was part of an unfathomable yet providential order ultimately under the sovereignty of God and revealed through celestial beings such as Guadalupe.

Three published sermons from the early 1850s exemplify how these orators drew on biblical notions of covenant to understand the contemporary fortunes of Guadalupe's chosen nation. One preacher was Joaquín Ladrón de Guevara, a priest who also served as a senator from the state of Guanajuato. Reflecting a growing practice extant since at least the end of the previous century—commemorating Guadalupe on the twelfth day of each month to extend the celebration of her December 12 feast throughout the year—Ladrón de Guevara offered his oration at the Guadalupe shrine on February 12, 1852. He began with a solemn declaration that the Guadalupe image at Tepeyac is the "singular emblem of our dear homeland." He reminded his hearers that Guadalupe had protected them in troubled times ranging from drought to epidemic to revolution, and he affirmed that "her adored name is the sign of triumph that the Mexican warrior invokes to sound the trumpet of battle." In an indirect reference to the U.S. military defeat of Mexico four years earlier, however, Ladrón de

Guevara went on to acknowledge that "if on some occasion the enemy of our republic was able to blaspheme, like the Philistine, asking where is the God who defends the Hebrews, it has been a salutary lesson so that we recognize, prostrating ourselves, the Lord of armies, abjuring pride, egoism, and avaricious aspirations."[28]

Thus Ladrón de Guevara saw no heavenly breach of the Guadalupan covenant in Mexico's loss of war and territory to the "Philistines" north of their border. Indeed, he invoked "the patriarchs, prophets, and other illustrious personages of the old covenant" to demonstrate that their "intimate relations [with God] enable us to glimpse his incomparable magnificence" (202–203). Summarizing such covenant relations with God's chosen people of old, Ladrón de Guevara noted the promise to Noah that a flood would never again destroy the earth, to Abraham that he would father a multitude of descendants, to Moses that he would liberate the enslaved Israelites, and to Joshua that he would conquer Jericho. He also recalled how God aided biblical women of old, enabling Judith to lead her people to triumph over the Assyrians, Abigail to placate David's ire and prevent vengeful bloodshed (1 Samuel 25), and Esther to foil a plot to annihilate the Jews living in Persia. Above all, Ladrón de Guevara underscored God's "irrevocable election" (200) of Mary to be the mother of the savior. Drawing in particular on the imagery of the covenant with Noah, Ladrón de Guevara stated that on the hill of Tepeyac "appears the most beautiful rainbow, perpetual sign of the firm compact of our beliefs, the most pure mother who does not forget from her throne in the heavens the indigence of her needy children, [and who] constructs this fortress [shrine], in which like the most vigilant advocate she admits, valorizes, and recommends their vows" (205). If God had used the U.S. military victory to teach Mexicans humility before the divine will, Ladrón de Guevara's proclamation insisted that Guadalupe's faithfulness as the "protector of our nation" (208) was by no means extinguished. Rather, it continued to shroud her Mexican elect with the pledge of divine favor previously given to Noah and his descendants.

Ladrón de Guevara's contemporary Fray Pablo Antonio del Niño Jesús, a Carmelite priest at their Guadalajara priory, similarly lauded Guadalupe in gratitude, in his case for relief from the severe cholera epidemic of 1850. Fray Pablo chose as his text for the occasion Psalm 90:15: "My people will invoke me, and I will listen to them; I will be with them in their tribulation and remove them from it." Reminding his hearers of the "cruel and heartbreaking scenes" among their friends and family just a few months previously, he contended that this scripture passage had been fulfilled in their presence: it was the "mother of God, mother of sinners . . . mother of mercy and life" who, now as in the past, "from her throne on Tepeyac listens benignly to the people who invoke her, assists them in their tribulation, and liberates them from it."[29]

Fray Pablo marveled at the way Guadalupe remained steadfastly committed to her chosen Mexican people despite their unfaithfulness. He contrasted Guadalupe's gratuitous election of her Mexican children with their ungrateful wickedness. Hyperbolically underscoring his point, he even went so far as to claim "we are worse sinners than all other peoples, because even as the most privileged in the approbation of the Most Holy Virgin, it seems like we have studiously tried to commit our sins in direct proportion with the benefits we have received from God, with those benefits for which we are never thankful, with those benefits that we positively abuse" (308–309). More concretely, he cited decaying morality and social changes like impious publications in Mexico City. He concluded that the residents of the capital city had "almost lost their Catholic conscience" and that it was only Guadalupe's intercession that saved them from "a punishment similar to [the destruction of] Jerusalem" (309).

This charged rhetoric was the basis for Fray Pablo's articulation of Guadalupe's covenant with Mexico. Like Ladrón de Guevara, he posited that her promise of protection was unconditional. But while Ladrón de Guevara called on the biblical precedent of God's covenant with Noah, Fray Pablo focused on the Davidic covenant, God's promise that King David's descendants would succeed him and that from his lineage would come the Messiah. The preacher accentuated the utterly unrestricted character of God's allegiance to this covenant, introducing it with the statement that "God conserved the reign of Judah among the sons of Solomon, despite their aberrations, out of respect for the holiness of their father David" (310). Similarly, "since she descended from heaven in the miraculous way that we all know, since she said to her indulged son Juan Diego: 'I desire that you build me here a temple so I can be with you every day' . . . since then she has constituted herself our special mother in a way she has not done with any other nation" (312).

Guadalupe, Fray Pablo continued, had remained utterly faithful to her unfaithful children amid floods, plagues, hunger, earthquakes, and in times of discord and war. Echoing a notion that dated back to predecessors such as Laso de la Vega, Fray Pablo attested that in every instance she "placated the Lord's ire" (313) toward the sinful Mexican people. Thus it came as no surprise that, like the Israelites who prayed throughout Judea but offered their most solemn vows and pleas to God at the Temple in Jerusalem, during the cholera epidemic the Mexican faithful called on various saints and invocations of Mary throughout the land but ultimately turned their gaze to the Guadalupe shrine at Tepeyac. In the end, Fray Pablo contended, "Mary of Guadalupe was the one who made the epidemic disappear, who visited us with her consolation in the days of tribulation" (314). And as with the wayward Davidic kings, their mother of mercy showed that God is "more disposed to forgive than we ourselves are to implore pardon" (315). The alleviation of the cholera epidemic, in other words, was one more in a long succession of graced occurrences that revealed Guadalupe's unqualified covenantal love and protection initiated with Juan Diego and, like King David, passed on to those who inherited his promise.

A third 1850s preacher who underscored the Guadalupan covenant with Mexico was Father Francisco Javier Miranda, a prominent leader of the Conservative Party. Miranda's primary text for the 1852 Guadalupe feast at Tepeyac was from Revelation 11:19: "And the temple of God in the heavens was opened, and in the middle of it could be seen the ark of the testament." In Mexico this promise of Revelation was made manifest in "the apparition of Guadalupe, descended from the heavens as the Ark of the Covenant between God and the Mexican people." Miranda referred to the holy image on Juan Diego's *tilma* as the ark of the Guadalupan covenant seven times during the course of his oration. He deemed the venerated *tilma* "the ark of reconciliation of the New World" and "the holy ark, from which proceeds graces and blessings." Miranda also emphasized the intimacy of the bond between Guadalupe and Mexicans through a reflection on the Song of Songs about the longing a beloved has for her spouse. He asked rhetorically: "When the Mother of God appeared on a *tilma* that hung from the shoulders of an Indian, do we not observe that it seems the queen of heaven chose the heart of the Mexican as the place for her love to rest, in the same way that the spouse slept over the heart of her lover?" Guadalupe's tender approach enticed an equally fervent response on the part of her beloved Mexican people, whom Miranda sought to animate to greater gratitude, even as he noted with satisfaction their fervent celebration of the Guadalupe feast "from the shores of the Pacific Ocean, to the borders of New Mexico, and from the coasts of the Gulf of Mexico to the limits of Guatemala."[30]

The Ark of the Covenant, of course, is associated with the Mosaic, or Sinai, covenant, since it was the tabernacle in which the Decalogue, or the Ten Commandments, was kept. Also known as the Holy of Holies, it signified the presence of Yahweh among the chosen people of Israel, as well as the pact between them: God would be their God and protector and the people would in turn obey God's commands. Sánchez was the first of many theologians and preachers who named Guadalupe the Ark of the Covenant. He echoed the ancient Christian claim that the Virgin Mary is the Ark of the New Covenant, since she is the tabernacle that bore the incarnate Word just as the Hebrew ark bore the Ten Commandments. In Miranda's terms, she is "the living ark where Jesus Christ was enclosed" (298). Miranda did not explicitly treat the Mosaic covenant in his sermon, but he implicitly presented it through his emphasis on the Ark of the Covenant.

Unlike the covenants with Noah and David, the Mosaic covenant is conditional. It entails mutual obligations, and the possibility that God could withdraw his support if the people fail to fulfill their responsibilities. Miranda underscored this conditional quality in his rendering of the covenant established with Mexico through Guadalupe. Speaking just four years after the U.S. defeat of Mexico, he insisted that "when Catholic reason attends to the work of regeneration among Mexicans, it does not consider the science of man nor the valor of warriors; it does not calculate the power of arms, nor the adroitness of captains" (297). Rather, "it only looks upon and adores the invisible hand of the Almighty . . . which values equally the triumphs of some nations and the conquest of others, and even the aberrations of princes and of peoples, in order to achieve immortal ends in the world" (297). Miranda avowed that, because the mother of God had "planted roots" among them, their native land was "a thousand times more fortunate than the Promised Land" (302) to which Moses led the Israelites. Through Guadalupe's intercession Mexico enjoyed "the most appreciated goods of a people" (301): abundance, peace, and security. Yet he also recognized that "in light of the great evils that we suffer" some might be inclined to ask "what good is this abundance [of natural resources] that we don't enjoy, and where are peace and security?" (302) To such interrogators Miranda offered what he considered the more fundamental question: "Where are the Christian virtues that would make us deserving of the gifts of heaven?" (302)

The fortunes of the nation and its inhabitants, in other words, hinged on their faithfulness to the covenant established through Guadalupe.

Disobedience could lead to suffering and misfortune "with which the justice of the Lord chooses to punish us" (302). Defeat at war and other disasters should first and foremost be understood within the framework of celestial correction for faults and failings and a call to renew the people's commitment to live out the Guadalupan covenant. Surveying the tumultuous history of Mexico, especially over the three decades since independence, Miranda nonetheless confessed that "I will always recognize in this *ayate* [the cloth of Juan Diego's *tilma*] the only good that has remained with us after so many dissensions, so much blood spilled and so many civil upheavals, because the Ark of the Covenant is on it" (302). Like the chosen people of old, the people of Mexico enjoyed the favor of divine election but also the responsibilities incumbent on those who received so high a favor. Miranda did not specify what these responsibilities were, other than his general references to Christian virtue. Yet, like the prophets of old, he urged his fellow Mexicans to recommit themselves to those responsibilities, even as he assured them that, like the Ark of the Covenant, the *tilma* was an enduring sign of heaven's faithfulness.

Coronation

The month-long series of sermons during the 1895 coronation ceremonies illuminated the Mexican episcopacy's interpretations of Guadalupe in the wake of their exile, bitter struggles with liberal adversaries, and rebuilding efforts since the ascent to power of Porfirio Díaz. Collectively the orations emphasized thematic trends that had grown in prominence since independence. Preachers repeatedly spoke of Guadalupe's decisive role in the conversion of the natives and the subsequent history of Mexico. They likened the Guadalupe image to the Ark of the Covenant and Tepeyac to the holy mountains and sacred places of the Bible. Several of the discourses were directed at specific groups that had gathered for their designated day of the coronation celebrations. But the two principal sermons presented on the days of the coronation rituals, October 11 and 12, illuminated the Guadalupan covenant that organizers sought to enliven through their crowning of Guadalupe as the ultimate sovereign of the Mexican nation.

Bishop José de Jesús Ortiz of Chihuahua preached on October 11, setting the stage for the coronation with an historical assessment of the national vocation initiated in the Guadalupe event. Ortiz posed the central question for his sermon at the outset: "What were the secret designs of God in permitting that the Immaculate Virgin came from the heights of heaven to visit the poor inhabitants of this until then unknown land?" To answer this question, he averred that "in the works of God one can clearly distinguish three different phases that correspond to three periods of their history: humility and at times scorn in their beginning, slowness in their development, and admirable fertility in their results." He likened this process to Jesus's parable in which a mustard seed, despite being among the smallest of seeds, produces an inordinately immense tree (Mark 4:30–32 and parallels). First comes the phase "of the vocation or of the sowing," when God does the work of planting the seed, preparing the hearts of future believers and then sending the missionaries who announce the word of God. Next comes a period of testing in which God desists from intervening and allows humans the freedom to cultivate the planted seeds of faith. In the final phase God collects the abundant fruits of the harvest, while also meting out rewards and punishments according to the merits of the laborers in the fields. Ortiz stated that this process was true not only of God's dealings with individual persons but also with countries, since "nations have their special vocation, their period of testing, their rewards and punishments."[31]

The bishop then spent the bulk of his sermon applying this schema to the history of Mexico. He correlated the first phase of that history with the three centuries of Spanish rule and evangelization, claiming that Spain was "called by God to plant the grain of mustard seed in this uncultivated and vast field" (19). Guadalupe's appearance to Juan Diego catalyzed Spain's evangelizing vocation. Yet, reflective of the clerical prominence in his congregation and in the coronation project, Ortiz made the atypical claim that Guadalupe initiated a covenant with Bishop Juan de Zumárraga. Just as God made a pact to bless the patriarch Abraham and his progeny, so too, through Zumárraga, Guadalupe confirmed "the providential mission of the conquering nation and cover[ed] the conquered race under the mantle of her protection" (19). Extending this notion of covenant, Ortiz went on to outline three key elements of the pact between God and Israel: the temple of Jerusalem where the faithful offered their national gratitude to God, the promise of God to save the people, and God's pledge of security to the people—namely, the tablets of the Ten Commandments and the Ark of the Covenant. These same three elements were now evident in the Guadalupe shrine, covenant, and *tilma*. Furthermore, "in every pact there are obligations and reciprocal rights" (19), which in Ortiz's estimation Spain performed admirably after Zumárraga "solemnly ratified the pact of covenant in the name of his country" and thus "accepted the mission to evangelize these [native] peoples" (20). Indeed, "the heroic nation [Spain] planted the grain of mustard seed in this virgin field, and at the end of three hundred years the minute seed was transformed into a robust tree that extends the shade of its branches to the most remote regions" (20).

The second phase of national history, the time when the planted seed is cultivated, corresponded in Ortiz's rendering to the period since independence. In his words, "When we emancipated ourselves from the mother country the period of testing began for us, at the same time that we received the double providential mission to continue the civilizing work among the indigenous race and conserve among ourselves the purity of the Catholic faith" (20). In contrast to Spain, Ortiz continued, Mexico had failed miserably on both counts. With regard to the natives, he exclaimed that "as an independent nation we have done nothing, absolutely nothing, on behalf of Mary's favored race!" (20). Furthermore, while the heroes of independence and the early formation of Mexico maintained a clear link between Catholic faith and the nation, since then "the heritage [of faith] we received from our elders has suffered most sad and unforgettable losses" (20). Novel teachings and discord had infected all areas of Mexican life, Ortiz continued, from schools to courtrooms to the press, and even to families.

Fortunately the third stage of Mexican history had now dawned, a time of harvest that Ortiz associated with the Díaz regime and especially the current revival of the Catholic faith and hierarchy. Ortiz triumphantly declared that "the Catholic faith, which according to our enemies had been extinguished beyond recourse, not only lives in the heart of those faithful to the ancient standard of independence, but also in these days has given unequivocal proof that it is now as powerful in works, as firm and solicitous in its integrity, as it was in the best of times" (21). The coronation that would take place in just a few hours provided an exceptional opportunity to further advance this religious revival. On this sacred occasion, Guadalupe "who was the support of the faithful in the days of tribulation and trial, once again returns to appear in the heaven of our hopes, offering true peace to all the children of Mexico, as if she desired to renew the ancient pact of covenant and pour out new blessings upon her chosen people" (21). Ortiz recognized that Mexicans' collective commitment to renew the Guadalupan covenant, and the favors or punishments that would follow upon that fateful choice, was by no means guaranteed. Yet he trusted in Guadalupe's benevolence in whatever was to come. He concluded his sermon with the supplication that, should persecutions of the church recur, Guadalupe would "return to us together with our deserved punishment the abundance of your blessings, the courage and Christian fortitude that we need to persevere until the end! Amen" (21).

The following afternoon the chosen speaker for the day of the coronation ceremony was Bishop Crescencio Carrillo y Ancona of the diocese of Yucatán. Though illness prevented Carrillo y Ancona from publicly delivering the sermon, Abbot Plancarte y Labastida proclaimed it from the bishop's prepared text. The scripture passage Carrillo y Ancona chose for the sermon was a paraphrase from the Song of Songs: "Come from Lebanon, my bride, come from Lebanon and you will be crowned" (4:8). He set the context for the occasion in cosmic terms: the coronation was an event that joined heaven and earth, a claim reinforced in the imposing scene of the coronation ceremony (see figure 4.2). From the heavens, Carrillo y Ancona avowed, the Holy Trinity, the patriarchs, prophets, apostles, martyrs, virgins, and all the angels and saints joined with the sun and moon, the stars, and all creation to honor Mary of Guadalupe as Divine Spouse, Co-Redemptrix, Immaculate, gloriously assumed into heaven, celestial Princess, and Universal Queen. The bishop was careful to state that Catholics "owe adoration only to God." But in keeping with the prevailing maximalist Marian theology and devotion of the occasion and of the epoch more generally, he contended that the coronation was in fact a means to offer such homage to the Almighty God and Creator of Mary, the sublime one whose "soul magnifies the Lord" (Luke 1:46).[32]

Carrillo y Ancona summarized at length the popes and bishops who had promoted the Guadalupe cult down to the present. This litany of prominent devotees led him to extol Guadalupe not only as the "Queen of Mexico" but also as the "Empress and Patroness of all America" (14). Honoring the presence of the episcopal visitors from Panama, Cuba, Canada, and the United States, he called for wider recognition of her hemispheric patronage. He also underscored the sacred duties that devotees incurred: "in crowning Our Lady of Guadalupe we fulfill a sweet obligation, very sweet for us; we recognize and confess ourselves blessed vassals of so great a Queen; we pledge her obedience" (14).

Mexican history provided for Carrillo y Ancona a firm justification for the coronation and the recommitment of the nation and its inhabitants to live as Guadalupe's loyal subjects. Though he eschewed direct criticism of the Mexican government, his theological reading of Mexican history encompassed an implicit but unmistakable advocacy for the church's leadership in Mexican society. He boldly asserted that "Mexican history is

FIGURE 4.2. Gonzalo Carrasco, *La coronación canónica de la Virgen de Guadalupe, 12 de octubre de 1895.* The archbishops Próspero María Alarcón and José Ignacio Árciga solemnly crown the Guadalupe image in a scene intended to incite awe at the uniting of heaven and earth. Courtesy Archivo del Museo de la Basílica de Guadalupe.

Guadalupan history. The Mexican people are the people of Holy Mary of Guadalupe" (15). Paraphrasing Luke 22:25 with no small degree of irony, he then stated that "the kings of nations, even though they call themselves the benefactors and fathers of their people, make themselves their tyrants" (15). By contrast, he argued, Guadalupe halted both the cruelties of the former Aztec rulers and "the horrible and barbaric calamities of the warlike [Spanish] invaders," and through the Catholic faith she "united and constituted into one people the two diverse castes, indigenous and Spanish, and thus was born the present race that is truly American" (15). Previously expounded in works such as figure 4.3, the belief that Guadalupe affected harmony in colonial society led Carrillo y Ancona and several of his contemporaries to modify perspectives that lauded *criollismo* or the Spanish colonial enterprise. Instead they accentuated the flourishing of a *mestizo* society and nation. Furthermore, Carrillo y Ancona contended

FIGURE 4.3. Anonymous, *Virgen de Guadalupe como fuente de la Divina Gracia con las alegorías de Nueva España y Castilla*, c. 1755. Paintings frequently portrayed Guadalupe as effecting harmony between natives and Spaniards, in this case with a depiction of royalty from both groups. Courtesy Archivo del Museo de la Basílica de Guadalupe.

that had it not been for the "worldly obstacles" that the Catholic religion faced in subsequent centuries, "how much greater, more advanced and more blessed would be today all the peoples of the New World, and very particularly the Mexican people!" (15). In the final analysis, just as the presence of the Lord had accompanied Israel in the Ark of the Covenant and "made from an enslaved people a free and great nation," so too Guadalupe accompanied Mexico through her image as the "true Ark" that "guarantees us in the bosom of the true Church, with the presence of the Lord, the possession of the promised land" (16).

The sermon concluded with allusions to some concrete steps that would alleviate contemporary social ills. Guadalupe's preference of Juan Diego as her chosen messenger and her speaking with him in his native tongue provided an example for just treatment of the indigenous peoples. Carrillo y Ancona's words of prayer called for religious renewal in Mexico: "Oh Most Holy Mother, Virgin Mary of Guadalupe, Ark of the Divine Mexican Covenant, grant that through you and under your protection the Mexican Republic will be ever fortunate to remain and live each day more constant and firm in inalterable faith in Christ" (16). His final admonition was that the Guadalupe coronation initiate a covenant renewal in which Mexicans not merely crown her with a tiara of precious jewels but also with the living crown of her faithful children in fulfillment of the (once again paraphrased) counsel given in Proverbs 17:6: "Good children are the crown of their parents" (16).

Guadalupe and the Mexican Nation

Nationalist interpretations of Guadalupe continued to predominate into the twentieth century and particularly during the turmoil of the Mexican Revolution (1910–1917) and the Cristero Rebellion (1926–1929), conflicts that reignited antagonisms between government and church officials and resulted in another period of exile for Mexican bishops, along with numerous priests, religious, and laity. Exiled Mexicans reinvigorated existing Guadalupan traditions in communities such as San Antonio's San Fernando Cathedral, where in 1931 devotees celebrated the four hundredth anniversary of the Guadalupe apparitions with a novena, including a daily sung Mass offered in solidarity "for the persecuted church in Mexico." San Fernando clergy stated that the immense crowds and their devotional fervor were a fitting tribute to Guadalupe for the countless favors she had granted "her chosen people, the beautiful Mexican nation."[33]

The public discourse of exiled Mexican clergy revealed the ongoing conviction about the intrinsic link between Guadalupe and their homeland. In a 1914 sermon for the Guadalupe feast at San Fernando, the Linares archbishop Francisco Plancarte y Navarrete (the nephew of Abbot Plancarte y Labastida) urged "the people of Mexico to return to an adoration and supplication of Our Lady of Guadalupe as a means of obtaining peace in their country." In the wake of the Cristero Rebellion two decades later Archbishop Leopoldo Ruiz y Flores, the ordinary of Morelia and the pope's apostolic delegate to Mexico, issued a press release from exile on the Guadalupe feast, assuring his fellow refugees that Guadalupe "will save Mexico from the claws of atheism, the plague of materialism, and the hate of Bolshevik socialism." Yet another clergyman of the early twentieth century contended that the Mexican government had brought a "severe and just punishment" down from heaven by its misguided efforts to banish God from schools, persecute the church, profane sacred temples, and mock the clergy in press reports that fomented paganism. To remedy the horrific conditions in Mexico, he called his compatriots to a spiritual renewal that included the rich sharing their goods with the poor, a return to mutual love as the basis of social life, parental insistence on religious instruction in their children's schools, greater respect for the things of God, and the clergy's diligence in fulfilling their duties of propagating Christian doctrine and consoling the afflicted.[34]

Thus in exile Guadalupan proclamations encompassed protest against political and religious conditions in Mexico, the claim that Mexico's social upheaval was a divine punishment for national infidelity to the Guadalupan covenant, and pleas for covenant renewal to remedy these ills. The nineteenth-century transformation of Guadalupan theologies was clearly evident. Sánchez's *Imagen de la Virgen María* and colonial-era preachers assessed Guadalupe's meaning within the context of biblical, patristic, and subsequent theological sources. Ita y Parra and his contemporaries spoke of the reciprocal relationship between Guadalupe and her devotees, but they primarily underscored the inescapabilty of divine providence as a principle of Christian faith and the foundation of New Spain society. Postindependence preachers modified the colonial-era theological project of linking the Guadalupe tradition with the premier sources and doctrines of Christianity as they increasingly engaged Guadalupe in Catholic interpretations and critiques of Mexican national life. While these preachers frequently drew from scriptural texts and especially the biblical notion of covenant, their application of that notion to Mexicans as God's chosen people narrowed their theological focus from the history of salvation to the history of the nation.

Little is known about the contours of Guadalupan preaching in more isolated settlements. Mier's 1794 sermon and Altamirano's observations nearly a century later confirm that veneration of Guadalupe was New Spain's most pervasive devotional expression by the late eighteenth century and became even more deeply ingrained following independence. Newcomers such as the French émigré Berlandier noticed immediately the common association of Guadalupe with the Mexican people and nation. Communities throughout the country organized celebrations of the Guadalupe coronation and her annual feast. Surely such celebrations encompassed variations in devotional culture and in sermonic discourse attuned to particular local circumstances and the inclinations of the resident preacher. At the same time, seminary training, improvements in transportation and publishing technology, and the repeated acclamation of Guadalupe as the national emblem no doubt embedded elements of Guadalupan covenant theology in many parish sermons.

Guadalupe's role in the rise of an independent Mexico illuminates the malleability of national symbols. Sánchez applauded her as Spain's "assistant conqueror" and attested that the "heathenism of the New World" was "conquered with her aid."[35] Colonial preachers underscored that the divine election of New Spain and its residents was made manifest in the Guadalupe event, an ongoing emphasis evident in the early nineteenth-century sermon of Heredia y Sarmiento. The often-repeated assertion that Guadalupe chose the people of New Spain as her own resounded in the struggles to free Mexico from Spain under the banner of Guadalupe, most eminently in Hidalgo's cry for independence. Both royalists and insurgents—political leaders and devotees from all strata of society—called on Guadalupe as their protector and advocate. Preachers such as Canal and Bárcena epitomized these sentiments in their conflicting claims about Guadalupe's allegiance to opposing sides in the war of independence. The eventual insurgent victory sealed Guadalupe's identification with Mexico, in effect replicating the self-justifying theological conclusion of Spanish conquistadores that victory in battle was a sign of celestial approbation and accompaniment.

Thereafter the engagement of Guadalupe as a symbol of national identity remained prone to cooptation. As Mexico's first national leader, Iturbide conscripted her image and stature to buttress his standing as emperor. Subsequent leaders followed suit in forging links between

Guadalupe and the cult of nationalism. Liberals and conservatives disagreed on the role of the church and their overall political philosophies, but both retained a national holiday for the Guadalupe feast and a prominent place for her in the national ethos. Catholic officials also called on Guadalupe as the standard-bearer of the church, mirroring their detractors in enlisting Guadalupe's support for their side in church-state conflicts. Their deployment of Guadalupe was especially evident in the coronation ceremony. The prelates drew on her renown to personify their revived public standing, advocate for the church's essential role in society, and bolster their proposals for moral and religious renewal. Numerous Catholics endorsed their vision, if not the implicit episcopal claim for sole interpretive authority vis-à-vis Guadalupe. But the coronation initiative also emboldened critics who insisted that it undermined a more authentically Christian—and Guadalupan—focus on dignity, justice, and the uplift of the poor. The advent of Guadalupe as a symbol of national patrimony facilitated such disagreements, since Mexicans of varied persuasions portrayed their national manifestos not only as the most patriotic but also as the most faithful to the divine establishment of the nation through the Guadalupan covenant.

Guadalupan preachers' application of biblical covenants to the Mexican people reveal another potentially contentious aspect of national symbols: asserting celestial patronage of one nation can weaken or even contradict biblical assertions of God's universal care for all. Bárcena and Ladrón de Guevara amalgamated the Noahic covenant with the unconditional Guadalupan promise to protect her sons and daughters. They compared the Guadalupe image on the *tilma* to the rainbow, both of which served as signs of these respective covenants. But they did not mention the biblical avowal that God's promise was not just to Noah, nor just to his clan, but to all peoples and indeed to all living creatures and all the earth (Genesis 9:8–17). Fray Pablo utilized the Davidic covenant to explain celestial aid during a cholera epidemic. But he did not cite the claim in the scriptures of his own Christian faith that the messiah born of the Davidic line was the savior of all humanity, not just the chosen people whom he and his fellow preachers audaciously identified with the inhabitants of Mexico. Miranda deemed his compatriots heirs of the Mosaic covenant, proposing a correlation between the Mexican people's obedience and God's blessings. His emphasis on the conditional Mosaic covenant became more dominant among Guadalupan preachers as they confronted what they perceived as rising immorality and irreligion. Even as Carrillo y Ancona lauded Guadalupe as the empress of the entire American hemisphere, he and Ortiz typified the growing number of preachers who employed such notions of covenant in assessments of Mexican history and contemporary realities. Yet none of these preachers alluded to biblical pronouncements such as the call in the prophet Isaiah (see e.g. 49:6) that Israel become a light to all the nations. Instead, they largely limited the horizon of their analyses to the internal dynamics of Mexico as the presumptive new Israel, leaving themselves open to critiques of obscuring Christian universalism. As Colleen Cross concluded in her study of Guadalupe and covenant, "Guadalupe does not make her covenant just with the Mexican nation or solely with Christian believers. She makes it with all of her children. In this manner, the universal and unconditional nature of the Noahic cove-nant is echoed. She truly becomes the mother of all."[36]

Nonetheless, the focus on Guadalupe's covenant relation with her Mexican daughters and sons enabled preachers and devotees to engage her as a force that disrupted social hierarches. Guadalupe's established status facilitated her ongoing appeal across divergent groups: insurgents and royalists, natives and Spaniards, *criollos* and *mestizos*, liberals and conservatives, clergy and laity. Seeking to embody such a unifying ap-peal, Catholic outreach efforts such as those of the Ladies of Charity and the formation of worker circles in the spirit of *Rerum Novarum* sought to create harmony across the class and social divides of Mexican society. Altamirano's exuberant description of the Guadalupe shrine and feast day as the sole instances of genuine unity and collective equality articulated a common perception of Guadalupe's power in Mexican society. Ortiz and Carrillo y Ancona echoed Altamirano in highlighting that power in their renderings of Mexican history, anointing Guadalupe as the true founder of their homeland through her enactment of peace between conquered natives and conquering Spaniards.

To be sure, such claims are contestable in various ways. The glorifica-tion of the Spanish Catholic past elided the inhumanity of conquest and the colonial caste system. The glorification of present Guadalupan devo-tion did not account for the persistence of social division and increased national discord since independence. Nor did it explore how the harmony of political factions and diverse castes in venerating Guadalupe could be extended to other arenas of Mexican life. Yet it is striking that such diverse figures as a former anticlerical turned writer and the bishop preachers of the coronation ceremony concurred that the Guadalupan covenant pro-vided a potent moral imperative to advocate for a renewed social order.

While Guadalupe did not provide an easy antidote for all of Mexico's ills, in a divisive century she was the common reference point for calls to break barriers of separation and construct egalitarian social relations.

The devotion of natives further illustrates the social implications of the Guadalupan covenant. Assuming the mantle of Laso de la Vega and his *Huei tlamahuiçoltica,* in the second half of the eighteenth century clergy initiated the most intense program of Guadalupan outreach among the indigenous peoples to date. Their strategy of inciting faith through natives' ethnic identification with Guadalupe and Juan Diego received visual support from artists who increasingly depicted the apparition scenes and portraits of the saintly Juan Diego himself. Yet natives did not merely accept their catechetical lessons passively. From community to community they appropriated the Guadalupe tradition in ways that were most meaningful and advantageous for perceived local interests, a dynamic particularly evident in the diverse ways natives engaged Guadalupe during the crucible of war for Mexican independence.

Meanwhile, among political and religious leaders the treatment of natives became the touchstone for assessing national renewal and faithfulness to the Guadalupan covenant. Assertions of clergy such as Ortiz that Spanish missioners uplifted the natives while Mexicans had done "absolutely nothing" for them since independence were motivated in part by the desire to demonstrate the superiority of the church over the state. Liberals countered with allegations that expenditures for religious celebrations exacerbated the plight of the poor and insisted their own modernizing programs provided the best means for social improvement. Yet all these claims provided motivation for church and state officials to demonstrate in practice their stated convictions about imitating Guadalupe through the uplift of Juan Diego's indigenous descendants. For natives themselves, the foundation of the national covenant on the encounter between the Nahua-appearing Mary of Guadalupe and her Nahua chosen messenger was a source of pride and a potential inducement to assertions of dignity and self-determination. Though most natives continued to suffer from poverty and dehumanization, the Guadalupan covenant provided an alternative imaginary that focused greater attention on their just treatment.

Guadalupan theologies of covenant arose amid political and social disruptions during the century following Mexican independence. Catholic preachers tended to find the relative stability of hegemonic Spanish colonial rule more congenial to their ideal of societal harmony. Thus it is not surprising that they deemed colonial society more providentially ordained, while they more easily objected to changing conditions in Mexico as evidence of a faltering or broken covenant. Yet the recognition of Guadalupe as the emblem and conscience of the nation provided hope and direction to many in troubled times. Despite its potential association with an uncritical nationalism, the Guadalupan covenant enabled devotees, preachers, and their critics to forge visions of a more united and just homeland. The prophetic dimension of covenant theologies—the conviction that faith can challenge and transform the social order rather than merely sacralize it as providential—has become even more prevalent in present-day interpretations that examine the Guadalupe tradition from the perspective of the poor and the marginalized, women, and evangelization.

5

Transforming America

CONTEMPORARY THEOLOGIES OF GUADALUPE

THE FIRST POPE from the American hemisphere visited Mexico and the Guadalupe shrine at Tepeyac in February 2016. Pope Francis's homily compared Mary of Nazareth's encounter with her cousin Elizabeth to the encounter between Mary of Guadalupe and Juan Diego. "Just as she went along the paths of Judea and Galilee, in the same way she walked through Tepeyac," the Holy Father proclaimed. As Mary had made her visitation to Elizabeth centuries before, so too she "wished also to come to the inhabitants of these American lands through the person of the Indian St. Juan Diego." Pope Francis then went on to meditate at some length on the purposes of God in the Guadalupan encounter:

> On that morning, at that meeting, God awakened the hope of his son Juan, and the hope of a People. On that morning, God roused the hope of the little ones, of the suffering, of those displaced or rejected, of all who feel they have no worthy place in these lands. On that morning, God came close and still comes close to the suffering but resilient hearts of so many mothers, fathers, grandparents who have seen their children leaving, becoming lost or even being taken by criminals. On that morning, Juancito experienced in his own life what hope is, what the mercy of God is.

The pope explained that the "preferential" love offered to Juan Diego and all the downtrodden "was not against anyone but rather in favor of everyone." He urged his hearers to realize that in "visiting this Shrine, the same things that happened to Juan Diego can also happen to us." Then he commissioned them in the name of Our Lady of Guadalupe to be the Juan Diegos of today: "Today, she sends us out anew; as she did Juancito, today, she comes to tell us again: be my ambassador, the one I send to build many new shrines, accompany many lives, wipe away many tears . . . Go and build my shrine, help me to lift up the lives of my sons and daughters, who are your brothers and sisters."[1]

Pope Francis's proclamation reflects several shifts in the Guadalupe tradition over the course of the twentieth and twenty-first centuries. One is the emergence of systematic treatments of Juan Diego's life and holiness. In tandem with a growing national adulation of Mexico's indigenous past following the Mexican Revolution, Catholic leaders initiated a movement to promote Juan Diego's cause for canonization. One important promoter was Bishop José de Jesús Manríquez y Zárate, who wrote a 1939 pastoral letter calling on Mexican church leaders to champion Juan Diego's cause. Later that year he published ¿Quien fue Juan Diego? (Who was Juan Diego?), a short book that provided the rationale for declaring Juan Diego a saint. Father Lauro López Beltrán's numerous writings on Juan Diego over the ensuing six decades, to the end of the century, included the small journal Juan Diego, which he founded and edited for nearly thirty years. In the decades before and after Juan Diego's 2002 canonization, an increasing number of publications examined the saint's inspiration for aspects of discipleship such as evangelization, lay ministry, and the call to holiness.[2]

The Guadalupan homily of an Argentinian pope also reflects the growing acclaim of Guadalupe across the Americas. Pope Francis is the first pope from the global south. He embodies the global restructuring of Christianity from the northern to the southern halves of the planet that has been noted by scholars such as Philip Jenkins. Though most conspicuous in demographic shifts—Jenkins asserts that by the year 2050 only 20 percent of the world's Christians will be non-Latino whites[3]—this restructuring has facilitated trends such as the increasing international interest in Guadalupe. As more Mexicans emigrated abroad and more non-Mexicans venerated Guadalupe, Bishop Crescencio Carrillo y Ancona's 1895 sermonic acclamation of Guadalupe as the patroness of the whole American hemisphere came to greater fruition. Reverence for Guadalupe has continued in Mexico even as it expanded throughout and beyond the hemisphere. Moreover, while gender, class, ethnic, and racial diversity among devotees has shaped the Guadalupe tradition since its inception, since the 1980s the range of backgrounds among published Guadalupan writers is unprecedented. In previous generations these writers were overwhelmingly male clergy from New Spain and later Mexico. In contemporary times, women, laity, and those from beyond the bounds of Mexico have joined in the effort to create critical theological discourse on Guadalupe, along with a growing number of popes and bishops who have offered their reflections. Guadalupe's devotional stature and the increasing availability of publication venues and lay opportunities for theological formation facilitated this multiplication of authors, who collectively have composed more theological writings on Guadalupe than in any previous era.

Pope Francis's homily illustrates a common contention in these writings: while for most devotees Guadalupe remains primarily a mother and celestial advocate, from the perspective of contemporary theologians she is at the same time a force for personal as well as social transformation. Prominent among contemporary theological works are attempts to examine the *Nican mopohua* apparition account from an indigenous perspective. In contrast to the colonial and nationalistic interpretations of previous centuries, these more recent analyses emphasize the narrative of Guadalupe's solidarity with the conquered indigenous peoples and, by extension, her ongoing solidarity with the downtrodden in other times and places. Women scholars have extended these analyses to the situation of patriarchy and its oppressive effects. Church leaders have joined a number of pastors and theologians who expound Guadalupe's role in evangelization. Though this thematic emphasis echoes a number of previous Guadalupan preachers and writers dating back to Miguel Sánchez and Luis Laso de la Vega, today's theologians and pastors propose an understanding of evangelization broader than a process of merely converting natives to Christianity. Indeed, they contend that marginalized persons such as Juan Diego are called to be evangelizers themselves, and even to convert the powerful through their evangelizing witness. While the range of themes in contemporary theologies of Guadalupe is extensive—from the doctrine of creation to a rich resource for theological aesthetics, among others[4]—the most frequent perspective is Guadalupe's authority to effect change, particularly on behalf of the suffering and the oppressed. Even critiques of these liberationist perspectives reinforce their prevalence in contemporary theologies of Guadalupe.

The bend toward transformation in Guadalupan theologies reflects wider trends in the Catholic Church and in theology. Beginning with *Rerum Novarum* in 1891, popes have developed a rich tradition of Catholic social encyclicals, expanding from an initial focus on workers' rights to broader concepts such as Pope Paul VI's introduction of integral human development in his 1967 encyclical *Populorum Progressio*. The Second Vatican Council, the "ecumenical" or worldwide council of Catholic bishops that met each fall from 1962 to 1965, emphasized the need to engage and transform the modern world as a constitutive element of Christian life and discipleship. Subsequently the Latin American episcopal conferences at Medellín (1968), Puebla (1979), Santo Domingo (1992), and Aparecida (2007), as well as the 1997 Special Assembly for America of the Synod of Bishops, were key events through which church leaders sought to enact the teachings of Vatican II and renew the church and its commitment to the poor. Post–Vatican II theological analyses have increasingly addressed dramatic changes such as the deep longing of marginalized people for dignity and justice. In the oft-quoted words of Gustavo Gutiérrez, a Peruvian theologian widely regarded as the founder of liberation theology, a defining characteristic of our era that theologians must confront is the "irruption of the poor" in human history.[5]

Guadalupe continues to hold sway as a symbol of Mexican nationality and pride. But simultaneously new understandings of her meaning have emerged, juxtaposing a construal of the protection she bestows on the Mexican people with broader visions of her defense of marginal persons everywhere. Like their predecessors, contemporary theologians engage as primary sources the narrative of the encounter between Juan Diego and Guadalupe, her image, and the devotion of her faithful. But these more recent analysts focus more intently on how Juan Diego and contemporary grassroots believers have related to Guadalupe's living presence. Studies of Guadalupe through the lens of Juan Diego and the marginalized, women, and evangelization illustrate the trajectory of the most recent chapter in the development of Guadalupan theologies. These theologies have addressed a more diverse and even conflictive domain of devotees as the veneration of Guadalupe has expanded globally.

An Expanding Devotion

Expressions of Guadalupan devotion beyond Mexico are not a new occurrence. Her image spread to Spain by the mid-seventeenth century, when the first dated painting of Guadalupe with her apparition scenes was enshrined at a convent in Agreda, Spain. Guadalupan devotion and images expanded considerably in Spain during the remainder of the colonial era. The first Guadalupe church beyond the bounds of present-day Mexico was in Ponce, Puerto Rico. Devotees dedicated a chapel to her there in 1670 and retained her name through successive reconstructions down to the current Cathedral of Our Lady of Guadalupe. In what is now the southwest United States, Guadalupan devotion also dates from the colonial era and continued to develop after 1848 when the U.S. defeat of Mexico forcibly altered the national residency of Mexicans now on the U.S. side of the reconfigured border. The 1895 coronation ceremony at Tepeyac was the first international celebration of Guadalupe, attracting the participation of bishops from Canada, Cuba, Panama, and the United States.

But during the twentieth and twenty-first centuries Guadalupe became an international phenomenon in unprecedented ways. Like other pervasive religious traditions, devotee enthusiasm stimulated the development of her ever wider circles of influence. Globalizing trends such as advancements in communications and travel technologies also facilitated the geographic expansion of her cult beyond the bounds of Mexico. One sign and cause of her widening impact was that popes increasingly recognized and promoted devotion to her. While Benedict XIV had named her patroness of New Spain in 1754, since 1895 when Leo XIII authorized her coronation popes have validated and extended the Guadalupe tradition. Pius X gave the Guadalupe shrine the official status of a basilica in 1904. Six years later he declared Guadalupe patroness of Latin America, a geographic extension of her patronage that successive popes confirmed and expanded down to John Paul II's avowal that she is the patroness of the entire American hemisphere. Pius XII was the first pope to transmit a Guadalupan reflection to Mexico, which he did via radio in 1945 on the occasion of the fiftieth anniversary of the Guadalupe coronation. Twenty-five years later Paul VI spoke via television to devotees celebrating the seventy-fifth anniversary of the coronation. In 1979 one of John Paul's initial acts on his first of five papal visits to Mexico was to celebrate the Eucharist at the massive new Guadalupe basilica, which had been dedicated three years earlier. He was the first pope to visit Mexico and to celebrate the Eucharist at Tepeyac. During his 2016 pastoral visit, Pope Francis was the second pope to preside over the Eucharist at the Guadalupe basilica.[6]

Papal approbations occurred in tandem with initiatives in numerous locales to advance Guadalupe's acclaim, particularly during the latter decades of the twentieth century and down to the present. These initiatives did not arise from a systematic plan or a single organization but rather from a variety of local circumstances and leaders whose efforts spanned national and even religious boundaries. Moreover, while instances of Guadalupan promotion clearly inspired one another, the links between them and the patterns of their diffusion defy easy generalization. Today shrines dedicated to Guadalupe are as far south as the Basilica of Our Lady of Guadalupe in Santa Fe, Argentina, and as far north as Johnstown, Cape Breton, Nova Scotia. Native American groups in North America—both Catholic and non-Catholic—have increasingly engaged her as a source of indigenous spirituality. Supporters of the prolife movement revere her as the patroness of the unborn, particularly in the United States. Her presence among Catholics is now a global phenomenon, as evidenced in worship spaces such as an altar dedicated to her at the Cathedral of Notre Dame de Paris; a chapel next to the tomb of Saint Peter at Saint Peter's Basilica in the Vatican; and a Guadalupe parish church in Puchong, Malaysia. Devotees and artists from a variety of backgrounds revere her, as the Korean image of Guadalupe and Juan Diego in figure 5.1 demonstrates. In 1989 the Dalai Lama delighted his Mexican hosts when he asked to be taken to the Guadalupe basilica during a visit to Mexico City.[7]

The influence of Guadalupe extends even beyond the bounds of official religion, especially in Mexico and the United States. She regularly appears in scenes of *telenovelas* (soap operas), other television programs, and films. While poets and other creative writers have written about Guadalupe since the colonial era, in more recent times their Guadalupan literary output has substantially increased. Murals depicting her are publically displayed in parks, housing complexes, and business establishments such as the one shown in figure 5.2. Business owners credit her image both with attracting "the desired clientele" and "preventing unwanted loitering outside of the store by local youths and inebriated customers." The devout and other observers have reported seeing her in settings that range from a water leak on the floor of a Mexico City metro station to a tree bark on the far north side of Chicago. She also appears in the daily lives of her faithful on objects such as T-shirts, tattoos, medals, refrigerator magnets, and wall hangings. Referencing Guadalupe's pervasive presence and renown among the devout, the irreligious, and people of all social classes, the distinguished Mexican thinker Octavio Paz quipped that "the Mexican people, after more than two centuries of experiments and defeats, have faith only in the Virgin of Guadalupe and the National Lottery."[8]

The association of Guadalupe with movements for social change, memorably expressed in Miguel Hidalgo's cry for independence, provided further impetus for the growth of Guadalupan devotion. Like Hidalgo, Emiliano Zapata and the peasants who joined him in the fight for land reform during the Mexican Revolution carried Guadalupe as their

FIGURE 5.1. Catherine Kwon, *Our Lady of Guadalupe*, 2016. Guadalupe's growing international appeal is illuminated in this painting of a Korean Guadalupe and Juan Diego. Courtesy Catherine Kwon.

banner into battle. Cesar Chavez, Dolores Huerta, and the United Farm Workers marched under Guadalupe's image and invoked her assistance for the farmworkers' cause for justice. The renowned Ejército Zapatista de Liberación Nacional (Zapatista National Liberation Army), a group that launched an uprising in the Mexican state of Chiapas in 1994, formed a "mobile city" they named Guadalupe Tepeyac. Beginning in 2002 the Asociación Tepeyac de New York organized for over a decade the annual Carrera Internacional de la Antorcha Guadalupana (International Guadalupan Torch Run), an event that linked Guadalupe to the struggles

FIGURE 5.2. A mural on a local business establishment shows Guadalupe watching over the skyline and the people of San Antonio, Texas. Negative #txsau_ ua15_01_13_b6_CR93-24-1, Collection UA 15.01.13, UTSA Special Collections, Institute of Texan Cultures.

and rights of immigrants. Over a two- to three-month period runners relayed a torch and the image of Guadalupe nearly three thousand miles from the Guadalupe basilica in Mexico City; up Mexico's eastern seaboard; across the U.S. border into Texas; through communities in the southern United States; past the White House; and then to New York City, where the torch and image arrived at Saint Patrick's Cathedral for the Guadalupe feast-day celebration on December 12. Thousands of runners participated each year and were received in churches and community centers for local celebrations along the way. Runners wore shirts with messages such as those declaring themselves *mensajeros de un pueblo dividido por la frontera* (messengers of a people divided by the border). Leaders such as María Zúñiga, the first female *capitana* (captain) for the torch run, attested that "we go out to take her message like the Indian Juan Diego did . . . [we] struggle in search of a more just and dignified life, where we can walk together as a great human community."[9]

Guadalupe's increased renown is evident in controversies about her image and tradition, which have become more visible and often more rancorous. The Vatican decision to beatify and then canonize Juan Diego incited renewed debate about the historicity of the Guadalupe apparitions.

Six years after the 1990 beatification, Monsignor Guillermo Schulenburg Prado, who had been the abbot of the Guadalupe basilica at Tepeyac for over three decades, commented that the account of Guadalupe's apparitions to Juan Diego was "only a symbol." Reports of his statement sparked such a storm of protest that a few months later Schulenburg Prado resigned his post as abbot. Subsequently Schulenburg Prado allied with other Mexican scholars of Guadalupe, as well as with Father Stafford Poole of the United States, in a joint letter to the Vatican Congregation for the Causes of the Saints. Signees questioned the existence of Juan Diego and declared that "if this canonization is carried out, it would cast doubt before all these scholars, Mexican or non-Mexican, believing Catholics, on the seriousness and credibility of our Church, to which we belong and which we defend in an absolutely resolute way." When Schulenburg Prado and his colleagues examined the *positio*, the official dossier explicating Juan Diego's heroic virtues for the canonization case, they sent another letter claiming it "was filled with inaccuracies and pure suppositions."[10]

Conflicts about Guadalupe have also arisen between Catholics and Protestants. Many Protestant congregations, particularly among the Pentecostals and evangelicals, accuse Catholics of worshiping idols and images, fostering "Mariolatry" instead of faith in Jesus Christ, and relying on church tradition rather than the sole truth of the Bible. Often they take a disparaging view of Guadalupe. One Mexican American Catholic devotee attested that a relative who converted to Pentecostalism "sparked a family feud that has pitted brother against brother" when he "started bad-mouthing Catholic symbols such as Our Lady of Guadalupe." Other Protestant groups, especially among the mainline denominations, are more welcoming of Hispanic traditions such as Guadalupe. Some have even celebrated the Guadalupe feast. But in various instances Catholic officials have accused such groups of "deception" when Mexicans unwittingly worshiped in Protestant churches, in part because the worship services are similar to Catholic rites and the churches contain "holy water dispensers and an icon of the Virgin of Guadalupe." Apologists for Catholicism often enlist Guadalupe as a bulwark for defending their faith. Encouraged by their pastors, many Catholics prominently place placards near their front door advising visitors that "este es un hogar católico" (this is a Catholic home); these posters frequently include a Guadalupe image to punctuate their expression of denominational loyalty.[11]

In yet other instances religious believers have clashed with public officials about the Guadalupe image, as in 1998 when parents were outraged that a Santa Fe elementary school principal, Bobbie Gutiérrez, banned on school property "any outerwear that is deemed gang-related, for example, Our Lady of Guadalupe shirts." Though local law enforcement officers supported the principal, the Santa Fe archbishop Michael Sheehan summarized the opposing view of Guadalupe devotees, who convinced Gutiérrez to rescind her policy: "Mary is Our Lady of Peace, not Our Lady of the Gang, and I think we shouldn't allow gang members or anyone else to take away the symbols that are sacred. I don't think this sacred image, which is so important to Catholics, should be discouraged because a few people abuse it." Another incident in Santa Fe a decade later involved Father Tien-Tri Nguyen and parishioners of Our Lady of Guadalupe parish, who were shocked to discover that U.S. border authorities had "detained" a Guadalupan image they commissioned from Mexican sculptor Georgina Farias. The border officials were concerned that contraband might be concealed in the two-ton, twelve-foot-tall statue, so they confiscated it and took it to a warehouse to conduct X-rays. For several days devotees' questions about the whereabouts of their Guadalupe went unanswered, until finally Father Nguyen led a delegation down to the border, found the statue, loaded it on a flatbed trailer, and processed it to its new parish home.[12]

Guadalupan controversies have not diminished—indeed, in many cases they augment—the devotion of multitudes who put their trust in their loving mother. Nor have controversies deterred the expanding celebrations of Guadalupe's feast in Catholic parishes. Over the past century this expansion is especially evident in the United States, where the Mexican-descent population has grown to more than thirty-five million, about one fourth of all people of Mexican descent in the world. A widespread parish devotion for the Guadalupe feast is *las mañanitas* (literally, "morning songs"), a tribute usually begun before dawn. Ritual enactments of the apparition narrative are also popular. Other devotions include prayer of the rosary, scripture readings, flower offerings, and testimonies or meditations about Guadalupe. In a number of places *matachines* dances are offered to honor Guadalupe and her Nahua origins. The passion devotees have for Guadalupe, along with church officials' growing approbation of her cult, have drawn non-Latinos to increasingly seek her presence and assistance. Saint Mark the Evangelist parish in San Antonio is one of a number of primarily Euro-American parishes that now celebrate the Guadalupe feast. Within a few years of beginning this annual celebration, the parish Guadalupana devotional society grew from 12 mostly

Hispanic members to nearly 140, both men and women, nearly half of them European Americans.[13]

Pastoral leaders contend that the widening of the Guadalupe tradition also magnifies a perennial challenge: the tendency of devotees to focus on Guadalupe as a miraculous protector rather than on the life of discipleship to which she summons her faithful. At the very outset of Guadalupan devotion in New Spain, Fray Francisco de Bustamante warned that native focus on the miraculous would cause them to lose their faith in God if their pleas for Guadalupe's intercession failed to produce the desired effect. Echoing his concern, some contemporary pastors have bemoaned that devotions such as those for Guadalupe "are nothing more than 'a Catholicism of a day' . . . stressing great but isolated moments of fervor, yet failing to translate into deep and lasting spiritual transformation and sustained participation in the life of the church." One priest with half a century of experience in Hispanic ministry asserted that many devotees seem "locked into" their "attraction to the Virgin [of Guadalupe] as a source of favors" and pay scant attention to the conversion of life and evangelization that church leaders proclaim as Guadalupe's call to her devotees.[14]

Conversely, the pervasiveness of Guadalupan devotion has led a number of pastors and theologians to contend that Guadalupe provides a graced opportunity for pastoral engagement of devotees, extending the concern for what they call "pastoral Guadalupana." Many claim that the texts of the four canonical gospels and the Guadalupe apparition narrative mutually illuminate one another, especially in core themes such as justice, conversion, and reconciliation. They also recall that Guadalupe has been a transformative force in the lives of many devotees, and they seek to further accentuate her evangelizing presence and message. Pastoral leaders at the Jesuit-run Dolores Mission in East Los Angeles, for example, have prepared Guadalupe celebrations at a juvenile detention center in which inmates present the Guadalupe apparition drama to their peers and offer reflections on how their visiting mothers remind them of the Virgin Mary. Dolores Mission leaders have also conducted a similar ritual at their parish center, with homeless guests from the parish-run Guadalupano Shelter program taking on major roles in the apparition narrative. Participants in these rituals attest that Guadalupe induces healing and fosters faith.[15] The dynamism of contemporary Guadalupan devotion is a catalyst for the recent surge of interest in Guadalupe among theologians who seek to unveil and cultivate her transformative power in people's lives.

Through the Eyes of Juan Diego

One of the most widespread contemporary interpretations of the Guadalupe event is that it is a counternarrative to the subjugation of the natives and other marginalized peoples, a claim usually rooted in the attempt to examine the *Nican mopohua* within the context of Nahua language and culture during the colonial era. Theologians who have proposed this interpretation and approach have often drawn on the work of Monsignor Ángel María Garibay Kintana, whose illustrious career included service as a canon of the Guadalupe basilica at Tepeyac and as a professor at the National University of Mexico. Garibay was the first expert to assess the *Nican mopohua* as a work of classical Nahuatl literature. He averred that the Nahua language "in its abundant ancient literary productions manifests two styles." The first is what he deemed *difrasismos*, the juxtaposition of parallel terms as a metaphoric expression, such as the combination "night and wind" to reference the transcendence of the divine. The second "is the abundance and profusion of expressions to elaborate one single thought," a motif evident in the *Nican mopohua* in passages such as Juan Diego's first words to Guadalupe serially addressing her as "my patron, noble lady, my daughter." Garibay's student, Miguel León-Portilla, extended his teacher's analysis with his studies of the Nahuas' philosophical thought and way of life. He concluded that the *Nican mopohua* encompasses "an exposition of core ideas in Christian thought, clothed in the Nahua peoples' language and form of conceiving the world."[16]

Insights such as these from Garibay and León-Portilla have had a wide impact. The contention that the *Nican mopohua* fuses elements from the Christian and Nahua worldviews and articulates them in Nahua idiom is now commonplace. Echoing Garibay, many contemporary theologians note the importance of understanding *difrasismos* within the *Nican mopohua*, especially the structuring of the narrative around the *difrasismo* of *flor y canto* (flower and song). For the Nahuas, God was not primarily known through rational discourse but through the poetic beauty of *flor y canto*. It was predominantly through poetry that the Nahua wise ones spoke of the mysteries of God and of life beyond our present earthly existence. Thus it is striking that the *Nican mopohua* begins with the beautiful music Juan Diego heard that attracted him to ascend the hill of Tepeyac and ends with Juan Diego gathering exquisite flowers and presenting them to Bishop Juan de Zumárraga. From the Nahua perspective, the bracketing of flower and song in the narrative signaled that the events of Tepeyac were divinely ordained. Similarly, contemporary theologians follow Garibay in exploring the multiple expressions conjoined to communicate a thought. Garibay observed that Guadalupe asks that a temple be built for her where she could exercise "four activities essentially maternal: to love, to have compassion, to aid, to defend." Then Guadalupe unites this series of thoughts into a single declaration: "I am your merciful Mother."[17] While not all theological authors accentuate this particular passage, nor its gendered delineation of "essentially" maternal actions, many imitate Garibay's hermeneutical approach of focusing attention on the Nahua style of speech as a means to understand the *Nican mopohua* more deeply.

The theologians who have employed this approach illustrate the growing international interest in Guadalupe. Though these thinkers are too numerous to examine here, the writings of three of them from different countries, each of whom has authored at least one major work on Guadalupe, illuminate this new trend in theologies of Guadalupe. Clodomiro Siller Acuña is a priest from the diocese of Tehuantepec, Oaxaca, Mexico, with extensive pastoral experience among indigenous communities. His various leadership positions include service as director of the National Center for Indigenous Missions in Mexico City. Virgilio Elizondo was a Mexican American priest in the Archdiocese of San Antonio, Texas and is widely considered the founder of U.S. Latino theology. He was also the first Latino theologian to write extensively on Guadalupe. Richard Nebel is a professor of missiology at the University of Würzburg in Germany, where he also completed his habilitation thesis on Our Lady of Guadalupe.[18]

The attempts of thinkers such as these to reassess the *Nican mopohua* from the perspectives of Nahuas after the conquest is evident in their most frequently enunciated theme—namely, justice or liberation, the breaking in of God's reign that upends the status quo of the world. They note the significance of Guadalupe's first words to Juan Diego: "dear Juan, dear Juan Diego." Contrary to the Spanish conquerors and even the missioners, Guadalupe does not address Juan Diego in a generic or derogatory way. Rather, she calls him by name and offers a tender greeting, communicating her inner attitude of respect and esteem. She then goes on to give him the mission of communicating to Bishop Zumárraga her desire that a temple be built on the hill of Tepeyac. Her words of comfort and calling are given effect in the narrative's dramatic reversals. At the beginning of the story only Guadalupe has trust in Juan Diego; by the end the bishop and his assistants believe he is truly her messenger. At the outset of the account Juan Diego kneels before the bishop; in the end the stooped *indio* stands erect while the bishop and his household kneel before him and venerate the image on his *tilma*. Throughout the account Juan Diego must journey to the center of the city from Tepeyac some three miles to the north; at the end of the narration the bishop and his entourage accompany Juan Diego to the periphery of Tepeyac, where they will build the temple that Guadalupe requested. Symbolically—and physically—the presence of the ecclesial leadership and the church they are constructing are thus moved from the center of their capital city out to the margins among the indigenous people. From this perspective, Guadalupe reveals a new vision, one in which the lowly are entrusted with a mission and the powerful are instructed to accompany them. Guadalupe, in other words, manifests God's preferential love for the poor and the transformation of church and society that such a love of preference demands.

A correlative claim is the central role of Juan Diego, a perspective particularly evident in the works of Siller Acuña. In his view, "the poor peasant [Juan Diego] is, in the *Nican mopohua*, the key that initiated and made comprehensible the event of Tepeyac." Moreover, in this sacred text Juan Diego speaks "the theology of the poor." Seeking to understand the presence of God among his people, Juan Diego acts out of a conviction that "the difficulties of the poor are the difficulties of God." While Guadalupe asks for a temple where she can show her love and compassion to the marginal and to all peoples, in serving as her messenger Juan Diego implicitly asks in her name for a new society in which the poor will be believed and respected as Guadalupe is believed and respected. Thus Juan Diego models the poor as protagonists for transforming divisive social codes. Siller Acuña repeatedly accentuates that no one can claim to love Our Lady of Guadalupe unless they also love the poor embodied in her chosen emissary, Juan Diego. He even goes so far as to make the novel claim that the final lines of the *Nican mopohua*, which state that the bishop enshrined Juan Diego's *tilma* with its miraculous image in the cathedral where many devotees gathered to "see and admire her precious image as something divine," appear to be later additions that contradict the central meaning of the text. Siller Acuña laments that, in this passage and in numerous subsequent instances of Guadalupan pastoral initiatives and devotion, "everything is centered on the image, on the devotion" even though "the Virgin had placed her message and her promise and her intention apart from herself, in the service of the poor natives." He poignantly concludes that "the image, separated from a commitment with the poor, has no Guadalupan significance." These are radical claims: nearly all

Mexicans maintain they are devoted to Guadalupe, yet Mexican society has long been marked by poverty and inequality. Siller Acuña asserts that, no matter what their contestations to the contrary, those who are not actively involved in the struggle to transform this situation are not true devotees of their mother Guadalupe.[19]

The urgency of a Guadalupan commitment to confront poverty and injustice is intimately conjoined with another theme that Elizondo uncovers in the *Nican mopohua*: the theology of conversion that it narrates.[20] Bishop Zumárraga seemingly presumes he is not in need of conversion, that his life is already right with God. Yet unlike Juan Diego, who put his faith in Guadalupe unreservedly, it was the bishop who required a sign before he would believe. Elizondo explicates how Zumárraga was called to go beyond the blindness of ethnocentrism and pride that was so imbedded in the mentality of the Spanish conquerors. He underscores what the *Nican mopohua* depiction of Zumárraga teaches: those who struggle most to accept God's call to conversion are the religious and the righteous. To his credit, the bishop comes to recognize the truth of the message Juan Diego announces and the *indio*'s dignity as a child of God called by Guadalupe. In the end, his conversion enabled the bishop to confront the biases and limitations of his Spanish culture and hear the voice of God's mother speaking to him through an unanticipated messenger.

Juan Diego, on the other hand, did not need to be converted from excessive pride. On the contrary, in the *Nican mopohua* his greatest sin is a lack of self-worth, an internalization of the effects of the conquest, particularly the conquerors' presumption that the natives were inferior or even subhuman. Ultimately Juan Diego's internalization of these judgments weakened his conviction that he too was made in God's image and likeness. After his first unsuccessful interview with Bishop Zumárraga, he tells Guadalupe that he is too lowly and unimportant. He pleads with her to choose another messenger with greater social status. But Guadalupe insists that it is essential he be her spokesperson. The call to complete her mission is an invitation to restore his dignity and humanity.

The conversion of Juan Diego—and by extension the call to conversion of all the rejected and anyone who doubts their own fundamental goodness as a creation of God—is not a call from sinful pride to humble acceptance of God's will and ways. It is a call from debilitating self-abasement to a healthy embrace of God's love and the mission of living for God and others to which that love beckons. Thus the pathway of conversion is not the same for all, though the call to conversion is extended to everyone.

As Elizondo states, Christian conversion demands that believers follow both the pathways of Juan Diego and of Juan de Zumárraga. All are called to confront sinful pride and spiritual blindness, the Juan de Zumárraga tendencies that lurk inside every human. But all are also called, and especially the rejected and the marginalized, to see themselves and others as God and Mary of Guadalupe see them: as precious, dignified, and made in God's own image and likeness.

Elizondo also probes the ways Juan Diego's encounter and the Guadalupe image itself have uplifted his own Mexican American people, whom he identifies as *mestizos* born from two dramatic clashes: first, that of Mesoamericans with the conquistadores of sixteenth-century Catholic Spain and then, following the U.S. takeover of northern Mexico, Mexican-descent residents with other peoples of the United States. Elizondo's expansive vision of his people's history and Guadalupe's impact is reflected in artistic works like figure 5.3. He builds on the nineteenth-century claim of figures such as Ignacio Manuel Altamirano and Bishop Carrillo y Ancona that Guadalupe united conquering Spaniards with the conquered natives, adding that she also enables borderlands Mexican Americans to integrate their Mexican and U.S. experiences despite the painful effects of conquest and ethnic prejudice. Elizondo posits that Our Lady of Guadalupe is a "mestiza," one who "is neither an Indian goddess nor a European Madonna; she is something new. She is neither Spanish nor Indian and yet she is both and more . . . She is the first truly American person and as such the mother of the new generations to come." Thus Elizondo professes that Guadalupe provides hope and inspiration for *mestizo* Mexican Americans who, in imitation of Juan Diego, are called to confront rejection, synthesize the richness from their parent cultures, and lead the way to construct a society in which the barriers between peoples are broken.[21]

Intentionally or not, the arguments of those who criticize such theological claims substantiate their growing influence. Stafford Poole offers one critique, extending the implications of the long-standing historicity debate about the Guadalupe apparition tradition to the works of "some liberation theologians." He contends that without a documented "objective historical basis" for the apparitions "the symbolism [of Guadalupe] loses any objectivity it may have had and is at the mercy of propagandists and special interests."[22] In this view, unless there is evidence to verify the events narrated in the *Nican mopohua*, analyses of its evangelical messages are illegitimate. Poole's detractors admit that, like any attempt to articulate the meaning of a faith tradition, theologies of Guadalupe are susceptible

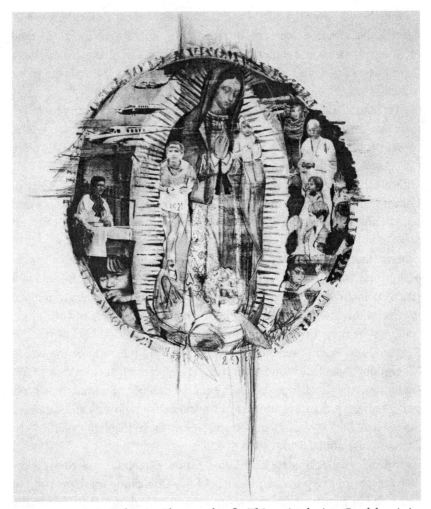

FIGURE 5.3. Anita Valencia, *El sexto sol*, 1981. This artist depicts Guadalupe's influence in everyday lives, surrounding Guadalupe with her own family members, including her brother Virgilio Elizondo on the far left of the drawing. The intimacy of Guadalupe with her devotees is juxtaposed alongside her cosmic impact: the inscription encircling the image cites the Revelation 12 text "a great sign appeared in the sky . . . " and the title of the work, *El sexto sol* (The sixth sun), draws on Nahua cosmology to signal the dawn of a new age. Courtesy Anita Valencia.

to misappropriations of the Christian message and even to cooptation. But they insist that such potential pitfalls loom whenever a religious tradition has a wide-ranging sphere of impact, regardless of the extant textual evidence underlying the tradition's historical origins. The key factor that leads to manipulative interpretations, in other words, is a religious tradition's sway over the hearts and minds of believers, not its lack of historical substantiation. Far from inducing theologians to abandon the field of Guadalupan interpretation, such potential pitfalls make critical theological assessment in light of the wider Christian tradition all the more urgent.

A related critique posits that some attempts at reading the *Nican mopohua* from the perspective of native or other marginalized peoples present a liberationist view of Guadalupe that merely disguises a political agenda in religious language and practices. Those who propose this critique include Carl Anderson, the supreme knight of the Knights of Columbus, the world's largest Catholic fraternal service organization, and Monsignor Eduardo Chávez, the postulator of the canonization cause of Saint Juan Diego. Echoing Vatican criticisms of "liberation theology," they contend that "today some see liberation as a political solution to a variety of spiritual and ethical problems" and "thus reduce liberation itself to a strictly political concept that can only be achieved through strictly political means." Conversely, they assert "the message of Our Lady of Guadalupe could not be more different: her solution was not political but spiritual."[23] Responses to such criticisms revolve around the meaning of the words "liberation," "political," and "spiritual." They encompass the claim that, while it is true Guadalupe does not endorse one political system or party over another, spiritual realities are not detached from poverty and suffering in everyday life, as well as the efforts—even those involving politics—to liberate those afflicted with such maladies.

Indeed, theologians such as Siller Acuña, Elizondo, and Nebel avow that we cannot grasp the significance of the Guadalupe tradition without knowing her transformative presence among her faithful today, especially the most vulnerable. As Nebel puts it, "The truth of the *Nican mopohua*, whose edifying, pedagogical, and admonitory functions are clearly evident, is not inferred so much from a perspective of historical knowledge, but rather from a Christian experience of life."[24] As with the gospels or any sacred text, he contends, enacting the call to transformation in the *Nican mopohua* reveals its deeper meanings. From this perspective, the life struggles and religious practices of Guadalupan devotees are important resources for theological investigations. Like Juan Diego, many of Guadalupe's contemporary devotees come from the lower strata of society. And like Juan Diego many recall being ignored or rejected and are tempted to perceive themselves as inferior. On her feast day, they encounter Guadalupe in rituals and devotions such as the enactment of the apparition narrative. Though they recognize that their veneration does not eliminate the rejection and social ills that beset them, such devotees attest that Guadalupe uplifts them as she did Juan Diego, strengthening them in their trials and difficulties. They resonate with the ritual enactment of Juan Diego's encounter with a loving mother, his election as an unexpected hero, his rejection, his unwavering faith, and his final vindication. In a word, they confess that the Guadalupe narrative is true: it reveals the deep truth of their human dignity and exposes the lie of experiences that diminish their fundamental sense of worth. Theologians' encounters with such grassroots believers shape their conviction that, through the eyes of Juan Diego, the ultimate significance of the *Nican mopohua* and the wider Guadalupe tradition is discovered in the way they are lived out among the poor today.

Women and Guadalupe

The increasing number of Catholic women theologians since the Second Vatican Council encompassed the first women authors of theological works on Guadalupe. Several of them propose a liberationist perspective akin to that of Siller Acuña, Elizondo, and Nebel. The Brazilian theologians Ivone Gebara and Maria Clara Bingemer assert that "the appearance of the Virgin of Guadalupe and growing devotion to her had the important role of restoring to an exploited people a religious identity." Ada María Isasi-Díaz, a Cuban exile to the United States who developed a liberationist discourse she called *mujerista* theology, observed similar dynamics among contemporary U.S. Latinas and Latinos: "Living in a society that does not value them, their conviction that Guadalupe and her divine son love them satisfies the need we all have to be precious for someone."[25]

Scholars from various fields, artists, and creative writers offer critical analyses of Guadalupe, particularly her power in the lives of women: the power both to transform women's lives and to sanction their subordination in family, church, and society. Women theologians have engaged such works and concerns in their investigations. They have also drawn on women's experience and devotion as primary sources to articulate three issues for women who seek to develop an empowering relation with Guadalupe: the need to critique Guadalupe and the wider Marian tradition in light of patriarchal influences, Guadalupe's relation to the historical person Mary of Nazareth, and a critical understanding of her liberating potential.

Contemporary women's analyses are grounded in long-standing female engagement with Guadalupe. The limitations placed on women in church, society, and educational institutions resulted in a dearth of women authors during the first three centuries of Guadalupan theologies. But by no means did women lack influence on Guadalupan devotion, nor did Guadalupe lack a corresponding influence on women. Primary sources from the colonial era, the vast majority of which men produced, do not tend to focus on the role women played in preparing and celebrating religious feasts. Nonetheless, there is sufficient documentation to demonstrate that, especially as Guadalupan devotion expanded toward the end of the colonial era, planning local Guadalupe celebrations and directing prayers such as the rosary provided opportunities for women to exercise community leadership. These opportunities increased during the nineteenth century. In feast-day processions across numerous locales, girls dressed in white and bearing candles and flowers served as the immediate attendants of the Guadalupan image. Yet throughout these centuries such leadership roles were constrained. They reflected an extension of household responsibilities into ritual, often sanctifying women's domesticity. Over time they reinforced the notion that piety was primarily the responsibility of women, bolstering male-female distinctions shaped by gender-specific stereotypes. They symbolically linked the purity of girls with the Virgin Mary, a communal accentuation of feminine chastity that provided divine sanction for the strong association of virginity with feminine virtue and lacked a corresponding association between boys and Jesus. Thus women's leadership illuminates what Ana María Díaz-Stevens calls the "matriarchal core" of Latino Catholicism—that is, women's exercise of authority in communal devotions despite the ongoing patriarchal limitations of institutional Catholicism and Latin American societies.[26]

Drawing on the experience of their foremothers, contemporary women writers insist on the need to critically reformulate understandings of Mary that can reinforce long-standing notions of women's subservience. María Pilar Aquino, a theologian from Mexico who has spent many years teaching in the United States, contends that one debilitating view "is the exalted and idealized image of Mary as the supreme symbol of purity and virginity, which neutralizes her human integrity and her sexuality as a woman." Such an image has been employed to establish a double standard, with chastity regarded as the defining characteristic of feminine morality while being unnecessary or even contradictory to social codes of masculinity. The focus on virginity can also foster attitudes that celibacy is more holy than the vocation of marriage, sometimes with the implication that sexual expression reveals a lack of self-control or is even evil, rather than a gift from God. Theologians such as Gebara and Bingemer also contest such attitudes: "Mary's virginity . . . does [not] entail disdain for sexuality and marriage." Rather it "is about the glory of the almighty God made manifest in what is poor, impotent, and disdained in the eyes of the world."[27] Thus Mary's virgin motherhood is not intended to pedestalize her and impose on other women an unattainable ideal. Indeed, her virginity has implications for single and married believers, for women and men alike. It is an expression of her intimate and single-hearted relation with the God who favors all, but especially those the world sees as insignificant, such as Mary the peasant woman of Galilee.

Another contested view is that Mary's fiat response to her call to be the mother of God—"I am the servant of the Lord; let it be done to me as you say" (Luke 1:38)—means women have a more passive type of discipleship modeled on Mary's submission to God's will, while men have a more active form of discipleship modeled on Jesus. Mary is seen as mother, homemaker, and supporter of her son, Jesus, while he is seen as engaged in the work of redemption in the public spaces of life. These perceptions can lead to the presumption that Mary reinforces the confinement of women to the privacy of their homes and that consecrated virginity or all-absorbed motherhood are the sole worthy vocational options for women. Historically some who propose such gendered limitations have argued that women should leave political, activist, or other public roles to men, since in a far more fundamental sense as homemakers women are already the foundation and binding source of society and their community. In Aquino's words, these gender stereotypes are based on "the image of Mary as obedient and passive, resigned and suffering, humbly dedicated to domestic tasks in accordance with the *role* that is naturally hers in the private sphere."[28]

Scholars such as Evelyn Stevens sum up the debilitating expectations placed on women in the term *marianismo* which, in the words of Rosa Maria Gil and Carmen Inoa Vazquez, "defines the ideal role of woman. And what an ambitious role it is, taking as its model of perfection the Virgin Mary herself. *Marianismo* is about sacred duty, self-sacrifice, and chastity." At its worst this understanding of womanhood divulges into an adulation of the long-suffering woman. As the theologian Nancy Pineda-Madrid avers, "the ideology of 'marianismo' idealizes suffering as integral to what it means to be a woman." Latina women have even seen suffering itself as inherently honorable or virtuous. Pineda-Madrid notes that the repressive social imaginary that undergirds such perspectives "largely functions at a subterranean level." But she articulates the following explanation for this valuation of misery: "If a Latina bears her suffering in silence, then she somehow becomes morally and spiritually superior. It is *as if* this is her calling by virtue of her sex and God's design."[29] Intentionally or not, depictions of Mary as self-sacrificing, sorrowing, and subordinate can sanctify this oppressive view of women.

Women theologians propose a different view of Mary. Commenting on the Magnificat, the canticle of Mary of Nazareth in which she praises the God who "has deposed the mighty from their thrones and raised the lowly to high places" (Luke 1:52), Gebara and Bingemer state that Mary, "whom traditional catechesis has over and over again presented as the passive and silent mother of the Child Jesus, comes out as someone who stands up and clearly and valiantly takes on as her own this God's 'no'" to the forces of subjugation. These and other theologians insist on the need to examine anew the gospel witness to Mary's life of faith as a poor woman of Galilee. From this perspective, Mary's fiat was not a passive act of submission, but an active cooperation with divine initiative and a courageous acceptance of an adventurous and perilous calling. She shared her wondrous experience of election and the bonds of sisterhood with her kinswoman Elizabeth in the biblical event of the visitation. She journeyed miles and gave birth in a stable in Bethlehem, barely escaped King Herod's cruel slaughter of the innocents, and fled as a refugee to Egypt. With her husband, Joseph, she protected, educated, and formed the child Jesus in Egypt and in Nazareth upon their return from exile. Later she followed and believed in her son as one of his disciples, suffered the agony of witnessing his crucifixion, and stood in faith with the nascent Christian community in the upper room at Pentecost.[30]

Women theologians assert that, from this perspective, the key to understanding Mary is to recognize it is a courageous peasant woman that the church and its faithful laud as the mother of God. Litanies dedicated to Mary in Latin American communities encompass traditional invocations such as "mother of God" and "queen of heaven," but they also call on her as the mother of the oppressed, the mother of the forgotten, a widowed mother, the mother of a political prisoner, and a seeker of sanctuary. This linkage of blessed Mary with the poor women of the world provides hope and strength to many struggling women. In the words of Gebara and Bingemer, Mary's exalted state "is the glorious culmination of the mystery of God's preference for what is poor, small, and unprotected in this world, so as to make God's presence and glory shine there."[31]

Like such claims about Mary of Nazareth, contemporary interpretations of Guadalupe accentuate her liberating potential for women, despite on-going struggles and limitations. In her study of the Guadalupanas of Kansas City, Missouri, Theresa Torres relates these women devotees' reluctance to engage in activism beyond the confines of parish life, as well as their tendency to only indirectly represent their concerns to hierarchical church authorities. Still, these same women successfully blocked the decision of diocesan officials to close their church, revealing how Guadalupe helps them "to move beyond the limits of their socially constructed images of themselves both individually and collectively." Similarly, in her study of ethnic Mexican women devotees across three stages of the life cycle, María del Socorro Castañeda-Liles notes that mothers employ Guadalupe's authority to socialize their daughters into strict Catholic gender expectations. But she also avows that within the "network of relationships" central to the daily existence of these women "Our Lady of Guadalupe arises as the most significant female sacred symbol and as a force that moves women to transgress subjugation." Women even enlist Guadalupe's support in their efforts to contest domestic violence and male privilege in the home and the wider community. As one devotee observed, "Guadalupe gives you dignity to go places you haven't been before."[32]

Among Latina theologians, Jeanette Rodriguez was the first to explore systematically women's relationships with Guadalupe. Drawing on interviews conducted among Mexican American women, she details the comfort, peace, and ability to sustain relationships that Guadalupe embodies and inspires in their lives. She narrates her interviewees' varied perceptions and personal experiences of Guadalupe. As the title of her major study, *Our Lady of Guadalupe: Faith and Empowerment Among Mexican-American Women*, suggests, Rodriguez's primary focus is Guadalupe's fortifying presence. One of her interviewees summarized well this emphasis: "Our Lady of Guadalupe represents to me everything we as a people should strive to be: strong yet humble, warm and compassionate, yet courageous enough to stand up for what we believe in." Asserting that much of Guadalupe's capacity to empower women is still untapped, Rodriguez posits that women need to be more profoundly "challenged by the message of Our Lady of Guadalupe" to work for transformation in their lives and their surroundings and thus embody more fully "the liberating call of mission as experienced by Juan Diego."[33]

Theological writings such as those of Rodriguez engage and enhance the growing number of works in which women attempt a critical reappraisal of Guadalupe. The creations of Chicana artists such as Yolanda López exemplify this stance. López created a series of Guadalupe images in mixed media, collage, and paintings. None gained greater attention than her 1978 triptych of Guadalupan paintings depicting her grandmother, her mother, and herself. As the Chicana/o studies scholar Karen Mary Davalos has stated, López's depictions are in tension with the traditional Guadalupe image in which "each aspect of the figurative composition is symbolic of her humility and obedience: her head is covered, her eyes cast down, and her face turned slightly away from the viewer." In López's *Portrait of the Artist as the Virgin of Guadalupe*, for example, she presents herself with muscular legs in running shoes, draped in Guadalupe's mantle, surrounded by the traditional rays of light, looking directly out at the viewer, leaping over the moon and the angel at the bottom of the Guadalupe image, and gripping in her right hand the snake often associated with Mary in Catholic iconography. Davalos is one of various interpreters who see in this depiction an invitation to women to "step away from oppressive social codes" and "take charge of one's life, especially one's sexuality." López's portrait of her mother, *Margaret F. Stewart: Our Lady of Guadalupe*, similarly adapts Guadalupe's primary features into a new image frame, in this case her mother at her sewing machine. Davalos and other analysts assert that this painting of a dignified mother whose brown body is worn through hours of dedicated labor contests the superficial glamorization of women as young, slender, and white. *Guadalupe: Victoria F. Franco*, López's portrait of her grandmother, shows the elderly woman seated amid the prominent features of the Guadalupe image with a snake in one hand and a knife in the other. In this image, López states, "the snake is flayed. It symbolizes the end of life. She's holding the knife herself, because she's no longer struggling with life and with sexuality. She has her own power." Significantly, the name for each of the women depicted is given, emphasizing their distinctive personhood, but the grouping of the trio of images underscores the connection between women across generations.[34]

Chicana literature such as the writings of Sandra Cisneros has reconsidered Guadalupe in parallel fashion. Cisneros presents Guadalupe as an advocate for counteracting the "traditional" gender roles and expectations that she purportedly buttresses. During her childhood and young adult years in Chicago, Cisneros learned to perceive Guadalupe as a source of divine sanction for a familial and cultural code of silence about women's bodies and sexuality, as well as a double standard of feminine purity and masculine promiscuity. Only after a series of experiences such as her visit to the Guadalupe basilica in Mexico City was she able to reclaim Guadalupe. These experiences and her association of Guadalupe with the pre-Columbian antecedent Tonantzin enabled her to embrace Guadalupe as a brown-skinned, feminine manifestation of divine power who dwells "inside each Chicana and *mexicana*" and can enable them to see the totality of their corporeal existence as created in the divine image. Describing herself as someone "obsessed with becoming a woman comfortable in her skin"—brown skin she sees reflected in the divine pantheon through Guadalupe—Cisneros sums up her view of Guadalupe by paraphrasing an invocation of the Hail Mary, "Blessed art thou, Lupe, and, therefore, blessed am I."[35]

The theologian who has most extensively engaged Chicana works such as these is Pineda-Madrid. She maintains that "if the full humanity of Chicanas and all Latinas is a central concern of U.S. Latino/a theology, Chicana feminist discourse must be engaged particularly when its theorists put forward critical readings of Guadalupe."[36] Pineda-Madrid examines the Guadalupan writings of Elizondo in conversation with the interpretations of Norma Alarcón, Gloria Anzaldúa, and Laura Elisa Pérez, each of whom offers a reappraisal of Guadalupe. These writers concur that such a reappraisal is crucial since, in the words of Alarcón, "Guadalupe is a symbol that continues to exist for the purpose of 'universalizing' and containing women's lives within a discrete cultural banner."[37] Pineda-Madrid explicates that "for the Chicana feminist theorists, a liberative interpretation of Guadalupe needs to create space and support for Chicanas as speaking subjects, needs to heal and transform Chicanas so as to deepen their self-esteem, and needs to enable Chicanas (and others) to know even more deeply the interconnectedness of all humankind and of all creation." Yet she cautions that Chicana theorists tend to define Guadalupe "in strictly utilitarian, instrumental terms" and thus do not articulate a comprehensive vision of Guadalupe's redemptive potential. Pineda-Madrid's analysis offers direction for the ongoing development of Guadalupan theologies that critically assess and integrate insights from Chicana feminist discourse and from Latino/a theologies that emphasize themes such as justice.[38]

Evangelizer of America

The works of contemporary theologians have drawn on official Catholic sources that examined anew the Marian and Guadalupan traditions. Vatican II was the first ecumenical council of the Catholic Church to articulate a systematic treatment of Mary, primarily in the eighth and final chapter of the council's dogmatic constitution on the church, *Lumen Gentium* (1964). Like women theologians in the postconciliar era, the council authors underscored the biblical witness to Mary of Nazareth, stating that "she stands out among the poor and humble of the Lord, who confidently hope for and receive salvation from Him." They also observed that God enlists Mary's cooperation "not merely in a passive way, but as freely cooperating in the work of human salvation through faith and obedience."[39]

More broadly, *Lumen Gentium* examines Mary within the context of the Christ event and the ongoing life and mission of the church, extolling the witness of "her pilgrimage of faith" as a model for all believers. This claim shaped the subsequent teaching of popes and Latin American bishops on Mary—and specifically on Guadalupe—as an animator of discipleship and evangelization. In his 1975 apostolic exhortation *Evangelii Nuntiandi* (On evangelization in the modern world), Pope Paul VI declared: "On the morning of Pentecost she watched over with her prayer the beginning of evangelization prompted by the Holy Spirit: may she be the Star of the evangelization ever renewed which the Church, docile to her Lord's command, must promote and accomplish." At their conference in Puebla the Latin American bishops noted "the *mestizo* countenance of Mary of Guadalupe, who appeared at the start of the evangelization process"[40] on the American continent. Echoing John Paul II's theme of the new evangelization,[41] at their subsequent conferences at Santo Domingo and Aparecida, the bishops invoked Guadalupe as the "Star of the New Evangelization" and acclaimed her appearance as "a decisive event for the proclamation and recognition of her Son." Similarly, in various presentations and texts John Paul and Benedict XVI called Mary the "Star of the New Evangelization." In his 2013 apostolic exhortation *Evangelii Gaudium* (On the proclamation of the gospel in today's world), Francis reiterated this title and also deemed Mary the "mother of evangelization" and "a model of evangelization."[42]

Pastors and theologians who urge devotees to heed Guadalupe's evangelizing call have noted that the theme of evangelization is doubly present in the *Nican mopohua*: first Our Lady of Guadalupe evangelized Juan Diego and then he became her agent in evangelizing others. Guadalupe is not presented as an evangelizer who scares or coerces but instead as one who wins Juan Diego's heart with the love and compassion of God, calls him to a mission, and then supports him and assures him that he can do great things for her and for God. Because of Juan Diego's testimony, the bishop, his assistants, and other residents also came to know and believe in Guadalupe. Juan Diego is transformed from one who hears Guadalupe's message to one who announces it, from one feels unworthy to one who boldly proclaims, from a neophyte to an empowered evangelizer.

The teaching of John Paul II underscores the link between Guadalupe, Juan Diego, and the evangelization of persons, cultures, and societies.[43] John Paul's ardent Marian and Guadalupan piety led him to make more pronouncements on Guadalupe than any other pope. During his first visit to Mexico, in his opening address at the Puebla conference of Latin American bishops he commented that "the fact that this meeting of ours is taking place in the spiritual presence of Our Lady of Guadalupe . . . is for me a cause for joy and a source of hope." He went on to pray: "May she, the 'Star of evangelization,' be your guide in your future reflections and decisions." His 1990 and 2002 trips to Mexico included the celebration of the beatification and canonization of Juan Diego, respectively. In 1999 he formally presented the apostolic exhortation *Ecclesia in America* to Guadalupe during a Eucharist celebrated at the Guadalupe basilica, "entrusting to the Mother and Queen of this continent the future of its evangelization." On all the aforementioned as well as other occasions he explicated and developed his Guadalupan thought in homilies and public addresses.[44]

John Paul acclaimed Guadalupe as the mother of God who proclaims Christ to the Americas. He taught that she announced the Christian gospel in a manner that respected native symbols and cultures. While he recognized that the arrival of Europeans in the New World was a process that entailed "discovery, conquest, and evangelization" and was "not without shadows," he contended that the legacy of evangelization in the New World "on the whole is luminous" among those who "discern in history God's loving intervention, despite the limitations of every human endeavor." Guadalupe amplified the efforts of the early missioners as her appearance "to the native Juan Diego on the hill of Tepeyac in 1531 had a decisive effect on evangelization." John Paul stated she had this singular influence because her image and message present "an impressive example of a perfectly inculturated evangelization," accentuating inculturation as the way "the Church makes the Gospel incarnate in different cultures and at the same time introduces peoples, together with their cultures, into her own community." In the case of Guadalupe, her very image integrates elements from both the Iberian Catholic and Nahua cultures. She is Mary the mother of God in Nahua appearance. Similarly, her encounters with Juan Diego creatively announced the gospel in a manner that respected and uplifted his dignity and that of his people and their culture. For John Paul, Guadalupe encapsulates "the great principle of inculturation: the deep transformation of genuine [Nahua indigenous] cultural values through their integration into Christianity and the rooting of Christianity in the various cultures."[45]

Indigenous leaders and other commentators question whether John Paul's depiction is too sanguine and does not adequately address the violence and pain natives endured. They also ask whether Juan Diego should be memorialized as an evangelizer, as a painful reminder of the oppression of the native peoples, or both. When church officials distributed the canonization image of Juan Diego depicting him with European features such as fair skin and a full beard—a portrait from the renowned eighteenth-century artist Miguel Cabrera (see p. 123) that the officials defended as the earliest known likeness of Juan Diego—even devout native Catholics such as Fausto Guadarrama questioned: "Are they trying to conquer us again through this image?" Francisco Ortiz Pedraza, a director at Mexico's Instituto Nacional de Antropología e Historia, opined there is "racism in the image" and in those who distributed it because "instead of looking like Juan Diego, it looks more like [the conquistador] Hernán Cortés." Some indigenous leaders deemed the canonization "a belated outreach to an indigenous world that Catholic missionaries have never fully penetrated."[46]

Nonetheless, John Paul's articulation of Guadalupe's presence and action in the initial evangelization of the continent has led many to join him in uplifting Guadalupe as an exemplar for the contemporary church in the ongoing work of evangelization. John Paul urged today's Guadalupan devotees to address "a great new challenge: the new evangelization." Like the missioners of yesteryear, John Paul contended, contemporary evangelizers face numerous obstacles, which today include secularization, agnosticism, consumerism, proselytism, a lack of involvement in the prayer of the church and in popular devotion, and an understanding of faith that devalues or dismisses solidarity with those who suffer. Given such immense challenges, he taught that evangelizing efforts must confront both personal and social sin. The presence of Mary "awakens in us the hope of mending our [personal] ways and persevering in good." She also "enables us to overcome the multiple 'structures of sin' in which our personal, family, and social life is wrapped." Confronting such structures—racism, economic injustice, the exploitation of women, and the like—is a necessary element of evangelization. Furthermore, in the call to the pathway of conversion Mary is "a model, the faithful accomplisher of God's will, for those who do not accept passively the adverse circumstances of personal and social life." Mary's example impels commitment to "the poorest and neediest ones, and for the necessary transformation of society." Thus John Paul charged Guadalupan devotees to show preferential concern for marginal persons in the same way Guadalupe takes such persons under her maternal care: young people, children, the unborn, the poor, the indigenous, peoples of African heritage, workers, immigrants, refugees, and the elderly. He implored Our Lady of Guadalupe that, like Juan Diego, today's evangelizers will "bring your image with us impressed on our journey of life and proclaim the Good News of Christ to all peoples."[47]

John Paul confirmed devotees' esteem for Juan Diego in his beatification and canonization as "the first indigenous [Native American] Saint of the American Continent." On both occasions the pope accentuated Juan Diego as Guadalupe's companion in evangelization. In the early stages of the proclamation of the gospel in Mexico, Juan Diego participated in the Guadalupan process of a "perfectly inculturated evangelization," for "in accepting the Christian message without forgoing his indigenous identity, Juan Diego discovered the profound truth of the new humanity, in which all are called to be children of God." Today Juan Diego's testimony issues *"a strong call to all the lay faithful of the nation* to assume all their responsibilities in the transmission of the gospel message and in the witness of a living and operative faith in Mexican society." This includes the laity confronting "poverty, corruption, contempt for truth and for human rights." Accentuating the ongoing plight of natives and other marginalized peoples, John Paul presented Juan Diego as their protector and as an inspiration in their struggles. Juan Diego exemplifies the evangelizing vocation of the laity, which encompasses their mandate to accompany and uplift the poor and the marginalized. They are called not only to be the recipients of evangelization, but to be the Juan Diegos of today and take up the task of evangelizing one another, as well as the task of evangelizing society. All are called to evangelize through emulating the holiness of Saint Juan Diego, which John Paul portrayed as shining forth through trust in God and in Guadalupe, humility, charity, moral integrity, and simplicity of life. Summarizing his teaching on Juan Diego, John Paul

ended his canonization homily asking the indigenous saint "to accompany the Church on her pilgrimage in Mexico, so that she may be more
evangelizing and more missionary each day" and "imbue every area of
social life with the spirit of the Gospel."[48]

Transforming America

The growing international veneration of Guadalupe over the course of the
twentieth century buttressed the claims of popes, bishops, theologians,
and devotees that her transformative and evangelizing presence extends
outside Mexico to the other nations of the hemisphere and beyond. In ret-
rospect, major historical events addressed through the lens of Guadalupan
theologies—conquest, attempts to Christianize natives, society building,
racial mixing, independence, and the demands for justice of marginalized
groups—were not only major events in Mexico. They also marked the history of nations throughout the Americas, accentuating the importance of
contemporary efforts to understand Guadalupe's transformative meaning
within a broader hemispheric and global context.

The theologian Mary Doak underscores that the current emphasis on
Guadalupe's transformative presence has deep roots in the past. Doak
recalls that "the image of Our Lady of Guadalupe has been venerated and
deeply cherished for hundreds of years now, especially by those who, like
Juan Diego, have been told that they are insignificant, unworthy, and of
little value to the powers of this world." Citing the core biblical text of
Revelation 12 first introduced into the Guadalupe tradition in Sánchez's
Imagen de la Virgen María, Doak reveals how that biblical text and the
Guadalupe apparition tradition mutually illuminate one another: "Our
passage from the book of Revelation can then lead us to an even deeper appreciation of the appearance of Our Lady of Guadalupe, since Revelation's
image of the woman giving birth in the face of a devouring dragon
confronts us with the fact that it is never an easy or a safe thing to side with
the poor and powerless ones." She goes on to state that "while the vision
of John of Patmos [in Revelation 12] focuses on the opposition between
the good that will win and the evil that will lose, the appearance to Juan
Diego emphasizes that we are all called to join in the community of self-
giving love that will be victorious in the end." Doak's analysis claims the
scriptural and Guadalupan foundations of the contemporary trend to urge
the peoples of Mexico, America, and beyond to commit themselves to a
Guadalupan vision of personal and social conversion. Whether that vision

is concentrated on concern for the indigenous, the unborn, immigrants, the homeless, farmworkers, the incarcerated and their families, or other people who struggle, today Guadalupe is frequently engaged as a force for transformation.[49]

Contemporary efforts to put that force into action have met various challenges. Pastors continue to lament that numerous devotees are more inclined to seek Guadalupe's maternal aid for personal needs—their daily sustenance, familial well-being, health, and a better life—than to be her instrument for advancing social transformation in a systematic fashion. And in many instances pastors themselves have encouraged devotees to see Guadalupe not as an agent of change but rather as a defender of their denominational loyalty and of Catholic doctrines and spiritual traditions. Moreover, like the text of the *Nican mopohua* itself, which only implicitly challenges the Spanish colonial order's domination of the indigenous peoples, Guadalupan devotion has not always—or even usually—led to direct action that combats social structures and power dynamics such as those that subjugated the natives. Even those who have struggled for justice with Guadalupe by their side—from Zapata's revolutionary movement for land reform to the Zapatista fight for native rights, from the United Farm Workers to the immigrant advocates of the Antorcha Guadalupana, from Chicana artists to their literary counterparts—have often achieved more symbolic victories than lasting systemic changes.

Yet Guadalupe's power cannot be solely or even primarily measured in the visible results of her devotees' initiatives for structural social change. Her power must also be comprehended in the hope her presence inspires among the most downtrodden. Women epitomize this hope as much as any other group. Despite their ongoing plight under patriarchy and all its deleterious effects, numerous women find strength to endure through Guadalupe. Many even thrive as animators of their families and communities. Their uncommon courage in the face of adversity reveals how Guadalupe enables hope to erupt in the most unexpected places— indeed, frequently among those who have suffered the most egregious injustices. As Pope Francis acclaimed, the hope Guadalupe engenders can empower those on the peripheries and all her faithful to live out her plea to "go and build my shrine, help me to lift up the lives of my sons and daughters, who are your brothers and sisters."[50]

Like activists, pastors, and devotees who propose divergent visions of Guadalupe's call for transformation, theologians disagree about which changes she urges her faithful to enact. The growing range of backgrounds among interpreters of the Guadalupe tradition has facilitated this diversity of deliberations. While varied perspectives on Guadalupe marked previous eras, particularly in the nineteenth-century debates about Guadalupe's role in the Mexican nation, the contestation of contemporary understandings of Guadalupe is even more extensive. Such differences underscore just how influential a phenomenon Guadalupe has become, as competing parties vie for a hermeneutical edge in delineating and channeling her potency. Today the increasing number of perspectives on the Guadalupe tradition presents what could be deemed the postmodern challenge to understanding Guadalupe: when the meanings and applications of traditions such as Guadalupe expand, their power to unite people around a common cause or vision can diminish.

Nonetheless, contemporary Guadalupan interpretations embody a vibrant conversation about personal and social transformation. Despite divergent emphases and even outright disagreements, for many Guadalupe and Juan Diego reveal a divine mandate to renew their lives, communities, and societies. Theologians maintain that Guadalupe is a force of uplift for marginal persons such as Juan Diego. With Guadalupe, they contend, the dignity of the lowly is restored, women are valued in their full humanity, and the love of a common mother incites an evangelizing mission that fosters a more Godly existence. Today more than ever the Guadalupan social imaginary is focused on the capacity of all—the mighty but especially the lowly—to forge social change and even a new social order.

Indeed, according to contemporary theologians Guadalupe reveals that God's plan not only includes but in fact begins with the poor and the forgotten. In this regard, Guadalupan theologies have come full circle from the Eurocentric approach of Sánchez, Laso de la Vega, and their colonial contemporaries. Beginning with Sánchez, theologians have argued that Guadalupe is deeply rooted in the New World, a proclaimer of the gospel who fostered Christian faith among natives as well as those of other backgrounds. But the default attitude of most theologians was that natives needed redemption from idolatry and barbarism, or at least from religious and social ineptitude. Today theologians increasingly insist that the natives of the New World and other marginalized peoples are not mere objects of evangelizing and civilizing initiatives with European origins. Rather, their God-given dignity precedes any such initiatives. From a biblical perspective, they are the subjects God turns to first in the divine-human encounter. In imitation of the God of the Bible and of Guadalupe's election of Juan Diego, contemporary theologians attest that Guadalupe calls her faithful to a preferential love and solidarity with those the world counts as least. This call is extended to all, but often is particularly challenging for those who, like Juan de Zumárraga, are in positions of authority and privilege. The primary motivation for this preferential love is not to assist those in need. It is to encounter the living presence of God and of Guadalupe in the Juan Diegos of today.

Moreover, theologies of Guadalupe are increasingly conjoined with theologies of Juan Diego—that is, they are theological reflections that examine Guadalupe in relation to the marginalized one who became her partner in achieving her purposes. This new approach is a crucial epistemic shift in Guadalupan theologies and the Guadalupe tradition. Theologians during the colonial and national periods focused on Guadalupe as an overseer of right order for their vision of church and society. When they made reference to Juan Diego, they typically presented him as a model for native conversion to Catholicism or as the symbolic recipient of the heavenly favor bestowed on his people and the wider populace. Today theologians have given substantial attention to Juan Diego as the chosen protagonist of Guadalupe in confronting the plight of the marginalized. Popes and bishops have extolled him as an empowered evangelizer. Women theologians, who tend to accentuate Guadalupe as a feminine manifestation of strength and liberation, have concurrently emphasized that she emancipates marginalized women as she did Juan Diego. These articulations of Guadalupe's meaning are not just new interpretations but also comprise a new approach to engaging Guadalupe as a source of hope for the downtrodden. They underscore that participation in the Guadalupe–Juan Diego encounter among the poor and abandoned of today's world is a constitutive element of Guadalupan theologies and devotion.

Theologians down through the centuries have endeavored to explicate Guadalupe's message and image—as well as the dynamic devotion that undergirds them—in light of the biblical accounts of events such as creation; the people of Israel's encounters and covenant with their God liberator; the words, deeds, death, and resurrection of Jesus of Nazareth; and the Revelation 12 vision of the woman clothed with the sun. As they sought to understand their lives and their times, theologians esteemed Guadalupe as a harbinger of salvation history, an evangelizer, a sign of divine providence, a maker of covenant, and a prophetic animator of personal and social transformation. Yet even the well-intentioned have at times interpreted Guadalupe in ways that are debatable, such as justifying an arguably anti-evangelical status quo in the social order or conscripting Guadalupe for nationalistic purposes. According to theologians today, the crux of the issue of authentically engaging Guadalupe is fourfold: encountering her through accompaniment of marginalized persons and communities; counteracting biases evident in the history of Guadalupan theologies such as Eurocentrism, nationalism, and patriarchy; participating in critical conversations about the various proposals for appropriating the Guadalupe tradition; and synthesizing those proposals in light of the long trajectory of exploring Guadalupe theologically vis-à-vis the wider Christian tradition. Contemporary theologians magnify a centuries-old venture to comprehend the relationship between Guadalupe and her faithful and channel her transformative power in their lives. Their analyses from the perspective of marginal persons introduce a bold new move into the ongoing evolution of Guadalupan theologies and the wider Guadalupe tradition.

Notes

INTRODUCTION

1. Virgilio Elizondo, "Mary and Evangelization in the Americas," in *Mary, Woman of Nazareth*, ed. Doris Donnelly (New York: Paulist, 1989), 160.
2. Luis Laso de la Vega, *Huei tlamahuiçoltica* . . . (Mexico City: Juan Ruiz, 1649), reprinted with an English translation in *The Story of Guadalupe: Luis Laso de la Vega's "Huei tlamahuiçoltica" of 1649*, ed. Lisa Sousa, Stafford Poole, and James Lockhart (Stanford, CA: Stanford University Press, 1998), 89.
3. William B. Taylor, *Theater of a Thousand Wonders: A History of Miraculous Images and Shrines in New Spain* (New York: Cambridge University Press, 2016), quote at 2; see discussion at chap. 9, "Pilgrims, Processions, and Romerías," esp. 509. Taylor lists New Spain shrines and miraculous images in appendix 1, "Colonial Image Shrines." See also Taylor, "The Virgin of Guadalupe in New Spain: An Inquiry into the Social History of Marian Devotion," *American Ethnologist* 14 (February 1987): 9–33; Taylor, *Magistrates of the Sacred: Priests and Parishioners in Eighteenth-Century Mexico* (Stanford, CA: Stanford University Press, 1996), 277–300; Taylor, *Shrines and Miraculous Images: Religious Life in Mexico Before the Reforma* (Albuquerque: University of New Mexico Press, 2010).
4. David A. Brading, *Mexican Phoenix: Our Lady of Guadalupe; Image and Tradition Across Five Centuries* (New York: Cambridge University Press, 2001), 366.
5. Jacques Lafaye, *Quetzalcoatl and Guadalupe: The Formation of Mexican National Consciousness, 1531–1813*, trans. Benjamin Keen (Chicago: University of Chicago Press, 1976); Francisco Raymond Schulte, *Mexican Spirituality: Its Sources and Mission in the Earliest Guadalupan Sermons* (Lanham, MD: Rowman and Littlefield, 2002); Carlos Herrejón Peredo, *Del sermón al discurso cívico, México, 1760–1834* (Zamora, Mich., Mexico: El Colegio de Michoacán, and Mexico City: El Colegio de México, 2003); Alicia Mayer, *Flor de primavera mexicana: La Virgen*

de Guadalupe en los sermones novohispanos (Mexico City: Universidad Nacional Autónoma de México, 2010); Jaime Cuadriello, *Maravilla americana: Variantes de la iconografía guadalupana, siglos XVII–XIX* (Guadalajara: Patrimonio Cultural del Occidente, 1989); Cuadriello, Carmen de Monserrat Robledo Galván, and Beatriz Berndt León Mariscal, *La Reina de las Américas: Works of Art from the Museum of the Basílica de Guadalupe* (Chicago: Mexican Fine Arts Center Museum, 1996); Cuadriello, "Cifra, signo, y artilugio: El 'ocho' de Guadalupe," *Anales del instituto de investigaciones estéticas* 39 (2017): 155–204; Jeanette Favrot Peterson, *Visualizing Guadalupe: From Black Madonna to Queen of the Americas* (Austin: University of Texas Press, 2014).

6. Ernesto de la Torre Villar and Ramiro Navarro de Anda, eds., *Testimonios históricos guadalupanos* (Mexico City: Fondo de Cultura Económica, 1982); Fidel González Fernández, Eduardo Chávez Sánchez, and José Luis Guerrero Rosado, *El encuentro de la Virgen de Guadalupe y Juan Diego* 4th ed. (Mexico City: Editorial Porrúa, 2001); de la Torre Villar and Navarro de Anda, *Nuevos testimonios históricos guadalupanos*, 2 vols. (Mexico City: Fondo de Cultura Económica, 2007).

7. Paolo Giuriati and Elio Masferrer Kan et al., *No temas . . . yo soy tu madre: Un estudio socioantropológico de los peregrinos a la Basílica de Guadalupe* (Mexico City: Plaza y Valdés Editores, 1998); Deidre Sklar, *Dancing with the Virgin: Body and Faith in the Fiesta of Tortugas, New Mexico* (Berkeley: University of California Press, 2001); Mary O'Connor, "The Virgin of Guadalupe and the Economics of Symbolic Behavior," *Journal for the Scientific Study of Religion* 28 (1989): 105–19; Elaine A. Peña, *Performing Piety: Making Sacred Space with the Virgin of Guadalupe* (Berkeley: University of California Press, 2011).

8. Norma Alarcón, "Traddutora, Traditora: A Paradigmatic Figure of Chicana Feminism," in *Scattered Hegemonies: Postmodernity and Transnational Feminist Practices*, ed. Inderpal Grewal and Caren Kaplan (Minneapolis: University of Minnesota Press, 1994), 110–33; Mary E. Odem, "Our Lady of Guadalupe in the New South: Latino Immigrants and the Politics of Integration in the Catholic Church," *Journal of American Ethnic History* 24 (Fall 2004): 26–57; Alyshia Gálvez, *Guadalupe in New York: Devotion and the Struggle for Citizenship Rights Among Mexican Immigrants* (New York: New York University Press, 2010); Davíd Carrasco, "The Virgin of Guadalupe and Two Types of Religious Experience: The Personal Illumination and the Ceremonial Landscape," in *Religionen: Die Religiöse Erfahrung* (Würzburg: Königshausen & Neumann, 2008), 99–113.

9. Orlando O. Espín, "Mexican Religious Practices, Popular Catholicism, and the Development of Doctrine," in *Horizons of the Sacred: Mexican Traditions in U.S. Catholicism*, ed. Timothy Matovina and Gary Riebe-Estrella (Ithaca, NY: Cornell University Press, 2002), 139–52, quote at 141; Espín, *Idol and Grace: On Traditioning and Subversive Hope* (Maryknoll, NY: Orbis, 2014).

10. Cuadriello, *Maravilla americana*; Cuadriello, Robledo Galván, and León Mariscal, *Reina de las Américas*; Cuadriello, "Cifra, signo, y artilugio"; Peterson, *Visualizing Guadalupe*.

11. Timothy Matovina, *Guadalupe and Her Faithful: Latino Catholics in San Antonio, from Colonial Origins to the Present* (Baltimore: Johns Hopkins University Press, 2005).

12. Luis Rivera Pagán, *A Violent Evangelism: The Political and Religious Conquest of the Americas* (Louisville: Westminster/John Knox, 1992); Gustavo Gutiérrez, *Las Casas: In Search of the Poor of Jesus Christ*, trans. Robert R. Barr (Maryknoll, NY: Orbis, 1993); Alejandro García-Rivera, *St. Martín de Porres: The "Little Stories" and the Semiotics of Culture* (Maryknoll, NY: Orbis, 1995); Claudio Burgaleta, *José de Acosta, S.J., 1540–1600: His Life and Thought* (Chicago: Jesuit Way, 1999); Michelle A. Gonzalez, *Sor Juana: Beauty and Justice in the Americas* (Maryknoll, NY: Orbis, 2003); Theresa A. Yugar, *Sor Juana Inés de la Cruz: Feminist Reconstruction of Biography and Text* (Eugene, OR: Wipf and Stock, 2014).

13. Alex Nava, *Wonder and Exile in the New World* (University Park: Pennsylvania State University Press, 2013); Michelle A. Gonzalez, *A Critical Introduction to Religion in the Americas: Bridging the Liberation Theology and Religious Studies Divide* (New York: New York University Press, 2014); Christopher D. Tirres, *The Aesthetics and Ethics of Faith: A Dialogue Between Liberationist and Pragmatic Thought* (New York: Oxford University Press, 2014).

14. Gonzalez, *Sor Juana*, 8.

15. Pablo Richard, ed., *Materiales para una historia de la teología en América Latina* (San José, Costa Rica: Departamento Ecuménico de Investigaciones, 1981); Josep-Ignasi Saranyana et al., *Teología en América Latina*, 3 vols. (Madrid: Iberoamericana, 1999–2008).

16. Jeanette Rodriguez, *Our Lady of Guadalupe: Faith and Empowerment Among Mexican-American Women* (Austin: University of Texas Press, 1994), 128.

CHAPTER 1

1. Miguel Sánchez, *Imagen de la Virgen María . . .* (Mexico City: Viuda de Bernardo Calderón, 1648), reprinted in Ernesto de la Torre Villar and Ramiro Navarro de Anda, eds., *Testimonios históricos guadalupanos* (Mexico City: Fondo de Cultura Económica, 1982), 152–267.

2. For an analysis of "Creolism" as an emerging and distinct identity of Spanish subjects in the New World, see Tamar Herzog, *Defining Nations: Immigrants and Citizens in Early Modern Spain and Spanish America* (New Haven, CT: Yale University Press, 2003), 143–52.

3. For critical examinations of these debates, see Luis Rivera Pagán, *A Violent Evangelism: The Political and Religious Conquest of the Americas* (Louisville: Westminster/John Knox, 1992); Elsa Cecilia Frost, "Indians and

Theologians: Sixteenth-Century Spanish Theologians and Their Concept of the Indigenous Soul," in *South and Meso-American Native Spirituality: From the Cult of the Feathered Serpent to the Theology of Liberation*, ed. Gary H. Gossen in collaboration with Miguel León-Portilla (New York: Crossroad, 1993), 119–39.

4. Martinus Cawley, "*Criollo* Patriotism in Guadalupe's 'First Evangelist' Miguel Sánchez (1594–1674)," *Marian Studies* 46 (1995): 41–70; Cawley, "The Four Loves of Miguel Sánchez (1594–1674), Guadalupe's 'First Evangelist,'" *Marian Studies* 53 (2002): 112–35; Miguel Sánchez, *Novenas de la Virgen María, Madre de Dios, para sus dos devotísimos santuarios de los Remedios y Guadalupe* (Mexico City: Viuda de Bernardo Calderón, 1665).

5. Miguel Sánchez, Testamento, Archivo Histórico de Notarías de la Ciudad de México, Registro de Bernabé Sarmiento de la Vera, 1671–1675. Sincere thanks to Father Martinus Cawley, OCSO, who provided me with a copy of this document. This and all further quotations in this volume from Spanish- language sources are my translations of the texts.

6. Luis Laso de la Vega, *Huei tlamahuiçoltica* . . . (Mexico City: Juan Ruiz, 1649); Luis Becerra Tanco, *Felicidad de México* . . . (Mexico City: Viuda de Bernardo Calderón, 1675); Francisco de Florencia, *La estrella del norte de México* . . . (Mexico City: Viuda de Juan Ribera, 1688). These three works are reprinted in de la Torre Villar and Navarro de Anda, eds., *Testimonios históricos*, 282–308, 309–33, 359–99. The Laso de la Vega reprint in *Testimonios históricos* is translated from Nahuatl to Spanish. Becerra Tanco's treatise in *Testimonios históricos* is called *Origen milagroso del Santuario de Nuestra Señora de Guadalupe*, the title of a 1666 pamphlet he authored, though the text reprinted is the later revised version from *Felicidad de México*. The Florencia reprint in *Testimonios históricos* only encompasses a portion of the text; for a full version see Francisco de Florencia, *La estrella del norte de México* . . . (Guadalajara: J. Cabrera, 1895). An English translation of Laso de la Vega's *Huei tlamahuiçoltica* is in Lisa Sousa, Stafford Poole, and James Lockhart, eds. and trans., *The Story of Guadalupe: Luis Laso de la Vega's "Huei tlamahuiçoltica" of 1649* (Stanford, CA: Stanford University Press, 1998). The first author to deem these four writers the Guadalupan evangelists was Francisco de la Maza, "Los evangelistas de Guadalupe y el nacionalismo mexicano," *Cuadernos Americanos* 6 (December 1949): 163–88.

7. Mateo de la Cruz, *Relación de la milagrosa aparición de la santa imagen de la Virgen de Guadalupe de México* . . . (Puebla: Viuda de Borja, 1660), reprinted in de la Torre Villar and Navarro de Anda, eds., *Testimonios históricos*, 267–81.

8. "Información por el sermón de 1556," reprinted in de la Torre Villar and Navarro de Anda, eds., *Testimonios históricos*, 36–72, quotes at 52–53, 58–59, 67, 70–71.

9. Martín Enríquez de Almanza, "Carta al rey Felipe II" (1575), reprinted in de la Torre Villar and Navarro de Anda, eds., *Testimonios históricos*, 148–49; Bernal Díaz del Castillo, *The History of the Conquest of New Spain*, ed. Davíd Carrasco (Albuquerque: University of New Mexico Press, 2008), 370; Juan

Suárez de Peralta, *Tratado del descubrimiento de las Yndias y su conquista*, ed. and trans. Giorgio Perissinotto (Madrid: Alianza Editorial, 1990), 248; Jeanette Favrot Peterson, *Visualizing Guadalupe: From Black Madonna to Queen of the Americas* (Austin: University of Texas Press, 2014), 140; William B. Taylor, *Shrines and Miraculous Images: Religious Life in Mexico Before the Reforma* (Albuquerque: University of New Mexico Press, 2010), 111. A print of the Echave Orio painting is in Peterson, *Visualizing Guadalupe*, 160.

10. Taylor, *Shrines and Miraculous Images*, 102.

11. Taylor, *Shrines and Miraculous Images*, 105.

12. Peterson, *Visualizing Guadalupe*, 112, 137–58, quote at 8.

13. Kate Macan, "Our Lady of Guadalupe in Art, 1606–1688: Growing the Devotion," in *New Frontiers in Guadalupan Studies*, ed. Virgilio Elizondo and Timothy Matovina (Eugene, OR: Pickwick, 2014), 39–64, quote at 39; Peterson, *Visualizing Guadalupe*, 197.

14. Stafford Poole, *Our Lady of Guadalupe: The Origins and Sources of a Mexican National Symbol, 1531–1797* (Tucson: University of Arizona Press, 1995), 71–73.

15. Enríquez de Almanza, "Carta al rey Felipe II," 148–49.

16. Taylor, *Shrines and Miraculous Images*, 103–10.

17. Jennifer Scheper Hughes, *Biography of a Mexican Crucifix: Lived Religion and Local Faith from the Conquest to the Present* (New York: Oxford University Press, 2010); María Elena Díaz, *The Virgin, the King, and the Royal Slaves of El Cobre: Negotiating Freedom in Colonial Cuba, 1670–1780* (Stanford, CA: Stanford University Press, 2000); Jalane D. Schmidt, *Cachita's Streets: The Virgin of Charity, Race, and Revolution in Cuba* (Durham, NC: Duke University Press, 2015); William A. Christian, *Apparitions in Late Medieval and Renaissance Spain* (Princeton, NJ: Princeton University Press, 1981), 15–16, quotes at 4; Christian, *Local Religion in Sixteenth-Century Spain* (Princeton, NJ: Princeton University Press, 1981).

18. Taylor, *Shrines and Miraculous Images*, quote at 65; see discussion esp. in part 2, "Our Lady of Guadalupe: Toward a History of Devotion"; Taylor, *Theater of a Thousand Wonders: A History of Miraculous Images and Shrines in New Spain* (New York: Cambridge University Press, 2016), 529–30, 554–55, quote at 182; Taylor, "The Virgin of Guadalupe in New Spain: An Inquiry into the Social History of Marian Devotion," *American Ethnologist* 14 (February 1987): 9–33; Taylor, *Magistrates of the Sacred: Priests and Parishioners in Eighteenth-Century Mexico* (Stanford, CA: Stanford University Press, 1996), 277–300.

19. Taylor, *Theater of a Thousand Wonders*, 47–48, 185–90, 571–73, 580–82; Taylor, *Shrines and Miraculous Images*, 29, 147–48.

20. The cause and epidemiological analysis of *matlazahuatl* is debated, but many commentators have associated it with typhus.

21. Poole, *Our Lady of Guadalupe*, 68, 98.

22. Taylor, *Shrines and Miraculous Images*, 148.

23. Luis de Cisneros, *Historia del principio y origen, progresos venidas a México y milagros de la santa imagen de Nuestra Señora de los Remedios* (Mexico City: N.p., 1621); Taylor, *Shrines and Miraculous Images*, chap. 5, "Guadalupe, Remedios, and Cultural Politics of the Independence Period."

24. Poole, *Our Lady of Guadalupe*, 98, 218.

25. Jacques Lafaye, *Quetzalcoatl and Guadalupe: The Formation of Mexican National Consciousness, 1531–1813*, trans. Benjamin Keen (Chicago: University of Chicago Press, 1976), 254; Poole, *Our Lady of Guadalupe*, 97–98, 163.

26. Juan Bautista, *Anales*, reprinted in Fidel González Fernández, Eduardo Chávez Sánchez, and José Luis Guerrero Rosado, *El encuentro de la Virgen de Guadalupe y Juan Diego*, 4th ed. (Mexico City: Editorial Porrúa, 2001), 325–26; Domingo Francisco de San Antón Muñón Chimalpahin Quauhtlehuanitzin, *Anales*, reprinted in González Fernández, Chávez Sánchez, and Guerrero Rosado, *El encuentro*, 326–27.

27. Sánchez, *Imagen de la Virgen María*, 158, as translated in Poole, *Our Lady of Guadalupe*, 102.

28. Juan Bautista Muñoz, "Memoria sobre las apariciones y el culto de Nuestra Señora de Guadalupe," *Memorias de la Academia de la Historia* 5, #10–12 (1817), reprinted in de la Torre Villar and Navarro de Anda, eds., *Testimonios históricos*, 689–701.

29. See, e.g., Edmundo O'Gorman, *Destierro de sombras: Luz en el origen de la imagen y culto de Nuestra Señora de Guadalupe del Tepeyac* (Mexico: Universidad Nacional Autónoma de México, 1986); Xavier Noguez, *Documentos guadalupanos: Un estudio sobre las fuentes de información tempranas en torno a las mariofanías en el Tepeyac* (Mexico City: Fondo de Cultura Económica, 1993); Poole, *Our Lady of Guadalupe*; Xavier Escalada, *Enciclopedia guadalupana: Apéndice códice 1548; Estudio científico de su autenticidad* (Mexico City: n.p., 1997); José Luis Guerrero, *El "Nican mopohua": Un intento de exégesis*, 2 vols. (Mexico City: Realidad, Teoría y Práctica, 1998); González Fernández, Chávez Sánchez, and Guerrero Rosado, *El encuentro*. For an examination of the history of the apparition debate from the Spanish colonial era to Juan Diego's canonization, see Stafford Poole, *The Guadalupan Controversies in Mexico* (Stanford, CA: Stanford University Press, 2006).

30. Poole, *Our Lady of Guadalupe*, 75, 219.

31. Poole, *Our Lady of Guadalupe*, 150, 223; Poole, *Guadalupan Controversies*, 202. For further analysis of the genesis of the Guadalupe apparition narrative and Sánchez's role in shaping it, see Timothy Matovina, "The Origins of the Guadalupe Tradition in Mexico," *Catholic Historical Review* 100 (Spring 2014): 243–70. A response from Stafford Poole and a rejoinder to that response are also in that same issue of the *Catholic Historical Review*.

32. Escalada, *Enciclopedia guadalupana*. See also González Fernández, Chávez Sánchez, and Guerrero Rosado, *El encuentro*.

33. Antonio de Robles, *Diario de sucesos notables (1665–1703)*, as cited in de la Torre Villar and Navarro de Anda, eds., *Testimonios históricos*, 1108, 1335.

34. José Patricio Fernández de Uribe, *Disertación histórica . . .* (Mexico City: Ontiveros, 1801), 71, as cited in de la Torre Villar and Navarro de Anda, eds., *Testimonios históricos*, 1158; Agustín de la Rosa, *Defensa de la aparición de Nuestra Señora de Guadalupe . . .* (Guadalajara: Luis G. González, 1896), reprinted in de la Torre Villar and Navarro de Anda, eds., *Testimonios históricos*, 1222–79, quotes at 1223–4, 1252.

35. Francisco de la Maza, *El guadalupanismo mexicano* (Mexico City: Porrúa y Obregón, 1953), 9.

36. Lafaye, *Quetzalcoatl and Guadalupe*, 250.

37. Poole, *Our Lady of Guadalupe*, 2, 100, 106.

38. Poole, *Our Lady of Guadalupe*, 107; Poole, "Stafford Poole Responds," *Catholic Historical Review* 100 (Spring 2014): 271–83, quote at 278–79.

39. Sánchez, *Novenas de la Virgen María*; Sánchez, *Imagen de la Virgen María*, 245–55. Further quotations from *Imagen de la Virgen María* in this chapter are cited in context with page numbers from the most accessible reprint version of the book in de la Torre Villar and Navarro de Anda, eds., *Testimonios históricos*.

40. Cawley, "*Criollo* Patriotism," 68.

41. Alicia Mayer, *Flor de primavera mexicana: La Virgen de Guadalupe en los sermones novohispanos* (Mexico City: Universidad Nacional Autónoma de México, 2010), 143–58, 165–77; Cornelius Conover, "Reassessing the Rise of Mexico's Virgin of Guadalupe, 1650s–1780s," *Mexican Studies/Estudios Mexicanos* 27 (Summer 2011): 251–79, quote at 255.

42. David A. Brading, *Mexican Phoenix: Our Lady of Guadalupe; Image and Tradition Across Five Centuries* (New York: Cambridge University Press, 2001), 73.

43. Quodvultdeus, *Sermo III de Symbolo*, ch. 1, ed. R. Braun, Corpus Christianorum, Series Latina (CCSL) 60 (Turnhout 1953ff.), 349. Editions of Augustine attributed this sermon to him until the early twentieth century, when the Belgian scholar Dom Germain Morin was the first to argue that the three sermons *De Symbolo* (along with nine other sermons) were the work of Quodvultdeus rather than Augustine. Dom Germain Morin, "Pour une future édition des opuscules de S. Quodvultdeus, évêque de Carthage au Vi siècle," *Revue Bénédictine* 31 (1914): 156–62. For the later stages of scholarly corroboration of this attribution, see CCSL 60, v–vii. It is worth noting that the association of the woman in Revelation 12 with Mary is quite rare among early Christian writers. Indeed, few patristic authors before the sixth century comment on the book of Revelation and those that do tend to link the woman in chapter 12 directly with the church rather than Mary. See, e.g., Hippolytus, *De Antichristo* 60–1 (J.-P. Migne, Patrologia Graeca [PG], Paris, 1857ff., 10.779–82); Methodius, *Symposium* 8.5–6 (ed. H. Musurillo; Sources chrétiennes, Paris, 1942ff., 95.212–6); Victorinus

of Poetovium, *Commentary on Apocalypse* 12.1–4 (Corpus Scriptorum Christianorum Orientalium, Louvain, 1903ff., 49.104–12).

44. The text of John 19 does not directly name the two figures standing beneath the cross as John and Mary. Sánchez follows a long-standing tradition in identifying the "disciple whom he loved" (John 19:26) as John.

45. The text Sánchez attributes to Augustine is from Ambrosius Autpertus, who wrote in the eighth or ninth century. Ambrosius Autpertus, *Sermo de Assumtione Sancte Marie*, ch. 5, ed. R. Weber, CCSL 27B, 1030.

46. Sánchez's quotation is an altered version of the text in Augustine, *Enarrationes in Psalmos*, Exposition on Psalm 26, para. 8, ed. E. Dekkers and J. Fraipont, CCSL 38, 153.

47. Peterson, *Visualizing Guadalupe*, 119–29.

48. Augustine, *In Johannis Evangelium Tractatus*, Tract 118.4, J.-P. Migne, Patrologia Latina (Paris, 1841ff.), vol. 35, col. 1949.

49. Cyril's authorship of this text is disputed, though it is attributed to him in S. Cyrilli Alexandrini Homilia contra Nestorium, PG, vol. 77, col. 992 B11–12. E. Schwartz questioned the authenticity of Cyril's authorship in the critical edition of this homily, but most scholars still accept it as genuine. E. Schwartz, ed., *Acta Conciliorum Oecumenicorum*, I, 1, 2, 102; Mark Santer, "The Authorship and Occasion of Cyril of Alexandria's Sermon on the Virgin (Hom. Div. IV)," *Studia Patristica* 12 (Texte und Untersuchungen 115; Berlin, 1975): 144–50.

50. Mayer, *Flor de primavera mexicana*, 98; Brading, *Mexican Phoenix*, 96–101, 146–68, quote at 165. See also de la Maza, *El guadalupanismo mexicano*; Francisco Raymond Schulte, *Mexican Spirituality: Its Sources and Mission in the Earliest Guadalupan Sermons* (Lanham, MD: Rowman and Littlefield, 2002); Carlos Herejón Peredo, *Del sermón al discurso cívico, México 1760–1834* (Zamora, Mich., Mexico: El Colegio de Michoacán, and Mexico City: El Colegio de México, 2003).

51. Sor Juana Inés de la Cruz, *Obras completas de Sor Juana Inés de la Cruz*, vol. 1, ed. Alfonso Méndez Plancarte (Mexico City: Fondo de Cultura Económica, 1951), 310; Virgilio Elizondo, *Guadalupe: Mother of the New Creation* (Maryknoll, NY: Orbis, 1997), ix.

52. David A. Sánchez, *From Patmos to the Barrio: Subverting Imperial Myths* (Minneapolis: Augsburg Fortress, 2008); Josefrayn Sánchez-Perry, "Theotokos of Byzantium and Guadalupe of Tepeyac: Patristics, Typology, and the Incarnation," *Apuntes: Reflexiones teológicas desde el contexto Hispano-Latino* 33 (Spring 2013): 18–33; Michael Anthony Abril, "Apocalypse at Tepeyac," in *New Frontiers in Guadalupan Studies*, ed. Elizondo and Matovina, 125–53, quote at 137.

53. Jean-Pierre Ruiz, "The Bible and U.S. Hispanic American Theological Discourse: Lessons from a Non-Innocent History," in *From the Heart of Our*

People: Latino/a Explorations in Catholic Systematic Theology, ed. Orlando O. Espín and Miguel H. Díaz (Maryknoll, NY: Orbis, 1999), 100–20, quote at 107.

CHAPTER 2

1. Luis Laso de la Vega, *Huei tlamahuiçoltica* . . . (Mexico City: Juan Ruiz, 1649), reprinted with an English translation in *The Story of Guadalupe: Luis Laso de la Vega's "Huei tlamahuiçoltica" of 1649*, ed. and trans. Lisa Sousa, Stafford Poole, and James Lockhart (Stanford, CA: Stanford University Press, 1998).

2. Miguel Sánchez, *Imagen de la Virgen María* . . . (Mexico City: Viuda de Bernardo Calderón, 1648), reprinted in Ernesto de la Torre Villar and Ramiro Navarro de Anda, eds., *Testimonios históricos guadalupanos* (Mexico City: Fondo de Cultura Económica, 1982), 152–267, quote at 263.

3. Francisco de Florencia, *La estrella del norte de México* . . . (Mexico City: Viuda de Juan Ribera, 1688), reprinted in de la Torre Villar and Navarro de Anda, eds., *Testimonios históricos*, 359–99, quotes at 364, 378.

4. Stafford Poole, *Our Lady of Guadalupe: The Origins and Sources of a Mexican National Symbol, 1531–1797* (Tucson: University of Arizona Press, 1995), 110–26; David A. Brading, *Mexican Phoenix: Our Lady of Guadalupe, Image and Tradition Across Five Centuries* (New York: Cambridge University Press, 2001), 81–88.

5. Michael E. Smith, *The Aztecs*, 3rd ed. (Malden, MA: Wiley-Blackwell, 2012), 61–64, 292.

6. Sabine MacCormack, "Human and Divine Love in a Pastoral Setting: The Histories of Copacabana on Lake Titicaca," *Representations* 112 (Fall 2010): 54–86, quote at 75.

7. Lisa Sousa, *The Woman Who Turned into a Jaguar, and Other Narratives of Native Women in Archives of Colonial Mexico* (Stanford, CA: Stanford University Press, 2017), chap. 3, "Marriage Encounters," quote at 83; Louise M. Burkhart, *The Slippery Earth: Nahua-Christian Moral Dialogue in Sixteenth-Century Mexico* (Tucson: University of Arizona Press, 1989); Burkhart, "Pious Performances: Christian Pageantry and Native Identity in Early Colonial Mexico," in *Native Traditions in the Postconquest World*, ed. Elizabeth Hill Boone and Tom Cummins (Washington, DC: Dumbarton Oaks, 1998), 361–81, quote at 362. See also Osvaldo F. Pardo, *The Origins of Mexican Catholicism: Nahua Rituals and Christian Sacraments in Sixteenth-Century Mexico* (Ann Arbor: University of Michigan Press, 2004); Jaime Lara, *City Temple Stage: Eschatological Architecture and Liturgical Theatrics in New Spain* (Notre Dame, IN: University of Notre Dame Press, 2004); Lara, *Christian Texts for Aztecs: Art and Liturgy in Colonial Mexico* (Notre Dame, IN: University of Notre Dame Press, 2008).

8. Katharine Mahon, "'May You Be Joyful, Oh Saint Mary': Translating and Transforming Marian Devotion in New Spain," in *New Frontiers in Guadalupan Studies*, ed. Virgilio Elizondo and Timothy Matovina (Eugene, OR: Pickwick,

2014), 19–38, at 22; Amy G. Remensnyder, *La Conquistadora: The Virgin Mary at War and Peace in the Old and New Worlds* (New York: Oxford University Press, 2014); Louise M. Burkhart, *Before Guadalupe: The Virgin Mary in Early Colonial Nahuatl Literature* (Albany, NY: University of Albany Institute for Mesoamerican Studies, 2001), 129 (quoted by Fray Juan de Mijangos), 149; Burkhart, "The Cult of the Virgin of Guadalupe in Mexico," in *South and Meso-American Native Spirituality: From the Cult of the Feathered Serpent to the Theology of Liberation*, ed. Gary H. Gossen in collaboration with Miguel León-Portilla (New York: Crossroad, 1993), 198–227, esp. 212–13.

9. Burkhart, *Before Guadalupe*, 115; Miguel León-Portilla, *Aztec Thought and Culture*, trans. Jack Emory Davis (Norman: University of Oklahoma Press, 1963), 123–28; J. Jorge Klor de Alva, "Aztec Spirituality and Nahuatized Christianity," in *South and Meso-American Native Spirituality*, ed. Gossen, 173–97, quote at 182.

10. William F. Hanks, *Converting Words: Maya in the Age of the Cross* (Berkeley: University of California Press, 2010), xvii, 5; James Lockhart, *The Nahuas After the Conquest: A Social and Cultural History of the Indians of Central Mexico, Sixteenth Through Eighteenth Centuries* (Stanford, CA: Stanford University Press, 1992), esp. chap. 7, "Language."

11. Bernardino de Sahagún, "Sobre supersticiones," appendix to *Historia general de las cosas de Nueva España*, Book XI (1576), reprinted in de la Torre Villar and Navarro de Anda, eds., *Testimonios históricos*, 142–44; Burkhart, *Before Guadalupe*, 11; Burkhart, "The Cult of the Virgin of Guadalupe in Mexico," 207–209; Jeanette Favrot Peterson, *Visualizing Guadalupe: From Black Madonna to Queen of the Americas* (Austin: University of Texas Press, 2014), 81–89. For an English translation and analysis of Sahagún's commentaries on the Guadalupe cult at Tepeyac, see Yongho Francis Lee, "Our Lady of Guadalupe in Bernardino de Sahagún's *Historia general de las Cosas de Nueva España*," in *New Frontiers in Guadalupan Studies*, ed. Elizondo and Matovina, 1–18.

12. Peterson, *Visualizing Guadalupe*, 71–81; Davíd Carrasco, *Religions of Mesoamerica*, 2nd ed. (Long Grove, IL: Waveland, 2014), 162.

13. "Información por el sermón de 1556," reprinted in de la Torre Villar and Navarro de Anda, eds., *Testimonios históricos*, 36–72, quotes at 51–52, 59, 67, 71.

14. Gregory XIII, *Ut deiparae semper virginis*, March 2, 1576, reprinted in Fidel González Fernández, Eduardo Chávez Sánchez, and José Luis Guerrero Rosado, *El encuentro de la Virgen de Guadalupe y Juan Diego*, 4th ed. (Mexico City: Editorial Porrúa, 2001), 557–60; Sahagún, "Sobre supersticiones"; Francisco Verdugo Quetzalmamalitzin, *Testamento* (Will), 2 April 1563, reprinted in González Fernández, Chávez Sánchez, and Guerrero Rosado, *El encuentro*, 363–64; Catalina de Sena, *Testament*, reprinted in *Beyond the Codices: The Nahua View of Colonial Mexico*, ed. and trans. Arthur J. O. Anderson, Frances Berdan, and James Lockhart (Berkeley: University of California Press, 1976), 54–57, quote at

55; Juan Bautista, *Anales,* reprinted in González Fernández, Chávez Sánchez, and Guerrero Rosado, *El encuentro,* 325–26.

15. Peterson, *Visualizing Guadalupe,* 217–18; William Taylor, *Shrines and Miraculous Images: Religious Life in Mexico Before the Reforma* (Albuquerque: University of New Mexico Press, 2010), 105, 109, 125; Martinus Cawley, *Anthology of Early Guadalupan Literature* (Lafayette, OR: Guadalupe Abbey, 1984), 79–80.
16. Poole, *Our Lady of Guadalupe,* 67, 70, 88.
17. Poole, *Our Lady of Guadalupe,* 70.
18. A facsimile and transcription of the official inquiry are in Eduardo Chávez Sánchez, *La Virgen de Guadalupe y Juan Diego en las informaciones jurídicas de 1666,* 2nd ed. (Mexico City: Ángel Servin, 2002).
19. Chávez Sánchez, *La Virgen de Guadalupe y Juan Diego,* 149–54.
20. Chávez Sánchez, *La Virgen de Guadalupe y Juan Diego,* 152.
21. Chávez Sánchez, *La Virgen de Guadalupe y Juan Diego,* 166, 178–79.
22. Patricia Harrington, "Mother of Death, Mother of Rebirth: The Mexican Virgin of Guadalupe," *Journal of the American Academy of Religion* 56 (winter 1988): 25–50, quote at 33; Donald V. Kurtz, "The Virgin of Guadalupe and the Politics of Becoming Human," *Journal of Anthropological Research* 38 (summer 1982): 194–210, quote at 206; Poole, *Our Lady of Guadalupe,* esp. 10–11; Taylor, *Shrines and Miraculous Images,* 125.
23. William B. Taylor, "The Virgin of Guadalupe in New Spain: An Inquiry into the Social History of Marian Devotion," *American Ethnologist* 14 (February 1987): 9–33, see esp. 19–21; Taylor, *Magistrates of the Sacred: Priests and Parishioners in Eighteenth-Century Mexico* (Stanford, CA: Stanford University Press, 1996), 291–93; Jeanette Favrot Peterson, "The Virgin of Guadalupe: Symbol of Conquest or Liberation?" *Art Journal* 51 (winter 1992): 39–47; Carrasco, *Religions of Mesoamerica,* 163.
24. Sousa, Poole, and Lockhart, eds. and trans., *Story of Guadalupe,* 18–43. For tables of loanwords and phrases, see 23, 25.
25. Miguel León-Portilla, *Tonantzin Guadalupe: Pensamiento náhuatl y mensaje cristiano en el "Nican mopohua"* (Mexico City: Fondo de Cultura Económica, 2000), 17–33, quote at 22. For opposing arguments on the authorship of the *Nican mopohua,* see González Fernández, Chávez Sánchez, and Guerrero Rosado, *El encuentro,* 171–74; Sousa, Poole, and Lockhart, eds. and trans., *The Story of Guadalupe,* 1–47, esp. 43–47.
26. Sousa, Poole, and Lockhart, eds. and trans., *The Story of Guadalupe,* 51. Further quotations from *Huei tlamahuiçoltica* are cited in context with page numbers from this same work, which is the first and only English translation of the entire treatise and is printed with the Nahuatl and English on facing pages.
27. Richard Nebel, *Santa María Tonantzin, Virgen de Guadalupe: Continuidad y transformación religiosa en México* (Mexico City: Fondo de Cultura Económica, 1995), 39–81, esp. 71; William A. Christian Jr., *Apparitions in Late Medieval*

and Renaissance Spain (Princeton, NJ: Princeton University Press, 1981), 87–93, quote at 92; William B. Taylor, *Theater of a Thousand Wonders: A History of Miraculous Images and Shrines in New Spain* (New York: Cambridge University Press, 2016), 560.

28. Sánchez, *Imagen de la Virgen María*, 245–55; Peterson, *Visualizing Guadalupe*, chap. 3 "A 'Book of Miracles.'" See also Peterson, "Canonizing a Cult: A Wonder-Working Guadalupe in the Seventeenth Century," in *Religion in New Spain*, ed. Susan Schroeder and Stafford Poole (Albuquerque: University of New Mexico Press, 2007), 125–56.

29. Peterson, *Visualizing Guadalupe*, 150, 152.

30. Peterson, *Visualizing Guadalupe*, 149, 157; Alison Fitchett Climenhaga, "The *Huei tlamahuiçoltica*: Responding to Pastoral Challenges in Light of Our Lady of Guadalupe," in *New Frontiers in Guadalupan Studies*, ed. Elizondo and Matovina, 65–87, quote at 78.

31. For the practice of children participating in Spanish penitential processions, see Christian, *Apparitions in Late Medieval and Renaissance Spain*, 217–18.

32. Orlando O. Espín, *The Faith of the People: Theological Reflections on Popular Catholicism* (Maryknoll, NY: Orbis, 1997), 59; Burkhart, "The Cult of the Virgin of Guadalupe in Mexico," 211. For a treatment of understandings of a stern God and compassionate Mary in the longer history of Christianity, see Elizabeth A. Johnson, *Truly Our Sister: A Theology of Mary in the Communion of Saints* (New York: Continuum, 2003), chap. 4, "Cul-de-Sac: The Maternal Face of God."

33. Sánchez, *Imagen de la Virgen María*, 184–86. Other biblical figures that Sánchez compares to Juan Diego include John the Evangelist, King David's friend Jonathan, Adam, and the patriarch Jacob, at 179, 193–94, 229–30, 237–38.

34. The Marian Library at the International Marian Research Institute at the University of Dayton provides an excellent overview of the Little Office of the Blessed Virgin Mary, originally authored by Chad Pfoutz and available at http://campus.udayton.edu/mary/prayers/LittleOfficeBVM.htm. The cited text is based on the antiphon for Psalm 95 from the Third Nocturn of matins.

35. Taylor, "The Virgin of Guadalupe in New Spain," 14–15; Taylor, *Magistrates of the Sacred*, 285–86; Taylor, *Shrines and Miraculous Images*, esp. 125.

36. Luis Laso de la Vega, *Se apareció maravillosamente la Reina del Cielo Santa María, nuestra Amada Madre de Guadalupe, aquí cerca de la ciudad de México en el lugar nombrado Tepeyácac*, ed. and trans. Primo Feliciano Velázquez (Mexico City: Carreño e hijo, 1926). The Velázquez translation of *Huei tlamahuiçoltica* is reprinted in de la Torre Villar and Navarro de Anda, eds., *Testimonios históricos*, 282–308.

37. Allan Figueroa Deck, "Seized and Saturated by Gift: Living for Others," in *The Treasure of Guadalupe*, ed. Virgilio Elizondo, Allan Figueroa Deck, and Timothy Matovina (Lanham, MD: Rowman and Littlefield, 2006), 11–17, quotes at 12, 13, 17.

CHAPTER 3

1. Carlos Herrejón Peredo, *Del sermón al discurso cívico, México 1760–1834* (Zamora, Mich., Mexico: El Colegio de Michoacán, and Mexico City: El Colegio de México, 2003), 17, 19. Herejón Peredo catalogs in chronological order extant published sermons from the colonial era in the appendix of his volume, 423–57. See also Francisco Raymond Schulte, *Mexican Spirituality: Its Sources and Mission in the Earliest Guadalupan Sermons* (Lanham, MD: Rowman and Littlefield, 2002), 169–209.

2. For a sample of a Guadalupe sermon from such a collection, along with other instructional material, see Ignacio de Paredes, *Prompturario manual mexicano: Que a la verdad podrá ser utilísimo a los parrochos para la enseñanza; a los necesitados indios para su instrucción . . .* (Compendium Mexican manual: Which in truth can be extremely useful for pastors in their teaching, to the needful Indians for their instruction . . .) (Mexico City: Bibliotheca Mexicana, 1759), lxxiii–xc.

3. See, e.g., David A. Brading, *Mexican Phoenix: Our Lady of Guadalupe, Image and Tradition Across Five Centuries* (New York: Cambridge University Press, 2001), chap. 7, "Divine Idea"; Schulte, *Mexican Spirituality*; Alicia Mayer, *Flor de primavera mexicana: La Virgen de Guadalupe en los sermones novohispanos* (Mexico City: Universidad Nacional Autónoma de México, 2010).

4. There is at least one earlier published sermon associated with the Guadalupe shrine at Tepeyac. The Augustinian friar Juan de Cepeda published a 1622 sermon given at the shrine on the feast of the Nativity of Mary, but his oration was a general Marian sermon and not specifically focused on Guadalupe. Fray Iuan de Cepeda, *Sermón de la Natividad de la Virgen María Señora Nuestra predicado en la Ermita de Guadalupe* (Sermon for the Nativity of Our Lady the Virgin Mary preached in the Hermitage [Chapel] of Guadalupe) (Mexico City: Bachiller Iuan de Alcaçar, 1622), reprinted in Vicente de P. Andrade, *Ensayo bibliográfico mexicano del siglo XVII,* 2nd ed. (Mexico City: Museo Nacional, 1899), 107–22.

5. José Vidal de Figueroa, *Teórica de la prodigiosa imagen de la Virgen Santa María de Guadalupe de México* (Mexico City: Juan Ruiz, 1661). Sermons exemplifying the latter two claims include, respectively, Juan de Goicoechea, S.J., *La maravilla immarcescible, y milagro continuado de María Santísima Señora Nuestra en su prodigiosa imagen de Guadalupe de México* (The unfading marvel and continuous miracle of Our Holy Mother Mary in her prodigious image of Guadalupe of Mexico) (Mexico City: Herederos de Juan Joseph Guiliena Carrascoso, 1709); Francisco Javier Lazcano, S.J., *Sermón panegyrico al inclyto patronato de María Señora Nuestra en su milagrosísima imagen de Guadalupe* (Panegyric sermon for the renowned patronage of Mary Our Lady in her most miraculous image of Guadalupe) (Mexico City: Bibliotheca Mexicana, 1759). Facsimile reprints of all three sermons are in David A. Brading, *Nueve sermones guadalupanos*

(1661–1758) (Mexico City: Centro de Estudios de Historia de México Condumex, 2005), 57–91, 95–123, 341–66.

6. Martín de Velasco, *Arte de sermones para hacerlos y predicarlos* (Mexico City: Imprenta Real del Superior Gobierno, 1728), 19.

7. Mayer, *Flor de primavera Mexicana*, part 2, "El sermón en la Nueva España: Siglos XVII y XVIII," quote at 66.

8. Domingo Terán de los Ríos, Diary, in *Boletín del Archivo General de la Nación* 28:1 (1957): 59–112, quote at 72. For an English translation of the Terán de los Ríos diary, see Mattie Austin Hatcher, "The Expedition of Don Domingo Terán de los Rios into Texas," in *Wilderness Mission: Preliminary Studies of the Texas Catholic Historical Society II*, ed. Jesús F. de la Teja (Austin: Texas Catholic Historical Society, 1999), 1–66, quote at 19.

9. Jorge E. Traslosheros H., "The Construction of the First Shrine and Sanctuary of Our Lady of Guadalupe in San Luis Potosí, 1654–1664," *Journal of Hispanic/Latino Theology* 5 (August 1997): 7–19, quote at 11; William B. Taylor, *Theater of a Thousand Wonders: A History of Miraculous Images and Shrines in New Spain* (New York: Cambridge University Press, 2016), 331.

10. For a chronological listing of the published Guadalupan sermons during these decades, see Schulte, *Mexican Spirituality*, 169–72.

11. Kate Macan, "Our Lady of Guadalupe in Art, 1606–1688: Growing the Devotion," in *New Frontiers in Guadalupan Studies*, ed. Virgilio Elizondo and Timothy Matovina (Eugene, OR: Pickwick, 2014), 39–64, esp. at 51–55; Jeanette Favrot Peterson, *Visualizing Guadalupe: From Black Madonna to Queen of the Americas* (Austin: University of Texas Press, 2014), 203–207, quote at 207. The full name of the 1653 painting is *Traslado de la imagen de la Virgen de Guadalupe a la primera ermita y representación del primer milagro* (Transfer of the image of the Virgin of Guadalupe to the first hermitage and representation of the first miracle), but it is commonly known as *El primer milagro*.

12. William B. Taylor, *Magistrates of the Sacred: Priests and Parishioners in Eighteenth-Century Mexico* (Stanford, CA: Stanford University Press, 1996), 287; Francisco de Florencia, *La estrella del norte de México . . .* (1688; reprint ed., Guadalajara: J. Cabrera, 1895), 133; Peterson, *Visualizing Guadalupe*, 237–38.

13. William B. Taylor, *Shrines and Miraculous Images: Religious Life in Mexico Before the Reforma* (Albuquerque: University of New Mexico Press, 2010), 109–10.

14. Taylor, *Shrines and Miraculous Images*, 109.

15. Taylor, *Magistrates of the Sacred*, 679–80n97; Taylor, *Theater of a Thousand Wonders*, 230n25.

16. Goicoechea, *La maravilla immarcescible*, as reprinted in Brading, *Nueve sermones guadalupanos*, 117, 122; Peterson, *Visualizing Guadalupe*, 238–51.

17. Cornelius Conover, "Reassessing the Rise of Mexico's Virgin of Guadalupe, 1650s–1780s," *Mexican Studies/Estudios Mexicanos* 27 (Summer 2011): 251–79, esp. 259–62.

18. Conover, "Reassessing," 256–62; Taylor, *Magistrates of the Sacred*, 278.

19. Taylor, *Shrines and Miraculous Images*, 122; Conover, "Reassessing," 263–65.

20. Cayetano de Cabrera y Quintero, *Escudo de armas de México . . .* (Mexico City: Viuda de D. Joseph Bernardo de Hogal, 1746), 70–71.

21. Cabrera y Quintero, *Escudo de armas de México*; Taylor, *Magistrates of the Sacred*, 283. For a summary of these events based on the contemporary account of Cabrera y Quintero in *Escudo de armas de México*, see Brading, *Mexican Phoenix*, 120–27.

22. Cayetano de Cabrera y Quintero, *El patronato disputado: Dissertación apologética* (Mexico City: Imprenta Real del Superior Gobierno, y del Nuevo Rezado de Doña Maria de Rivera, 1741); Brading, *Mexican Phoenix*, 127–28, 137. Cabrera y Quintero later reprinted the text of *El patronato disputado* in his *Escudo de armas de México*.

23. Taylor, *Magistrates of the Sacred*, 285–86; Taylor, *Theater of a Thousand Wonders*, 185–98, 208–14, chap. 4, "Advocations of the Virgin Mary in the Colonial Period."

24. Schulte, *Mexican Spirituality*, 186–200; Taylor, *Theater of a Thousand Wonders*, 113, 180–82, 338, 409; Taylor, *Shrines and Miraculous Images*, 117–20, quote at 117.

25. Matthew's genealogy was the typical gospel reading for the Guadalupe feast in New Spain until 1754. In that year Pope Benedict XIV promulgated the first Vatican-sanctioned liturgical texts for her feast, which encompassed the gospel reading of Mary's visitation to her kinswoman Elizabeth from Luke 1:39–45. For a study of these liturgical texts, see J. J. Salazar, "'¿No estoy yo aquí, que soy tu madre?' Investigación Teológica-Bíblica-Litúrgica acerca de la Nueva Liturgia de Nuestra Señora de Guadalupe" (S.T.D. diss., Rome, Pontificio Istituto Liturgico, 1981), vol. 1, pp. 141–202.

26. Bartolomé Felipe de Ita y Parra, *La imagen de Guadalupe, Señora de los tiempos* (Mexico City: Herederos de la Viuda de Miguel de Rivera, 1732). Quotation taken from the title page of this work. Further quotations from *La imagen de Guadalupe, Señora de los tiempos* are cited in context with page numbers from this original edition. My thanks to Father Thomas Thompson, S.M. of the Marian Library at the University of Dayton for providing me with a copy of Ita y Parra's *La imagen de Guadalupe* sermon.

27. For a presentation of this analysis in Augustine, see *Homilies on the Gospel of John 1–40*, trans. Edmund Hill (Hyde Park, NY: New City Press, 2009), Homily 10, no. 12.

28. Bartolomé Felipe de Ita y Parra, *La possessión en su esperanza* (The possession of her hope) (Mexico City: Joseph Bernardo de Hogal, 1730), 1, 7, 11.

29. Bartolomé Felipe de Ita y Parra, *Los pecados única causa de las pestes* (Madrid: Antonio Marin, 1740), 3, 6.

30. Ita y Parra, *Los pecados única causa de las pestes*, 12, 16.

31. Bartolomé Felipe de Ita y Parra, *La madre de la salud: La milagrosa imagen de Guadalupe* (Madrid: Antonio Marin, 1739), 1; reprinted in Brading, *Nueve sermones guadalupanos*, 163–82. Further quotations from *La madre de la salud* are cited in context with page numbers from the original edition.

32. The official approvals for the publication of both sermons are in the unnumbered opening pages of Ita y Parra, *Los pecados única causa de las pestes.*

33. Ita y Parra's contention that Guadalupe typifies the burning bush rather than the Ark of the Covenant is inconsistent with other colonial preachers and theologians such as Sánchez, whose association of Guadalupe with the Ark was noted in chapter 1. This minor discrepancy is not surprising, given the wealth of extant biblical imagery and its malleability in the preaching of New Spain orators. Ita y Parra undoubtedly knew the long-standing Christian acclamation of Mary as the Ark of the Covenant but accentuated the burning bush metaphor to illuminate his theological understanding of Guadalupe.

34. Michael Griffin, "Mother of Health, Remedy for the Plague: Preaching on Guadalupe in the Midst of Death," in *New Frontiers in Guadalupan Studies*, ed. Elizondo and Matovina, 88–107, quote at 96.

35. Griffin, "Mother of Health," 94.

36. Bartolomé Felipe de Ita y Parra, *La imagen de Guadalupe, imagen del patrocinio* (Mexico City: Viuda de D. Joseph Bernardo de Hogal, 1744), 1, 2; reprinted in Brading, *Nueve sermones guadalupanos*, 185–217. Further quotations from *La imagen de Guadalupe, imagen del patrocinio* are cited in context with page numbers from the original edition.

37. The first known publication that associates Guadalupe with Psalm 147:20 was a 1686 sermon of the Carmelite priest Manuel de San Joseph. However, the verse's citation in Francisco de Florencia's *La estrella del norte de México* two years later and on numerous subsequent artistic renditions of the Guadalupe image were more influential in disseminating the idea of the unique divine favor granted to New Spain in the Guadalupe event. Schulte, *Mexican Spirituality*, 171–72; Florencia, *La estrella del norte de México*, 132.

38. Bartolomé Felipe de Ita y Parra, *El círculo del amor formado por la América Septentrional jurando a María Santísima en su imagen de Guadalupe* (Mexico City: Viuda de D. Joseph Bernardo de Hogal, 1747), title page, 1; reprinted in Brading, *Nueve sermones guadalupanos*, 221–61. Further quotations from *El círculo del amor* are cited in context with page numbers from the original edition.

39. Bartolomé Felipe de Ita y Parra, *El arrebatado de Dios: El Señor D. Phelippe V, oración fúnebre* (Mexico City: Viuda de Don Joseph Bernardo de Hogal, 1747), 30–31.

40. Taylor, *Magistrates of the Sacred*, 293.

41. Juan José de Eguiara y Eguren, *María Santísima pintándose milagrosamente en su bellísima imagen de Guadalupe de México, saluda a la Nueva España y se constituye su patrona* (Mexico City: Bibliotheca Mexicana, 1757), reprinted in Ernesto de la

Torre Villar and Ramiro Navarro de Anda, eds., *Testimonios históricos guadalupanos* (Mexico City: Fondo de Cultura Económica, 1982), 480–93.

42. Eguiara y Eguren, *María Santísima*, 483.

43. William A. Christian Jr., *Local Religion in Sixteenth-Century Spain* (Princeton, NJ: Princeton University Press, 1981), 3; Ana María Díaz-Stevens, *Oxcart Catholicism on Fifth Avenue: The Impact of Puerto Rican Migration upon the Archdiocese of New York* (Notre Dame, IN: University of Notre Dame Press, 1993), 46; Ita y Parra, *La imagen de Guadalupe, imagen del patrocinio*, 2.

44. Augustine, *Sermones*, Sermo 130.1, J.-P. Migne, Patrologia Latina (Paris, 1841ff.), vol. 38, col. 725.

CHAPTER 4

1. Servando Teresa de Mier, *Sermón Guadalupano* (1794), in Ernesto de la Torre Villar and Ramiro Navarro de Anda, eds., *Testimonios históricos guadalupanos* (Mexico City: Fondo de Cultura Económica, 1982), 732–52, quotes at 733, 738. Page numbers for further quotations from *Sermón Guadalupano* are cited in context.

2. Alonso Núñez de Haro y Peralta, Response to Servando Teresa de Mier's *Sermón Guadalupano*, March 25, 1795, in Torre Villar and Navarro de Anda, eds., *Testimonios históricos*, 752–57. Various commentators have averred that Mier's sermon drew the ire of Spanish authorities such as Archbishop Núñez de Haro y Peralta because of its nationalist claims, since Saint Thomas's alleged evangelization gave Mexico the prerogative of its own apostolic origins in the faith and expunged the assertion that Spain established Catholicism in the region. Mier in fact later declared that the apostolic labors of Saint Thomas delegitimized the claims of the Spanish crown on New Spain. But at the time of his sermon he was still trying to provide a credible historical basis for the Guadalupe tradition that included her appearances to Juan Diego, apparently in response to unnamed detractors in New Spain. For an overview of secondary literature on the Mier sermon, see Alicia Mayer, *Flor de primavera mexicana: La Virgen de Guadalupe en los sermones novohispanos* (Mexico City: Universidad Nacional Autónoma de México, 2010), 202–205.

3. The most infamous nineteenth-century incident in these debates resulted in the public denunciation of the devout Catholic and acclaimed Mexican historian Joaquín García Icazbalceta. This episode is summarized in Stafford Poole, *The Guadalupan Controversies in Mexico* (Stanford, CA: Stanford University Press, 2006), 33–44, 75–78.

4. Carlos Herrejón Peredo, *Del sermón al discurso cívico, México 1760–1834* (Zamora, Mich., Mexico: El Colegio de Michoacán, and Mexico City: El Colegio de México, 2003), chap. 5, "La continua apoteosis guadalupana."

5. Pamela Voekel, *Alone Before God: The Religious Origins of Modernity in Mexico* (Durham, NC: Duke University Press, 2002), 1, 4, 5.

6. J. Michelle Molina, *To Overcome Oneself: The Jesuit Ethic and Spirit of Global Expansion, 1520–1767* (Berkeley: University of California Press, 2013), 203; William B. Taylor, *Theater of a Thousand Wonders: A History of Miraculous Images and Shrines in New Spain* (New York: Cambridge University Press, 2016), chap. 2, "Growth, Other Changes, and Continuities in the Late Colonial Period," quote at 95. For a study of these dynamics in one particular locale, see Roberto Aceves Ávila, "'Que es bueno y útil invocarles': Evolución de las prácticas y devociones religiosas en Guadalajara durante el período 1771–1900" (Ph.D. diss., El Colegio de Jalisco, Zapopan, Jalisco, 2017).

7. Narciso Bassols, ed., *Sermonario mexicano: Colección de sermones panegíricos, dogmáticos y morales, escritos por los oradores mexicanos más notables, ordenados por un eclesiástico de la Mitra de Puebla* (Mexican Sermonary: Collection of panegyric, dogmatic, and moral sermons, written by the most notable mexican orators, arranged by an ecclesiastic of the Diocese of Puebla) (Mexico City: Imprenta de Angel Bassols Hermanos, 1890), vol. 3; Victoriano Agüeros, ed., *Album de la coronación de la Sma. Virgen de Guadalupe* (Mexico: El Tiempo, 1895–1896), vol. 2, appendix, 1–75. The fourth volume of Bassols' *Sermonario mexicano* contains a collection of Marian sermons, two of which are also Guadalupan.

8. Taylor, *Theater of a Thousand Wonders*, 225; Taylor, *Shrines and Miraculous Images: Religious Life in Mexico Before the Reforma* (Albuquerque: University of New Mexico Press, 2010), 125–27, quote at 126; Taylor, "The Virgin of Guadalupe in New Spain: An Inquiry into the Social History of Marian Devotion," *American Ethnologist* 14 (February 1987): 9–33, quote at 30n35; Ignacio de Paredes, *Prompturario manual mexicano: Que a la verdad podrá ser utilísimo a los parrochos para la enseñanza; a los necesitados indios para su instrucción . . .* (Compendium Mexican manual: Which in truth can be extremely useful for pastors in their teaching, to the needful Indians for their instruction . . .) (Mexico City: Bibliotheca Mexicana, 1759), lxxiii–xc.

9. Taylor, *Shrines and Miraculous Images*, 127–28, 251n51, quote at 128.

10. Taylor, *Shrines and Miraculous Images*, 144–45; William B. Taylor, *Magistrates of the Sacred: Priests and Parishioners in Eighteenth-Century Mexico* (Stanford, CA: Stanford University Press, 1996), 294–96.

11. Cornelius Conover, "Reassessing the Rise of Mexico's Virgin of Guadalupe, 1650s–1780s," *Mexican Studies/Estudios Mexicanos* 27 (Summer 2011): 251–79, esp. 276–78.

12. In 1750, for example, *criollos* occupied nearly two-thirds of the bishoprics in Spain's New World colonies, but from 1751 to 1808 almost three-quarters of the new appointees to these posts were *peninsulares*. Mark A. Burkholder, *Spaniards in the Colonial Empire: Creoles vs. Peninsulars?* (Malden, MA: Wiley-Blackwell, 2013), esp. chap. 5, "Reforms, Commentaries, and Officials, 1750–1808," and chap. 6, "The Church, Complaints, and Social Change, 1750–1808."

13. Taylor, *Magistrates of the Sacred*, 296.

14. Jean Louis Berlandier, *Journey to Mexico During the Years 1826 to 1834*, trans. Sheila M. Ohlendorf, Josette M. Bigelow, and Mary M. Standifer (Austin: Texas State Historical Association, 1980), 1:127.

15. Carlos María de Bustamante, *Manifiesto de la Junta Guadalupana a los Mexicanos y disertación histórico-crítica sobre la aparición de Nuestra Señora en Tepeyac* (Mexico City: Alejandro Valdéz, 1831), in de la Torre Villar and Navarro de Anda, eds., *Testimonios históricos*, 1056–91, quote at 1090.

16. David A. Brading, *Mexican Phoenix: Our Lady of Guadalupe, Image and Tradition Across Five Centuries* (New York: Cambridge University Press, 2001), 289.

17. Terry Rugeley, *Of Wonders and Wise Men: Religion and Popular Cultures in Southeast Mexico, 1800–1876* (Austin: University of Texas Press, 2001), 82. While the *cofradías* Rugeley cites were not dedicated to Guadalupe, his study illustrates a wider pattern of women's increased participation and leadership that transcended the *cofradías* and the Yucatán region he studied.

18. Ignacio Manuel Altamirano, *Pasajes y leyendas, tradiciones y costumbres de México* (Mexico City: Imprenta y Litografía Española, 1884), excerpted in de la Torre Villar and Navarro de Anda, eds., *Testimonios históricos*, 1127–1210, quotes at 1129, 1131, 1210.

19. Silvia Marina Arrom, "Mexican Laywomen Spearhead a Catholic Revival: The Ladies of Charity, 1863–1910," in *Religious Culture in Modern Mexico*, ed. Martin Austin Nesvig (Lanham, MD: Rowman and Littlefield, 2007), 50–77; Mark Overmyer-Velázquez, "'A New Political Religious Order': Church, State, and Workers in Porfirian Mexico," in *Religious Culture in Modern Mexico*, ed. Nesvig, 129–56; Brading, *Mexican Phoenix*, 288–98.

20. Agüeros, ed., *Album de la coronación*, 2:49–99.

21. *El Regidor* (San Antonio), October 12, 1895. For an overview of the liberal vision to refashion religion in Mexican life, see Pamela Voekel, "Liberal Religion: The Schism of 1861," in *Religious Culture in Modern Mexico*, ed. Nesvig, 78–105.

22. Agüeros, ed., *Album de la coronación*, 2:99–146.

23. Joseph Ignacio Heredia y Sarmiento, *Sermón panegírico de la gloriosa aparición de Nuestra Señora de Guadalupe* (Panegyric sermon of the glorious apparition of Our Lady of Guadalupe) (Mexico City: Imprenta de Doña María Fernández Jáuregui, 1803), 20. Page numbers for further quotations from *Sermón panegírico* are cited in context.

24. The breaks in the text are per the original. This text combines parts of two passages from the traditional apparition account. See *The Story of Guadalupe: Luis Laso de la Vega's "Huei tlamahuiçoltica" of 1649*, ed. and trans. Lisa Sousa, Stafford Poole, and James Lockhart (Stanford, CA: Stanford University Press, 1998), 65–67, 77–79. Heredia y Sarmiento cited two sources for the respective parts of the passage, both of which were examined in previous chapters of this present work: Cayetano de Cabrera y Quintero's *Escudo de armas de México* (1746) and Francisco de Florencia's *La estrella del norte de México* (1688).

25. Jorge Cañizares-Esguerra, "Son las mujeres las que defienden al rey con espadas y son los liberales los que queman herejes: El antiguo testamento y las revoluciones de independencia en la Monarquía de España," *20/10 El mundo Atlántico y la Modernidad Iberoamericana, 1750–1850*, México 2 (2013): 8–25, quote at 24. For a summary of various non-Guadalupan sermons promoting the two opposing sides in the insurgency, see Herrejón Peredo, *Del sermón al discurso cívico*, 287–342.

26. José de la Canal, *Sermón que en la festividad de Nuestra Señora de Guadalupe de Méjico, celebrada por su real congregación en la iglesia de San Felipe el Real de este corte . . .* (Sermon for the festivity of Our Lady of Guadalupe of Mexico, celebrated with the royal congregation of the church of Saint Philip the King of this court . . .) (Madrid: Imprenta de Don José del Collado, 1820), 5, 11, 31–32.

27. Manuel de la Bárcena, *Sermón exhortatorio que en la solemne función anual, que hace la Imperial Orden de Guadalupe a su celestial patrona . . .* (Exhortative sermon which in solemn annual function, the Imperial Order of Guadalupe offers to its celestial patroness . . .) (Mexico City: Imprenta del Supremo Gobierno, 1823), 6–7. Page numbers for further quotations from *Sermón exhortatorio* are cited in context.

28. Joaquín Ladrón de Guevara, *Sermón que en la solemne función celebrada . . .* (Sermon in the solemn function celebrated . . .) (1852), in *Sermonario mexicano*, ed. Bassols, 3:199–208, quotes at 199, 207. Page numbers for further quotations from Ladrón de Guevara's *Sermón* are cited in context. The reference to the Philistine appears to be from the account of David and Goliath in 1 Samuel 17. Though Goliath insults "the armies of the living God" (1 Sam. 17:26), however, he never literally asks, Where is the God who defends the Hebrews? Ladrón de Guevara might have conflated the Goliath account with texts from Psalms in which pagans do question the presence and even existence of the God of Israel— e.g., Psalm 115:2.

29. Fray Pablo Antonio del Niño Jesús, *Sermón de la Santísima Virgen de Guadalupe . . .* (1850), in *Sermonario mexicano*, ed. Bassols, 3:304–16, quotes at 304, 306–307. Page numbers for further quotations from Fray Pablo's *Sermón* are cited in context. Psalm 90 is typically numbered Psalm 91 in modern translations of the Bible.

30. Francisco Javier Miranda, *Sermón panegírico que en aniversario de la gloriosa aparición de Santa María de Guadalupe . . .* (Panegyric sermon for the anniversary of the glorious apparition of Holy Mary of Guadalupe . . .) (1852), in *Sermonario mexicano*, ed. Bassols, 3:292–303, quotes at 292, 296, 297, 301, 303. Page numbers for further quotations from Miranda's *Sermón* are cited in context.

31. The sermon of José de Jesús Ortiz is in Agüeros, ed., *Album de la coronación*, vol. 2, appendix, 18–21, quotes at 18, 19. Page numbers for further quotations from Ortiz's sermon are cited in context. The preparatory list of daily functions for the coronation in the *Album de la coronación*, 2:50, listed Archbishop José Ignacio

Árciga of Morelia, Michoacán, as the assigned preacher for October 11, but this source does not state when or why the change was made to have Bishop Ortiz prepare and present the sermon for that day.

32. Carrillo y Ancona's sermon is in Agüeros, ed., *Album de la coronación*, vol. 2, appendix, 2:10–18, quotes at 10, 12. Page numbers for further quotations from the sermon are cited in context.

33. Timothy Matovina, *Guadalupe and Her Faithful: Latino Catholics in San Antonio, from Colonial Origins to the Present* (Baltimore: Johns Hopkins University Press, 2005), 96–97.

34. *San Antonio Light*, December 12, 1914; *La Prensa* (San Antonio), December 12, 1934; December 13, 1916.

35. Miguel Sánchez, *Imagen de la Virgen María . . .* (Mexico City: Viuda de Bernardo Calderón, 1648), in de la Torre Villar and Navarro de Anda, eds., *Testimonios históricos*, 152–267, quotes at 179, 191.

36. Colleen Cross, "The Guadalupan Covenant: An Evaluation of the *Nican mopohua* in Light of the Ancient Jewish Tradition," in *New Frontiers in Guadalupan Studies*, ed. Virgilio Elizondo and Timothy Matovina (Eugene, OR: Pickwick, 2014), 108–24, quote at 122.

CHAPTER 5

1. Francis, *Holy Mass at the Basilica of Our Lady of Guadalupe: Homily of His Holiness Pope Francis*, Mexico City, February 13, 2016, https://w2.vatican.va/content/francesco/en/homilies/2016/documents/papa-francesco_20160213_omelia-messico-guadalupe.html.

2. José de Jesús Manríquez y Zárate, *Carta pastoral que el Excmo. y Rvmo. Obispo de Huejutla dirige a sus diocesanos sobre las necesidades de trabajar ahincadamente por la Glorificación de Juan Diego en este mundo*, April 12, 1939, as reprinted in Lauro López Beltrán, *Manríquez y Zárate, primer obispo de Huejutla, sublimador de Juan Diego, heroico defensor de la fe: Obra conmemorativa del quinto centenario del natalicio de Juan Diego, 1474–1974* (Mexico City: Editorial Tradición, 1974), 40–47; Manríquez y Zárate, *¿Quien fue Juan Diego?* (1939), as reprinted in López Beltrán, *Manríquez y Zárate*, 24, 77–84, 155–61; López Beltrán, *La historicidad de Juan Diego y su posible canonización* (Mexico City: Editorial Tradición, 1981); Virgilio Elizondo, et al., *A Retreat with Our Lady of Guadalupe and Juan Diego: Heeding the Call* (Cincinnati: St. Anthony Messenger Press, 1998); Norberto Rivera Carrera, *Juan Diego: El águila que habla* (Mexico City: Plaza & Janés, 2002); Eduardo Chávez Sánchez, *Juan Diego: Una vida de santidad que marcó la historia* (Mexico City: Editorial Porrúa, 2002).

3. Philip Jenkins, *The Next Christendom: The Coming of Global Christianity*, 3rd ed. (New York: Oxford University Press, 2011).

4. Rubén Rosario Rodríguez, *Racism and God-Talk: A Latino/a Perspective* (New York: New York University Press, 2008), chap. 4, "Guadalupe: *Imago Dei* Reconsidered"; Alejandro García-Rivera, *The Community of the Beautiful: A Theological Aesthetics* (Collegeville, MN: Liturgical Press, 1999), esp. 39–40, 56–59, 194; Cecilia González-Andrieu, "Till There Was You," in *The Treasure of Guadalupe*, ed. Virgilio Elizondo, Allan Figueroa Deck, and Timothy Matovina (Lanham, MD: Rowman and Littlefield, 2006), 65–71. For a summary of some works on Guadalupe of Latina and Latino theologians, see Timothy Matovina, "Theologies of Guadalupe: From the Spanish Colonial Era to Pope John Paul II," *Theological Studies* 70 (March 2009): 61–91, at 79–80.

5. Gustavo Gutiérrez, *A Theology of Liberation: History, Politics, and Salvation*, trans. Sister Caridad Inda and John Eagleson (Maryknoll, NY: Orbis, 1988; orig. English ed., 1973), xx.

6. Richard Nebel, *Santa María Tonantzin, Virgen de Guadalupe: Continuidad y transformación religiosa en México* (Mexico City: Fondo de Cultura Económica, 1995), 128–29; Our Lady of Guadalupe website, "A Chronicle of Events Related to the Miracle," http://www.sancta.org/table.html.

7. Carla Zarebska and Alejandro Gómez de Tuddo, *Guadalupe* (Oaxaca, Mexico: Jacobo Dalevuelta, 2002), 302.

8. Roberto Ramón Lint Sagarena, *Aztlán and Arcadia: Religion, Ethnicity, and the Creation of Place* (New York: New York University Press, 2014), 147–58, quote at 153; Dario Gamboni, "The Underground and the Virgin of Guadalupe: Contexts for the *Virgen del Metro*, Mexico City 1997–2007," *Anales del Instituto de Investigaciones Estéticas* 31 (2009): 119–53; Elaine A Peña, *Performing Piety: Making Sacred Space with the Virgin of Guadalupe* (Berkeley: University of California Press, 2011), chap. 4, "Devotion in the City: Building Sacred Space on Chicago's Far North Side"; Octavio Paz, "Foreword: The Flight of Quetzalcóatl and the Quest for Legitimacy," in Jacques Lafaye, *Quetzalcoatl and Guadalupe: The Formation of Mexican National Consciousness, 1531–1813*, trans. Benjamin Keen (Chicago: University of Chicago Press, 1976), xi. For contemporary writers who have examined Guadalupe in their work, see, e.g., Ana Castillo, ed., *Goddess of the Americas/La Diosa de las Américas: Writings on the Virgin of Guadalupe* (New York: Riverhead Books, 1996); Theresa Delgadillo, *Spiritual Mestizaje: Religion, Gender, Race, and Nation in Contemporary Chicana Narrative* (Durham, NC: Duke University Press, 2011). For further analysis of Guadalupe in contemporary murals, see David A. Sánchez, "Guadalupan Iconography: A Postcolonial 'Signifier of Resistance' of the Chicano/a Civil Rights Movement," *Listening: Journal of Religion and Culture* 44 (Spring 2009): 88–99.

9. Alyshia Gálvez, *Guadalupe in New York: Devotion and the Struggle for Citizenship Rights Among Mexican Immigrants* (New York: New York University Press, 2010), chap. 6, "La Antorcha Guadalupana/The Guadalupan Torch Run: Messengers

for a People Divided by the Border," quotes at 149, 150. Gálvez used pseudonyms for nearly all her interviewees.

10. Sam Dillon, "Doubting Keeper of Mexico's Guadalupe Shrine Is Stepping Down," *New York Times*, September 8, 1996; Joint Letter to the Congregation for the Causes of the Saints, March 9, 1998, in Stafford Poole, *The Guadalupan Controversies in Mexico* (Stanford, CA: Stanford University Press, 2006), 239–43, quote at 241; Joint Letter of September 27, 1999, in Poole, *Guadalupan Controversies*, 244–48, quote at 245. See also Poole, *Guadalupan Controversies*, chaps. 6 and 7, "The Beatification of Juan Diego" and "History Versus Juan Diego."

11. Michael Hirsley and Jorge Casuso, "Hispanic Catholics Feel Pull of Protestant Fervor," *Chicago Tribune*, January 7, 1990; Maxwell E. Johnson, *The Virgin of Guadalupe: Theological Reflections of an Anglo-Lutheran Liturgist* (Lanham, MD: Rowman and Littlefield, 2002); Cathleen Falsani, "Lutherans Luring Hispanic Catholics? Families Feel Duped into Wrong Church; Priests Charge Deceit," *Chicago Sun-Times*, August 20, 2002; William Lobdell and Jennifer Mena, "Our Lady: Not Just for Catholics," *Los Angeles Times*, December 12, 2003.

12. Linda B. Hall, *Mary, Mother and Warrior: The Virgin in Spain and the Americas* (Austin: University of Texas Press, 2004), 284–85; Clarissa Pinkola Estés, "They Tried to Stop Her at the Border," *National Catholic Reporter*, April 28, 2009.

13. J. Michael Parker, "Lady of Guadalupe Crosses Cultural Lines," *San Antonio Express-News*, December 11, 2006.

14. Bishops' Committee on Hispanic Affairs, *Hispanic Ministry at the Turn of the New Millennium* (Washington, DC: United States Conference of Catholic Bishops, 1999), On-Site Interview section, no. 6; Father John Koelsch, letter to the author, September 22, 2009.

15. Michael E. Engh, "With Her People: The Barrio and 'La Virgen,'" *America*, January 6, 2003, 15–16.

16. Ángel María Garibay K[intana], "La maternidad de María en el mensaje guadalupano," in *La maternidad espiritual de María: Conferencias leídas en los Congresos Mariológicos 7–12 octubre 1957 y 9–12 octubre 1960* (Mexico City: Editorial Jus, 1961), 187–202; Garibay, "The Spiritual Motherhood of Mary," in *A Handbook on Guadalupe* (New Bedford, MA: Franciscan Friars of the Immaculate, 1997), 9–16, quote at 10; *The Story of Guadalupe: Luis Laso de la Vega's "Huei tlamahuiçoltica" of 1649*, ed. and trans. Lisa Sousa, Stafford Poole, and James Lockhart (Stanford, CA: Stanford University Press, 1998), 65; Miguel León-Portilla, *Tonantzin Guadalupe: Pensamiento náhuatl y mensaje cristiano en el "Nican mopohua"* (Mexico City: Fondo de Cultura Económica, 2000), chap. 2, "El 'Nican mopohua,' el pensamiento indígena y el 'tecpilahtolli,' lenguaje noble de las Nahuas," quote at 68.

17. Garibay, "Spiritual Motherhood of Mary," 11.

18. Clodomiro L. Siller Acuña, *Para comprender el mensaje de María de Guadalupe* (Buenos Aires: Editorial Guadalupe, 1989); Virgilio Elizondo, *La Morenita: Evangelizer of the Americas* (San Antonio: Mexican American Cultural Center, 1980); Elizondo, *Guadalupe: Mother of the New Creation* (Maryknoll, NY: Orbis, 1997); Richard Nebel, *Santa María Tonantzin, Virgen de Guadalupe: Religiöse Kontinuität und Transformation in Mexiko* (Immensee, Switzerland: Neue Zeitschrift für Missionswissenschaft, 1992) and Spanish translation, *Santa María Tonantzin, Virgen de Guadalupe.*

19. Siller Acuña, *Para comprender el mensaje de María de Guadalupe,* 60, 90, 93, 94. An earlier version of this work is Siller Acuña, *Flor y canto del Tepeyac: Historia de las apariciones de Santa María de Guadalupe: Texto y comentario* (Xalapa, Veracruz: Servir, 1981). Besides an updated commentary and introduction, the text of the *Nican mopohua* presented in *Para comprender el mensaje de María de Guadalupe* is based on the translation of Ángel María Garibay, while in *Flor y canto del Tepeyac* it is based on the earlier translation of Primo Feliciano Velázquez. *Para comprender el mensaje de María de Guadalupe* also includes a facsimile of the Nahua text.

20. See esp. Elizondo, *Guadalupe,* chap. 4, "Conversion."

21. Elizondo, *La Morenita,* 112; Elizondo, *The Future Is Mestizo: Life Where Cultures Meet,* 2nd ed. (Boulder: University Press of Colorado, 2000), 65.

22. Stafford Poole, *Our Lady of Guadalupe: The Origins and Sources of a Mexican National Symbol, 1531–1797* (Tucson: University of Arizona Press, 1995), 14, 225.

23. Carl A. Anderson and Eduardo Chávez, *Our Lady of Guadalupe: Mother of the Civilization of Love* (New York: Doubleday, 2009), 87, 90. One of the primary Vatican sources Anderson and Chávez cite regarding the widely discussed Vatican statements on liberation theology is Benedict XVI (Cardinal Joseph Ratzinger), *The Ratzinger Report,* trans. Salvator Attanasio and Graham Harrison (San Francisco: Ignatius, 1985).

24. Nebel, *Santa María Tonantzin, Virgen de Guadalupe,* 247.

25. Ivone Gebara and Maria Clara Bingemer, *Mary: Mother of God, Mother of the Poor* (Maryknoll, NY: Orbis, 1989), 153–54; Ada María Isasi-Díaz, *La Lucha Continues: Mujerista Theology* (Maryknoll, NY: Orbis, 2004), 28.

26. Ana María Díaz-Stevens, "The Saving Grace: The Matriarchal Core of Latino Catholicism," *Latino Studies Journal* 4 (September 1993): 60–78. For the role of women in communal devotion during the colonial era and the nineteenth centuries, see also Terry Rugeley, *Of Wonders and Wise Men: Religion and Popular Cultures in Southeast Mexico, 1800–1876* (Austin: University of Texas Press, 2001), 82–83; Timothy Matovina, *Guadalupe and Her Faithful: Latino Catholics in San Antonio, from Colonial Origins to the Present* (Baltimore: Johns Hopkins University Press, 2005), 58, 75–76, 81–82.

27. María Pilar Aquino, *Our Cry for Life: Feminist Theology from Latin America* (Maryknoll, NY: Orbis, 1993), 173; Gebara and Bingemer, *Mary,* 107.

28. Aquino, *Our Cry for Life*, 173 (emphasis in original).

29. Evelyn P. Stevens, "*Marianismo*: The Other Face of *Machismo* in Latin America," in *Female and Male in Latin America: Essays*, ed. Ann Pescatello (Pittsburgh, PA: University of Pittsburgh Press, 1973), 90–101; Rosa Maria Gil and Carmen Inoa Vazquez, *The Maria Paradox: How Latinas Can Merge Old World Traditions with New World Self-Esteem* (New York: G. P. Putnam's Sons, 1996), 7; Nancy Pineda-Madrid, *Suffering and Salvation in Ciudad Juárez* (Minneapolis: Fortress: 2011), 49, 58 (emphasis in original).

30. Gebara and Bingemer, *Mary*, chap. 3, "Mary in Scripture," quote at 168. A more extensive treatment of Mary in scripture and as a first-century peasant woman of Galilee is in Elizabeth A. Johnson, *Truly Our Sister: A Theology of Mary in the Communion of Saints* (New York: Continuum, 2003), esp. part 4, "Picturing a World," and chap. 10, "The Dangerous Memory of Mary: A Mosaic."

31. Gebara and Bingemer, *Mary*, 120–21.

32. Theresa L. Torres, *The Paradox of Latina Religious Leadership in the Catholic Church: Las Guadalupanas of Kansas City* (New York: Palgrave Macmillan, 2013), 160; María del Socorro Castañeda-Liles, *Our Lady of Everyday Life: La Virgen de Guadalupe and the Catholic Imagination of Mexican Women in America* (New York: Oxford University Press, 2018), 14; Matovina, *Guadalupe and Her Faithful*, 161.

33. Jeanette Rodriguez, *Our Lady of Guadalupe: Faith and Empowerment Among Mexican-American Women* (Austin: University of Texas Press, 1994), 128, 129, 162. See also Rodriguez, "Devotion to Our Lady of Guadalupe among Mexican Americans," in *Many Faces, One Church: Cultural Diversity and the American Catholic Experience*, ed. Peter C. Phan and Diana Hayes (Lanham, MD: Sheed and Ward, 2005), 83–97; Rodriguez and Ted Fortier, *Cultural Memory: Resistance, Faith, and Identity* (Austin: University of Texas Press, 2007), chap. 2, "The Power of Image: Our Lady of Guadalupe."

34. Karen Mary Davalos, *Yolanda M. López* (Los Angeles: UCLA Chicano Studies Research Center Press, 2008), esp. 80–100, quotes at 87, 91, 93.

35. Sandra Cisneros, "Guadalupe the Sex Goddess," in *Goddess of the Americas*, ed. Castillo, 46–51, quotes at 50–51; Cisneros, "Tepeyac," in *Woman Hollering Creek and Other Stories* (New York: Random House, 1991), 21–23.

36. Nancy Pineda-Madrid, "Interpreting Our Lady of Guadalupe: Mediating the Christian Mystery of Redemption" (Ph.D. diss., Graduate Theological Union, Berkeley, CA, 2005), 3. See also Pineda-Madrid, "Notes Toward a Chicana Feminist Epistemology (and Why It Is Important for Latina Feminist Theologies)," in *A Reader in Latina Feminist Theology: Religion and Justice*, ed. María Pilar Aquino, Daisy L. Machado, and Jeanette Rodriguez (Austin: University of Texas Press, 2002), 241–66; Pineda-Madrid, "Guadalupe's Challenge to Rahner's Theology of Symbol," in *Rahner Beyond Rahner: A Great Theologian Encounters the Pacific Rim*, ed. Paul G. Crowley (Lanham, MD: Rowman and Littlefield, 2005), 73–85;

Pineda-Madrid, "Traditioning: The Formation of Community, the Transmission of Faith," in *Futuring Our Past: Explorations in the Theology of Tradition*, ed. Orlando O. Espín and Gary Macy (Maryknoll, NY: Orbis, 2006), 204–26; Pineda-Madrid, "'Holy Guadalupe . . . Shameful Malinche?': Excavating the Problem of 'Female Dualism,' Doing Theological Spade Work," *Listening: Journal of Religion and Culture* 44 (Spring 2009): 71–87.

37. Norma Alarcón, "Traddutora, Traditora: A Paradigmatic Figure of Chicana Feminism," in *Scattered Hegemonies: Postmodernity and Transnational Feminist Practices*, ed. Inderpal Grewal and Caren Kaplan (Minneapolis: University of Minnesota Press, 1994), 110–33, quote at 129–30. See also Gloria Anzaldúa, *Borderlands/La Frontera: The New Mestiza*, 2nd ed. (San Francisco: Aunt Lute, 1999); Laura Elisa Pérez, "El Desorden, Nationalism, and Chicana/o Aesthetics," in *Between Woman and Nation: Nationalisms, Transnational Feminisms, and the State*, ed. Caren Kaplan, Norma Alarcón, and Minoo Moallem (Durham, NC: Duke University Press, 1999), 19–46; Pérez, *Chicana Art: The Politics of Spiritual and Aesthetic Altarities* (Durham, NC: Duke University Press, 2007).

38. Pineda-Madrid, "Interpreting Our Lady of Guadalupe," 91, 93.

39. Vatican II, *Lumen Gentium*, November 21, 1964, nos. 55, 56, http://www.vatican.va/archive/hist_councils/ii_vatican_council/documents/vat-ii_const_19641121_lumen-gentium_en.html.

40. Vatican II, *Lumen Gentium*, no. 58; Paul VI, *Evangelii Nuntiandi*, no. 82, http://w2.vatican.va/content/paul-vi/en/apost_exhortations/documents/hf_p-vi_exh_19751208_evangelii-nuntiandi.html; Third General Conference of Latin American Bishops, *Evangelization at Present and in the Future of Latin America: Conclusions* (Washington, DC: National Conference of Catholic Bishops, Secretariat, Committee for the Church in Latin America, 1979), no. 446.

41. The meaning of the "new evangelization" is examined in a number of papal statements—e.g., Benedict XVI's *Ubicumque et Semper* (2010), http://w2.vatican.va/content/benedict-xvi/en/apost_letters/documents/hf_ben-xvi_apl_20100921_ubicumque-et-semper.html, in which the pope established the Pontifical Council for Promoting the New Evangelization. For John Paul's most comprehensive treatment of the new evangelization in the American continent, see John Paul II, *Ecclesia in America* (1999), esp. chap. 6, "The Mission of the Church in America Today: The New Evangelization," http://w2.vatican.va/content/john-paul-ii/en/apost_exhortations/documents/hf_jp-ii_exh_22011999_ecclesia-in-america.html.

42. Message of the Fourth General Conference to the Peoples of Latin America and the Caribbean, in *Santo Domingo and Beyond: Documents and Commentaries from the Fourth General Conference of Latin American Bishops*, ed. Alfred T. Hennelly (Maryknoll, NY: Orbis, 1993), 63–70, quote at 70 (no. 48); *The Aparecida Document: V General Conference of the Bishops of Latin America and the Caribbean; Concluding Document; Aparecida, 13–31 May 2007*, no. 4, http://www.celam.org/

aparecida/Ingles.pdf; John Paul II, *Novo Millennio Ineunte* (2001), no. 58, https://
w2.vatican.va/content/john-paul-ii/en/apost_letters/2001/documents/hf_jp-
ii_apl_20010106_novo-millennio-ineunte.html; Benedict XVI, *Homily of His
Holiness Benedict XVI*, October 11, 2012, http://w2.vatican.va/content/benedict-
xvi/en/homilies/2012/documents/hf_ben-xvi_hom_20121011_anno-fede.
html; Francis, *Evangelii Gaudium*, nos. 284–88, http://w2.vatican.va/content/
francesco/en/apost_exhortations/documents/papa-francesco_esortazione-ap_
20131124_evangelii-gaudium.html.

43. These links and themes have been developed in works such as Nebel, *Santa
María Tonantzin, Virgen de Guadalupe*, esp. 295–304; Elizondo, *Guadalupe*,
esp. 119–22; Elizondo, "*La Virgen de Guadalupe* as Mother and Master Icon for the
New Evangelization," in *To All the World: Preaching and the New Evangelization*,
ed. Michael E. Connors (Collegeville, MN: Liturgical Press, 2016), 12–21;
Rivera Carrera, *Juan Diego*, esp. chap. 3, "Juan Diego evangelizador"; Anita de
Luna, "Juan Diego: The Empowered Evangelizer," in *Treasure of Guadalupe*, ed.
Elizondo, Figueroa Deck, and Matovina, 51–56.

44. John Paul II, *Address of His Holiness Pope John Paul II*, Puebla, Mexico, January
28, 1979, section IV.1, https://w2.vatican.va/content/john-paul-ii/en/speeches/
1979/january/documents/hf_jp-ii_spe_19790128_messico-puebla-episc-latam.
html; John Paul II, *Homily of Pope John Paul II*, Mexico City, January 23, 1999, no.
4, https://w2.vatican.va/content/john-paul-ii/en/homilies/1999/documents/
hf_jp-ii_hom_19990123_mexico-guadalupe.html. My thanks to Mariscela
Méndez, a McNair Scholar whose project I supervised at the University of Notre
Dame in summer 2004. Her research on Pope John Paul's statements about
Guadalupe provided a bibliography of primary sources for this analysis of his
thought.

45. John Paul II, *Homilía del Santo Padre Juan Pablo II*, Veracruz, Mexico, May 7,
1990, no. 1, https://w2.vatican.va/content/john-paul-ii/es/homilies/1990/
documents/hf_jp-ii_hom_19900507_veracruz.html; John Paul II, *Ecclesia in
America*, no. 11; John Paul II, *Redemptoris Missio: On the Permanent Validity of the
Church's Missionary Mandate* (1990), no. 52, http://w2.vatican.va/content/john-
paul-ii/en/encyclicals/documents/hf_jp-ii_enc_07121990_redemptoris-missio.
html#%242D; John Paul II, "Opening Address of the Holy Father," in *Santo
Domingo and Beyond*, ed. Hennelly, 41–60, quote at 56 (no. 24).

46. Richard Boudreaux, "Latin America's Indigenous Saint Stirs Anger, Pride," *Los
Angeles Times*, July 30, 2002; Poole, *Guadalupan Controversies*, 185.

47. John Paul II, *Discurso del Santo Padre Juan Pablo II a los sacerdotes, religiosos,
religiosoas, seminaristas y laicos comprometidos*, Mexico City, May 12, 1990, no. 2,
http://w2.vatican.va/content/john-paul-ii/es/speeches/1990/may/documents/
hf_jp-ii_spe_19900512_sac-messico.html; John Paul II, *Homily of His Holiness
Pope John Paul II*, Zapopán, Mexico, January 30, 1979, nos. 3–4, https://
w2.vatican.va/content/john-paul-ii/en/homilies/1979/documents/hf_jp-ii_

hom_19790130_messico-zapopan.html; John Paul II, *Homily of John Paul II*, Mexico City, January 24, 1999, no. 7, https://w2.vatican.va/content/john-paul-ii/en/homilies/1999/documents/hf_jp-ii_hom_19990124_mexico-autodromo.html.

48. John Paul II, *Beatificación de Juan Diego y de otros siervos de Dios: Homilía de su Santidad Juan Pablo II*, Mexico City, May 6, 1990, no. 5 (emphasis in original), https://w2.vatican.va/content/john-paul-ii/es/homilies/1990/documents/hf_jp-ii_hom_19900506_citta-del-messico.html; John Paul II, *Canonization of Juan Diego Cuauhtlatoatzin: Homily of the Holy Father John Paul II*, July 31, 2002, nos. 1, 3–4, 5, http://w2.vatican.va/content/john-paul-ii/en/homilies/2002/documents/hf_jp-ii hom_20020731_canonization-mexico.html.

49. Mary Doak, "Facing the Dragon's Fire," in *Treasure of Guadalupe*, ed. Elizondo, Figueroa Deck, and Matovina, 1–8, quotes at 5, 6.

50. Francis, *Homily of His Holiness Pope Francis*.

Index